Resistance to the
Spanish-American and
Philippine Wars

Resistance to the Spanish-American and Philippine Wars

Anti-Imperialism and the Role of the Press, 1895–1902

CHARLES QUINCE

McFarland & Company, Inc., Publishers
Jefferson, North Carolina

LIBRARY OF CONGRESS CATALOGUING-IN-PUBLICATION DATA

Names: Quince, Charles, author.
Title: Resistance to the Spanish-American and Philippine wars : anti-imperialism and the role of the press, 1895–1902 / Charles Quince.
Description: Jefferson, N.C. : McFarland & Company, Inc., Publishers, 2017. | Includes bibliographical references and index.
Identifiers: LCCN 2017026959 | ISBN 9781476669748 (softcover : acid free paper) ∞
Subjects: LCSH: Spanish-American War, 1898—United States—Public opinion. | Spanish-American War, 1898—Press coverage—United States. | Hawaii—Annexation to the United States—Public opinion. | Philippines—History—Philippine American War, 1899-1902—Public opinion. | United States—Territorial expansion—Public opinion. | United States—Foreign relations—1865–1921—Public opinion. | Imperialism—History—19th century—Public opinion.
Classification: LCC E721 .Q85 2017 | DDC 973.8/9—dc23
LC record available at https://lccn.loc.gov/2017026959

BRITISH LIBRARY CATALOGUING DATA ARE AVAILABLE

ISBN (print) 978-1-4766-6974-8
ISBN (ebook) 978-1-4766-2954-4

© 2017 Charles Quince. All rights reserved

No part of this book may be reproduced or transmitted in any form or by any means, electronic or mechanical, including photocopying or recording, or by any information storage and retrieval system, without permission in writing from the publisher.

Front cover image "Destruction of the U.S. Battleship *Maine* in Havana Harbor," February 15, 1898, Kurz & Allison, Library of Congress

Printed in the United States of America

McFarland & Company, Inc., Publishers
  Box 611, Jefferson, North Carolina 28640
    www.mcfarlandpub.com

Table of Contents

PREFACE	1
1. In the Shadow of the Past: The Development of Expansionist and Anti-Expansionist Sentiments	3
2. A Group of Many Shades: The Anti-Anti-Imperialists	28
3. The Cuban Rebellion and American Politics, 1895–1896	64
4. A Critical Dilemma in Spanish-American Relations	77
5. Sliding Toward War	87
6. Naval Capabilities	96
7. Land Warfare	101
8. The Sentiments of the European Press	105
9. Voices of Concern: The Business Community and the Spanish-American War	110
10. A War Without Benefits	133
11. A Shift in Public Opinion	136
12. Dissent, Alleged War Crimes and the Philippines War	141
CONCLUSION	155
SUGGESTED READINGS	159
CHAPTER NOTES	171
BIBLIOGRAPHY	187
INDEX	197

Preface

I have always been fascinated by the events influenced by the storms associated with the Spanish-American War. That may explain why, in the face of prolonged interruptions, I have persisted with this project for more than five years. My interest in the Spanish-American War has influenced my approach to the study of world events, both historical and contemporary. In many ways, the debates surrounding the events connected to the Spanish-American War mirror the debates that took place in U.S. society during the time of dramatic upheaval.

The intellectual roots of this book reach back to my undergraduate years. While exploring the U.S. landscape of the late nineteenth century, I realized that many sources of this era focused on the overpowering influence of expansionist ideology. I became aware that very few of these studies provided an in-depth analysis of the questions that anti-expansionists posed to the U.S. public. When I searched for secondary literature that explored this subject, I found very little.

What follows is this book. It has two goals. First, I hope to give a general though by no means comprehensive analysis of the crucial public debates concerning the strategic advantages and disadvantages of the United States going to war with Spain. Second, I will analyze the historical, political, social, military, and economic precepts that shaped the hearts and minds of late nineteenth century U.S. society. The book also identifies four factors that contributed to the failure of anti-imperialists' opposition to the Spanish-American War: (1) Congressional anti-war/anti-imperialists' lack of a clear argument for why the United States should not go to war with Spain, (2) the rising tide of war fever that engulfed U.S. society after the destruction of the USS *Maine*, (3) the nation's sense of exceptionalism and its desire to fulfill its manifest destiny, and (4) the anti-imperialists falling victim to the harsh realities of their times and the misconceptions of their arguments.

Preface

The book concentrates on the months and years before military action as the debates over relations with Spain grew more heated, and extends into the Philippine insurrection. It addresses two major questions: First, why did the opposition to war with Spain and in the Philippines become so formidable? And second, why did this opposition fail to achieve its goals? The official papers of William McKinley and those of his aides and the diplomatic corps shed very little light on the mechanics of U.S. progression toward war with Spain and U.S. involvement in the Philippines. Congressional documents and committee meeting minutes give only a coarse picture of the nation's motivation to fight Spain and its involvement in the Philippines.

A detailed study of the contemporary press of the late nineteenth century United States is one method of establishing a coherent explanation of the relationship among the press, anti-imperialism, and the events associated with the Spanish-American War and Philippine insurrection. The anti-imperialists presented their case consistently and centered their argument on two key points: the heavy toll that expansionist policies would exact on U.S. society and the limited benefits the war would bring to the United States. In developing this study, I conducted a qualitative content analysis of various newspapers and other contemporary sources of the period to decipher the relationship among the U.S. public, anti-imperialism, the events of the Spanish-American War, and the Philippine insurrection.

The intent here is to focus on a range of phenomena and evidence that would give more clarity to U.S. society during the stormy events associated with the Spanish-American War and the Philippine war. My deepest hope is that my efforts, beyond providing tentative answers to the questions raised in the text, will lead others to more fully explore the neglected relationship between anti-imperialism and the events of the Spanish-American War.

1

In the Shadow of the Past: The Development of Expansionist and Anti-Expansionist Sentiments

The origin of the debate over U.S. territorial expansion is a theme that is traceable back to the colonial era. As the United States grew, geographically and developmentally, some Americans seriously questioned whether territorial expansion was in the best interest of the country. The national discussion over continental expansion reached its climax during the U.S. war with Mexico. Influential political leaders questioned the legitimacy of a war they believed was fought primarily for territorial aggrandizement.

Even as the nation became geographically transformed by the Mexican war, leading statesmen had already expressed grave doubts about the acquisition of overseas territory. Cuba, the holy grail of the western hemisphere, became the first major overseas territory to be targeted as a possible addition to the republic by Americans. During the early 1800s, Thomas Jefferson felt that the overall security of the United States depended on annexing Cuba, and within a decade, John Quincy Adams echoed these sentiments.

During the turbulent years following the American Civil War, Secretary of State William H. Seward became the chief missionary to spread the gospel of overseas expansion. With an apocalyptic tone, Seward not only emphasized the future competing interests in Asian markets among industrial nations, but his actions in promoting a reciprocity treaty with Hawaii along with his attempts to establish exclusive rights to the Isthmian Canal for the United States indicated that the Secretary of State believed the United States should secure a place in the trade with Asia. Seward's efforts laid the ground work for what many later Americans would call the "open door" policy in China and Korea. Although the

Resistance to the Spanish-American and Philippine Wars

distinguish statesman succeeded, to a certain extent, regarding his plans for Asia, Seward's plan did not come to fruition in the Caribbean where he attempted to add the Danish West Indies and Santo Domingo to the U.S. empire.

Several factors played a key part in the anti-expansionists' campaign to defeat Seward's plans. The twin domestic problems of Southern Reconstruction and the development of the West occupied the thoughts of most Americans during the 1870s and 1880s. Most Americans of this period thought that there was enough land for future generations and that adding any outlying territory did not make sense.

Although some segments of U.S. society called for the annexation of any territory, the main focus of U.S. expansionism seemed to be directed at Canada. Even fervent anti-expansionists, who did not want the nation to seize foreign territory, showed a keen interest in the annexing of Canada. Such leading anti-expansionists as Carl Schurz and William B. Cochran constantly advocated the annexation of Canada from the end of the Civil War to the late 1890s. Ironically, one of Schurz's main arguments against U.S. overseas expansion involved the belief that such action would divert attention from the true target of U.S. expansionism: Canada.

For proponents who advocated annexing Canada, the benefits outweighed the negative aspects. Such annexation would stop the intractable disputes over fishing rights and boundaries. Annexing Canada would give the English-speaking people vast territory without the need to contend with native inhabitants. In essence, it would allow the people of the United States to naturally fulfill their "manifest destiny."

The first major debate over expansion in the decade prior to the 1890s occurred in 1889 involving the Samoa crisis. During the 1870s, the U.S. Navy had considered establishing a coaling station in the Samoan Islands, a plan that ultimately led to strained relations between the United States, Britain, and Germany. This delicate balance became even more unstable when Germany instigated a native revolt in the islands in order to place a figurehead on the throne that would support its position. In the ensuing turmoil, a vast amount of U.S. property was destroyed while the German Consul at Apia took the initiative and replaced the Samoan flag with Germany's flag.[1]

The reaction in the United States was both spontaneous and blunt.

1. In the Shadow of the Past

Americans insisted that the leaders of the country uphold their interests. The *San Francisco Examiner* declared that "Germany in this affair has simply played the highwayman." This arousal of patriotic fervor over U.S. overseas expansion was the first such display of emotions shown since the national interest shown in the Hawaii and Santo Domingo episode of the 1870s.[2]

Although the proponents of expansionism elucidated the positive aspects of annexing the Samoan Islands, President Grover Cleveland decided to let Congress handle the matter. In placing the controversy in Congress' hands, Cleveland insisted "that the autonomy and independence of Samoa should be scrupulously preserved." The ensuing debate illustrated the rising tide of nationalism that swept the country. Congressional leaders introduced and passed legislation that included $500,000 for the protection of U.S. property and lives in Samoa, and voted to approve another $100,000 for the development of the harbor located at Pago Pago.[3]

Cleveland had bipartisan support for his Samoan policy. One of the nation's leading political papers, *The Nation*, believed the United States should completely withdraw from Samoa because "the more the matter is looked into, the more plainly does it seem, on our part, an outbreak of sheer jingoism and meddlesomeness in other people's affairs." Astonished by the actions of the United States, German officials invited Carl Schurz to several conferences in order to stabilize the deteriorating relationship between the United States and Germany. Acting outside any official capacity, Schurz assured Germany's foreign minister that "the traditional policy of the country was most deadly averse to such distant annexations and to the entanglements certain to grow out of such protectorates; and that traditional policy was too deeply rooted in public opinion to be disregarded."[4]

When Benjamin Harrison assumed the duties of the presidency, much of the belligerency in the country regarding the Samoan crisis had subsided. James G. Blaine, Harrison's Secretary of State, decided to follow the conservative policy initiated by Cleveland regarding the controversy. Chancellor Otto von Bismarck, perturbed by the potential problems with the United States, requested a conference be immediately convened to find an answer to the crisis. An act of nature helped the ensuing negotiations when a hurricane destroyed the U.S. and German fleets anchored in the harbor of Apia in Samoa.

Resistance to the Spanish-American and Philippine Wars

After the clouds of hostility had lifted, a treaty among the United States, Germany, and Great Britain was signed that clearly defined who controlled the islands. Blaine considered this tripartite pact as a last resort, and the agreement itself resulted in perpetual agitation between the three nations. The United States thought the convention did not ensure U.S. control of the islands; Germany emphasized that the agreement represented a serious departure from the traditional U.S. policy of isolationism. Finally, after a decade of friction, the United States and Germany agreed to divide the islands between themselves while England received additional territory in Africa and the Pacific.[5]

The events surrounding the Samoan crisis bring to the surface two important points. The tripartite agreement did indicate America's departure from an ingrained policy of avoiding entanglement, and the grievances that inherently arose from the lack of complete control of the islands by the United States compelled U.S. political leaders to distrust similar future agreements. Thus, while the United States signed an agreement that established "an unprecedented collaboration with European countries on a distant South sea archipelago," such cooperation jeopardized the U.S. longstanding policy of avoiding entangling alliances with foreign nations.[6]

Those who vehemently opposed U.S. involvement in Samoa also knew of the future implications of the tripartite covenant. A leading international law expert, Professor Theodore Woolsey of Yale, raised some fundamental questions regarding the change in U.S. foreign policy. Rhetorically Woolsey asked, "What does this mean and what will it involve?" He answered his own questions by admonishing:

> It means in the first place a departure from the old and safe policy of the fathers. It means courting rather than avoiding foreign entanglements. It means one collision after another, each with its sulphurous war clouds above it. It means the violation of former precedents, setting up new ones in their stead which may prove awkward, even dangerous. It will encourage aggressions upon weaker neighbors. It will make this country hated and distrusted by its natural friends. It will weaken its commercial position on this continent, throwing trade into channels other than our own.[7]

By taking this new change in foreign policy, Woolsey pointed out that the United States must "be prepared to" sustain it. He asserted that security obligations would compel the nation to enlarge the army and navy, and change the policy of funding them. Woolsey concluded by

1. In the Shadow of the Past

noting that this "tendency ... is not one which will stand still. It must be checked at once or grow greater." The Yale Professor's presage about the direction of U.S. foreign policy is noteworthy because within six months of his comments, the United States would face a similar problem involving overseas expansion.[8]

The crisis that developed over the annexation of the Hawaiian Islands in 1893 provided a second problem involving overseas expansion. The U.S. interest in the Islands can be traced back to the 1840s. The Islands' strategic location piqued the interest of the nation and became a hot topic of interest by such leading expansionist as Seward. The real possibility that a European nation would eventually annex the Islands became the focal point of a senatorial debate concerning Hawaiian annexation in the early 1870s.

Although a reciprocity treaty between the United States and the Hawaiian Kingdom was finalized in 1875, the agreement had strong opposition from U.S. sugar interests. Many U.S. products found their way to the Hawaiian free list, but preferential treatment was given to Hawaiian sugar in U.S. markets. This preference facilitated the growth of the sugar industry throughout the Islands. It also showed that the reciprocity treaty created an imbalance in the economic and social spheres of the Hawaiian Islands.

The economic relationship became further damaged by the passage of the McKinley Tariff in 1890 that not only secured sugar's place on the free list but gave a gratuity of two cents a pound to domestic producers. The end result led to an Island-wide economic depression in Hawaii. Sugar farmers, many of them Americans, decided to take matters into their own hands. Within this framework, a U.S.-led revolution broke out against Queen Liliuokalani in January 1893.[9]

The U.S. planters who urged annexation did not do so purely for economic reasons. Queen Liliuokalani had made an unwavering effort to increase the power of the throne. The Queen's legislative supporters passed measures licensing the establishment of a lottery system and the sale of opium. The move that ultimately pushed the situation over the edge centered on the Queen's attempt to use a royal decree to promote a constitution that would restore the royal prerogatives that the legislature had slowly usurped from the throne over the years.

Economic disorganization and threats of an arbitrary government became the aggregates that caused the U.S. political organization, the

Annexation Club, to remonstrate against the Queen. Leaders in the annexation movement communicated their concern to the U.S. minister, John L. Stevens. On January 16 and continuing into the next day, the annexationists seized control of the government building and installed Judge Sanford Dole as head of the provisional government. As events deteriorated, Stevens ordered Marines from the U.S.S. *Boston* to land and provide a protective shield for U.S. property.[10]

After gaining control of the government, the revolutionists promptly sent a group of representatives to Washington to request annexation of Hawaii to the United States. President Benjamin Harrison, preferring a vote from the Hawaiian people, wanted to negotiate a treaty of annexation before his term of office expired. However, a strong opposition to Harrison's policy quickly materialized. The ensuring debate in Congress and in the nation's press over the advantages and disadvantages of annexing Hawaii in 1893 became the first confrontation of the 1890s over the issue of U.S. overseas expansion.[11]

The response of the anti-expansionist leaders varied. George Vest, Senator from Missouri, informed the press that he would support annexation "unless he had some reason to believe that in doing so he was performing a service agreeable to Mr. Cleveland." Representative James Blount, Chair of the House Committee on Foreign Affairs, remained silent about the Hawaii crisis. However, two leading Senators, George Gray of Delaware and Richard F. Pettigrew of South Dakota, vehemently opposed the treaty of annexation.[12]

The *New York Evening Post* and *The Nation* tenaciously attacked the policy of annexation. Lacking any detailed information about the specifics that sparked the revolution in Hawaii, both newspapers deemphasized the threat of European interference in Hawaiian affairs or the need for unilateral action by the United States. *The Nation* and The *Evening Post*'s fundamental argument centered on the fact that the United States would not materially benefit from the policy of annexation. Because of the predominant position of the United States in the Pacific islands, annexation would not increase U.S. trade with Hawaii but would create collateral political problems associated with defending the islands.[13]

By the time Grover Cleveland started his second term in office, annexation had not been accomplished and the President withdrew the treaty from the Senate. Although Cleveland favored a formal reciprocity

1. In the Shadow of the Past

agreement based on an economic bond, he informed Carl Schurz that "we ought to stop and look and think" when it came to annexation. The President's Secretary of State, Walter Q. Gresham, straightforwardly announced that the administration "would not favor principles and policy looking toward the acquisition of territory." Simultaneously, Cleveland appointed James Blount to investigate and report on the perplexing situation in the islands.[14] Before Blount's report became finalized in November of 1893, Carl Schurz wrote a compendious tract that clarified the anti-annexationists' position. Using the historical backdrop of the origins of manifest destiny, Schurz called into question the wisdom of the so-called "new manifest destiny" whose supporters' objectives was "not merely the incorporation in the United States of territory contiguous to our borders, but rather the acquisition of such territory, far and near, as may be useful, in enlarging our commercial advantages, and in securing to our navy facilities desirable for the operations of a great naval power."[15]

Schurz described three "demonstrative" groups that made up the bulk of the supporters for the new manifest destiny. The first group consisted of those individuals who hoped to establish and expand U.S. business in foreign lands. The second group included those who displayed "ardent" nationalism and believed U.S. foreign policy was out of touch with reality; they desired the United States to assume a more aggressive role in international affairs by taking advantage of every opportunity for territorial expansion. The final group represented those individuals who believed maritime power was the cornerstone of an aggressive foreign policy.[16]

Concerning these three groups, Schurz believed that the last two deserved special cogitation. The merchants, he noted, included individuals with highly regarded reputations whose interests should be protected by the U.S. government. What Schurz objected to involved the businessmen's demand to incorporate in a republic where they did business simply because they wanted to protect their economic interests. Schurz did not specifically mention any groups, but did caution that such a policy, camouflaged as patriotism, "should be received with due distrust," because "there would be no end of wild attempts to drive the American people into the most reckless enterprises."[17]

The group that Schurz felt the nation should take seriously among the expansionists were those whose "patriotic ardor" caused them to reiterate the need for a program of "indiscriminate territorial" expansion as a part of the plan to make the United States "the greatest of the great powers of the world." In essence, Schurz abhorred the jingoists more than the businessmen. The patriotic argument represented an emotional appendage that impeded a rational discussion concerning the issue of annexation:

> To see his country powerful and respected among the nations of the earth, and to secure to it all those advantages to which its character and position entitle it, is the natural desire of every American. In this sentiment we are all agreed. There may, however, be grave differences of opinion as to how this end can be most surely, most completely, and most worthily attained. This is not a mere matter of patriotic sentiment, but a problem of statesmanship.[18]

Schurz then analyzed the arguments against annexation of a tropical area that contained a large foreign population. His major concern centered on the collateral and direct effect that annexation would have on the political and social life of the United States. Under the Constitution of the United States, such territory would sooner or later be admitted into the union. For example, Canada would present no structural problems because the people shared similar characteristics with Americans, but Hawaii, with its high number of Asians, could not easily be assimilated into the political and social culture of the United States.[19]

On his discourse concerning the question of manifest destiny, Schurz included the Caribbean because expansionists during the nineteenth century argued that the United States should expand into that region. He commented that the underlying motives for annexation in this area involved a deep desire to gain commercial advantage: "to get possession of the resources ... and by exploiting them to increase our wealth." Inaugurating such a policy would only be the beginning, because "there will always be more commercial advantages to be gained, the riches of more countries to be made our own, more strategic positions to be occupied to protect those already in our hands. Not only a taste for more, but interest, the logic of the situation would push us on and on."[20]

Schurz believed America's long interest in the annexation of Cuba represented a perfect example of this process. If the United States annexed Cuba, "Puerto Rico will come as a matter of course with Cuba." Next, the United States would want Santo Domingo, followed by Haiti and Jamaica, until the entire Caribbean had come under U.S. control.

Schurz noted that each acquisition in the Caribbean would lead the way for the nation to demand additional territory.[21]

Although Schurz admitted that such a vision shone brightly for America's future, he contended that such illusions would lead to the weakening of U.S. democracy. Tropical locations seemed incompatible with democratic institutions. They required the local tropical population's acquiescence to the will and authority of the majority, because "such a state of society is not found where, on the one hand, nature is so bountiful as to render steady work unnecessary, and where, on the other hand, the climatic conditions are such as to render steady work especially burdensome and distasteful."[22]

Where some inhabitants understood the basic concept of democratic principles, the majority of them did not accept the democratic theory "and experience shows that the tropics will indeed breed individual men who know how to govern others, but not great masses of men who know how to govern themselves."[23] Schurz did not believe that this failure to develop a progressive civilization in the tropics had anything to do with inherent racial inferiority of the indigenous population.

Schurz believed that the harsh elements of the tropics played a defining role in limiting the advancement of civilization. The Anglo-Saxons had succeeded as a colonizer by transplanting democratic institutions into temperate zones, but their success had come under the umbrella of conqueror. There was not "a single instance of the growth of a strong Anglo-Saxon democracy in tropical latitudes.... The reason is that the tropical climate is not congenial to men of Germanic blood."[24]

If Americans became upset over the immigration of Slavs, Italians, and groups that came from southern Europe, they would become more so over the groups of people who migrated from the tropical regions into the United States. The annexation of Hawaii would raise the ire of Americans to new levels because the overwhelming majority of the inhabitants were Asians and other non–White groups: "[Hawaii] would be bound to this republic not by community of interest or national sentiment, but simply by the protection against foreign aggression given to it and by certain commercial advantages."[25]

Schurz concluded his analysis by discussing naval arguments. For years, a number of Americans had advocated the expansion of the nation's naval forces to make them "second to none." The debate took a more energetic turn when Captain Alfred Thayer Mahan published his famous work, *The Influence of Sea Power Upon History*, in 1890. Mahan argued that any great nation must have a large naval force, with distant naval bases, not only during a time of war but also to facilitate and protect the expansion of commerce.[26]

Schurz understood very well the cornerstone of Mahan's central thesis. He knew that the strength of Mahan's argument involved combining the naval expansionist argument with the commercial one so that Hawaii would represent the "key" to "something vast and important in that region." Would "the possession of such an outlying domain two thousand miles away ... really be an element of strength to us against other powers?" Schurz believed it would not.[27]

He looked at America's present global position to come to this conclusion. The United States, during this time, held strategic advantages over other world powers in geographic isolation and plentiful natural resources. "In other words, in our compact continental stronghold we are virtually unassailable ... [but] a vulnerable point will be presented by the Hawaiian Islands if we annex them, as well as by any outlying possession of importance." Schurz did not support the argument that the nation needed a large naval force to protect its commerce:

> Our commerce is not threatened by anybody or anything, unless it be the competition of other nations and the errors of our own commercial policy; and against these influences warships avail nothing. Nor do we need any warships to obtain favorable commercial arrangements with other nations. Our position of power under existing circumstances is such that no foreign nation will, at the risk of a quarrel with us, deny our commerce any accommodation we can reasonable lay claim to.[28]

In conclusion, Schurz made it a point to attack minor but still important arguments. He considered it ridiculous to say that if the United States refused to take Hawaii under its control, she would later be unable to object to another global power taking control of the island. "Having shown ourselves unselfish, we shall have all the greater moral authority in objecting to an arrangement which would be obnoxious to our interests." In Schurz's opinion, the United States could not take control of every country with internal turmoil simply because it would benefit the future of that country.[29]

The article that Schurz wrote for Harper's *New Monthly Magazine* is significant for a number of reasons. First of all, it represented a rational statement of the anti-expansionist position by a man who was considered the spiritual leader of the opponents of empire. Secondly, Schurz's views expressed in the article are used by scholars to highlight the complex challenges of overseas expansionism. In the work *From Colony to Superpower*, George Herring used Schurz's views to show the depth of American opposition to the incorporation of territory that contained a large non–White population.[30]

In November of 1893, James Blount gave a finalized version of the circumstances surrounding the Hawaiian crisis to President Grover Cleveland. The report implied that U.S. Minister John L. Stevens, as well as U.S. Marines, were deeply embroiled in the revolution. After analyzing the intricate details of the reports, Cleveland decided to let Congress tackle the question of annexation. Lacking much needed political support from the executive branch, the possibility of annexation became less certain and public debate on the issue subsided.[31]

In 1894, *The Forum* commissioned historian James Schouler to prepare an unbiased review of the Hawaiian crisis. Relying exclusively on information contained in Blount's official report, Schouler acknowledged that officials of the U.S. government had a hand in the Hawaiian revolution. He did not lay the blame entirely on the Harrison Administration, but suggested that the president was misled by representatives of the U.S. government in Hawaii and by Hawaiian annexationists. The most interesting point is that no one, neither in Congress nor in Harrison's administration, ever polled the Hawaiians about their feelings concerning annexation.[32]

Schouler believed that the United States could proceed along two paths: helping the Queen regain her throne or mediate the differences between the monarchists and the revolutionists to settle the dispute without violence. The provisional government, he noted, had announced it would stay in power only until annexation. This declaration indicated that the United States had to intervene in the crisis. What shape or form that U.S. intervention would take remained unclear.[33]

The Cleveland Administration did not achieve a resolution to the Hawaiian question. Although the Hawaiian issue never became a central political issue during the 1896 presidential elections, McKinley's electoral victory revived hopes of annexation and the newly elected president submitted a proposed annexation treaty to Congress for legislative consideration. This moved raised the ire of the anti-annexationists. High-

Resistance to the Spanish-American and Philippine Wars

lighting the fact that McKinley had distanced himself from any jingoistic policy, *The Nation* stated, "The country has found out, what students of McKinley's career were well persuaded of, that his faculty of adopting his words to his hearers does not at all imply that he has a will of his own against Congress or against the masterful leaders of his party."[34]

The anti-annexationists attempted to use the expansionists' argument against them. Consequently, even as *The Nation* expressed anti-expansionist sentiments, the paper did support the notion of U.S. control of the Hawaiian Islands. It criticized the President on the grounds that the Republican platform during the election firmly supported complete control of Hawaii and such a goal could come about without the need for annexation. *The Nation* fully supported Admiral Mahan's theory that Hawaii was a "key" component in the Pacific, and vital to U.S. security as a coaling station.[35]

The Nation also pointed out other elements of Hawaii's strategic position that were important to the welfare of the United States. The paper noted that Hawaii was a key to the Pacific. Even if the United States annexed the island, it had little value without a security "lock" in the form of naval forces. *The Nation* went on to express grave doubts about the country providing this lock. It editorialized, "we shall never have such a navy" because "Congress sometimes wants a navy and sometimes it does not."[36]

The Nation further stated that Mahan also knew the consequences of the U.S. people's revulsion about militarism: "There is, however, one caution to be given.... Military positions, fortified posts, by land or by sea, however strong or admirably situated, do not by themselves confer control. People often say that such an island or harbor will give control of such a body of water. This is utter, deplorable, ruinous mistake."[37]

Mahan expressed strong sentiments about the topic of annexing Hawaii. He believed annexing Hawaii might prove detrimental to U.S. security unless the annexation became the axis of a policy centered on territorial expansion and military development. Mahan's military tunnel vision provided opponents with ammunition for a much stronger argument because at the time an anti-militarist theme ran through the mind-set of most Americans.[38]

Attempting to reassure Americans that England did not want to control either Hawaii or Cuba, the British writer James Bryce added his voice to the debate on annexing Hawaii. Similar to the sentiments expressed by U.S. anti-annexationists, Bryce stated it would be useless for the United States to expand her naval forces just to protect the islands. He pointed out that his views varied greatly from the views associated with "my valued friends in the United States, such as Captain Mahan and Mr. Roosevelt." Annexation "would be a source not of strength but of weakness."[39]

The English author gave a detailed list of the many pitfalls that could occur if such a path was taken. The first problem, noted Bryce, centered on the logical question: who should govern the islands? He did not accept the notion that the values and principles associated with well-established U.S. institutions could be transposed into the cultural infrastructure of Hawaii or Cuba; nor could either ever become a state or a territory. The United States already has "a great and splendid mission," not built on the dogma of territorial expansion, but built on showing the world how prosperous she had become in "building" the American nation "up between the oceans."[40]

In spite of the Republican's campaign promises concerning Hawaii and the president's suggestion that his statements on the Hawaii issue were tentative at best, McKinley's submission of the annexation treaty to Congress soon after his election indicates that other matters were on the horizon, such as the mounting Japanese pressure on the Hawaiian Republic and the fear that a reciprocity agreement with Hawaii would not become finalized. Once the treaty of annexation reached Senate chambers, the President did not fight forcibly for the measure when it became apparent that the bill would not garner the required two-thirds majority for ratification. However, by submitting the treaty, the President did help salvage the reciprocity measure.

The senatorial discussions concerning the treaty of annexation began in January 1898. As the debates moved into February, the annexationist-backed measure lacked the four votes necessary for ratification. A month later the annexationists changed their political tactics. To circumvent the strategy of U.S. sugar interests and their cohorts, the Senate Foreign Relations Committee, following a precedent set during the annexation of Texas in 1845, reported a measure for annexation by joint resolution rather than by treaty.

Admiral Dewey's victory at Manila Bay on May 1 brought the Hawaiian annexation issue to the forefront. The House of Representatives introduced a new measure for annexation and the debate took on new life. The most entertaining speeches concerning the issue of annexation came in an exchange between Congressman James Sulzer of New York and Representative John F. Shafroth of Colorado. Sulzer opened the debate by announcing that the United States "should not only annex Hawaii" but also "should enter upon a policy of acquiring colonial possessions ... [and] should extend its power and dominion across the Pacific and forever hold possessions of the Philippine Islands."[41]

A reply from Shafroth came in the form of a speech entitled "An Imperial Policy Dangerous to the Republic." Although most of the anti-expansionists believed that the American people shared their aversion to an expansionist policy, the representative from Colorado did not. Shafroth thought a large percentage of the House of Representatives agreed with Sulzer's sentiments concerning Hawaiian annexation. A sample of his colleague's opinion on the issue of Hawaiian acquisition made Shafroth aware of the rising tide of jingoism, and he criticized this growing martial spirit in the harshest of terms:

> If any person six weeks ago had suggested that the policy which the government has pursued with such magnificent results for the last one hundred years should be reversed and that we should extend our dominion to the Asiatic Continent, he would have been regarded as a dreamer unfit to represent the people of any State in the Union. And yet the excitement of the war has produced such a desire for conquest that the Representatives set no limit or bound to the extent of our dominion.[42]

Shafroth made a point of contrasting the annexation of Hawaii with the acquisition of the Philippines. He considered the Philippines a prime example of imperialism and noted that "the question has gone beyond that of merely annexing Hawaii and is now whether we will adopt an imperial policy for this Republic." In most aspects, Shafroth's speech mirrored the same arguments that Carl Schurz had previously supported. These arguments centered on the belief that annexation, as a political concept, violated such U.S. traditions as the Monroe Doctrine and were commercially impractical.[43]

Attempting to block the annexation of Hawaii translated into an exercise in futility. The imaginations of the nation's political leadership and of the American people were aligned by the victories in the Spanish-American War. Following House Speaker Thomas B. Reed's acquiescence to the forces of expansionism, the debate on annexation was accomplished by a joint congressional resolution during the first week of July 1898. Even as the Hawaiian question came to a close, other issues in global affairs caught the attention of the American people.

The Venezuelan boundary dispute of the mid–1890s represents another example of U.S. imperialism. The dispute between Great Britain and Venezuela over the boundary of British Guiana started in 1841 and raged into the 1890s. Venezuela had broken off diplomatic relations with Great Britain when England, in 1887, increased the boundary line of their claim and simultaneously refused America's offer of arbitration. The issue resurfaced when Venezuela hired William I. Scruggs as a lobbyist on their behalf. The former U.S. foreign minister wrote a booklet entitled *British Aggressions in Venezuela, or the Monroe Doctrine on Trial*. Scruggs distributed the political tract to key congressional leaders, governors, and business leaders throughout the country. Through perceptive promotion, Scruggs persuaded a number of congressional leaders that action should be taken on the Venezuelan dispute.[44]

Scruggs also reached out to other influential leaders. He wrote to President Cleveland and the Secretary of State strongly suggesting they take a look into the matter. His lobbying finally worked. Scruggs received an invitation to meet the President and convinced Cleveland that he could use his influence to settle the issue. The President included the issue in his December 1894 annual message and in 1895 congressional leaders passed a measure calling for the issue to be arbitrated, but no action came as a result of this suggestion.

Congressional pressure made the Cleveland Administration aware that the United States had a duty, prescribed by the Monroe Doctrine, to submit the dispute to arbitration. On July 20, 1895, Secretary of State Richard Olney sent a communiqué to British officials demanding they submit the matter to arbitration. While the British delayed their reply to Olney's request, the news of the note became public in September. Just prior to Cleveland's December 1895 annual message, the British responded to the note.[45]

The Cleveland Administration received a reply from the British Prime Minister that it did not like at all. Lord Salisbury, speaking in a tone similar to that of a patient parent to a mischievous child, proceeded to recapitulate England's long-established position that Venezuela's boundary claims were without merit and that to allow an arbitration board decide the fate of British Guiana residents would be wrong. Salisbury further commented on the irrelevance of the Monroe Doctrine

Resistance to the Spanish-American and Philippine Wars

to the issues at hand and denied that England sought to impose her imperial will on Venezuela.[46]

If the Prime Minister's response bluntly stated England's position, Cleveland's reply also straightforwardly stated the U.S. position. The President sent Congress a reply that included a summary of America's previous position concerning the Venezuela issue and pointed out that the United States had its own interests in mind rather than the interests of Venezuela. Cleveland declared that British refusal to submit the matter to arbitration represented a serious threat to the Monroe Doctrine:

> If a European power, by an extension of its boundaries, takes possession of the territory of one of our neighboring Republics against its will and in derogation of its rights, it is difficult to see why to that extent such European power does not thereby attempt to extend its system of Government to that portion of this Continent which is thus taken. This is the precise action which President Monroe declared to be "dangerous to our peace and safety," and it can make no difference whether the European system is extended by an advance of frontier or otherwise.[47]

With this in mind, the United States must ensure that the boundary claims in dispute are equitably settled. The President informed Congress that he had decided to establish a commission to "make the necessary investigation," and requested that Congress initiate "adequate appropriation" to fund the commission. Cleveland further stated that when the commission finalized its report,

> It will in my opinion be the duty of the United States to resist by every means in its power as a willful aggression upon its rights and interests the appropriation by Great Britain of any lands or the exercise of governmental jurisdiction over any territory which ... we have determined of right belongs to Venezuela ... in making these recommendations I am fully alive to the responsibility incurred, and keenly realize all the consequences that may follow.
>
> I am, nevertheless, firm in my conviction that ... there is no calamity which a great nation can invite which equals that which follows from a supine submission to wrong and injustice, and the consequent loss of national self-respect and honor, beneath which are shielded and defended a people's safety and greatness.[48]

When Congress applauded Cleveland's message by passing a $100,000 appropriation bill for a boundary commission to arbitrate the dispute, the entire nation caught the fever of patriotic militarism. Talk of war with Great Britain filled all corners of U.S. society.

However, rational decisions worked for a peaceful solution to the problems. England did not want to go to war and welcomed arbitration of the dispute. These feelings were facilitated by German Kaiser Wilhelm's note to Paul Kruger congratulating the leader of the Transvaal Boers in South Africa on the surrender of Jameson's raiders. British hostile public opinion against the United States greatly diminished after the Germans' complimentary actions. Shortly before Cleveland left the presidency, England and Venezuela (aided by the United States) signed a binding agreement that was submitted to arbitration and finalized in 1899.

Many leading anti-imperialists opposed the antagonistic tone of Cleveland's 1895 annual message. The publisher of *The Anti-Imperialist*, Edward Atkinson, informed a reporter that the President's message was ludicrous. Andrew Carnegie believed just the opposite. He "was especially pleased, since the crisis provided him with the perfect opportunity to publicize two of his pet projects; the disposal by Great Britain of her colonial empire in the western hemisphere, and international arbitration." Refractory Democrats, allied with leading anti-imperialists such as John P. Altgeld and Clarence Darrow, outspokenly opposed Cleveland's actions.

The voices of the anti-imperialists' nemeses, the expansionists, was mixed. Theodore Roosevelt and Henry Cabot Lodge approved of Cleveland's actions while Whitelaw Reid, the publisher of the *New York Tribune*, viewed the president's actions as "an awful calamity not only for our country, but for all Anglo-Saxon communities."[49] An organized effort to formally protest Cleveland's policy seemed impossible because of the relatively short time period in which the President announced the policy. The most far-reaching opposition to the President's policy came from the ardent anti-imperialist George Boutwell in the form of a book entitled *The Venezuelan Question and the Monroe Doctrine*. Boutwell became apprehensive about "the war spirit ... aroused, especially among the youth of the country," and the calls to increase America's naval forces. "In these days war should not be undertaken except for the preservation of national honor, or the protection of public or private rights—rights not merely menaced, but actually invaded."[50] "The Monroe Doctrine," he asserted, "is not for the benefit, primarily, of Venezuela, or of any other American State, but first for the protection of the United States, and then in aid of the acceptance and maintenance of republican institutions on this continent."[51]

Boutwell clearly believed England did not want to undermine the Venezuelan government, nor did she wish to make unsubstantiated claims for additional territory. "If this were true, the controversy between Venezuela and Great Britain would not be touched by the application of the Monroe Doctrine ... [for] Great Britain does not aim at the establishment of a new government." He did not believe that the principle contained in the tenets of the Monroe Doctrine were "a law for anybody. It is a declaration of a public policy by and for the United States. We should not allow other nations to interpret it."[52]

Boutwell noticed that America's neighbors to the south seem to look toward the United States for safety and security. "These expectations are the first fruits of an erroneous policy—a policy which will be burdensome to us and injurious to the States that shall rely upon us for protection. The Monroe Doctrine is for us, and not for them." He inquired whether Great Britain violated the sovereign rights of the United States, and if she did, then why did the United States not seek a remedy to the injury? Boutwell criticized the establishment of an arbitration commission to settle the controversy and felt the British and Venezuelans should settle the disputes themselves.[53]

Even as events surrounding the Venezuelan–British controversy unfolded, a wave of new developments associated with the 1890s would soon reach its crest. In late February 1895, news reached the shores of the United States that an insurrection in Cuba against Spanish rule was imminent. Although the destruction of property and loss of life rose to horrendous levels in Cuba, the Cleveland Administration attempted to stay neutral until the President's term in office had expired. During his final two years in office, Cleveland opposed all efforts to annex Cuba to the United States. Cleveland had reasons to resist the efforts to annex the island. He believed that intervening in the Cuba crisis would eventually lead to war and would satisfy the ambitions of the jingoists. As the fighting raged, pressure from U.S. public opinion to recognize the Cuban rebels increased dramatically. Right up to his last day in office, Cleveland believed that the granting of autonomy to the rebels by Spain would end the hostilities.

The election of William McKinley to the presidency in 1896 did not indicate that this policy would change. Hoping for a peaceful resolution and alluding to the necessity of eventual intervention on the part of the United States, McKinley stated, "I cannot speak of forcible annexation, for that cannot be thought of, [in accordance with] our code of morality that would be criminal aggression." The newly elected President did believe that purchasing Cuba from Spain was a viable option. However, by the fall of 1897 the McKinley Administration had inched slowly toward U.S. intervention in the Cuban crisis.[54]

Since McKinley accepted the challenge of a war that ultimately involved the question of empire, the debate over imperialist and anti-imperialist policies became something of a model. This 360 degree circle calls for a comparative analysis between the arguments of the early 1890s and the arguments of the late 1890s. The anti-imperialist arguments used during the early years of the 1890s was vastly different from those used in 1898. Carl Schurz's arguments against Santo Domingo's annexation in the early 1870s had similarities to those he used to criticize the annexation of Hawaii in 1893, but the totality of these arguments did not contain the policy of self-determination as a virtuous concept.

The Boston anti-imperialist conference held on June 15, 1898, believed that gaining the Philippine Islands by military acquisition desecrated America's firm belief in the right of a people to self-determine their destiny. When the challengers talked about the imperialist policies of the United States, they meant a foreign policy that involved the military appropriation of overseas territory and repudiation of the concept of self-determination. The issue of self-determination did not define the case of Santo Domingo during the early 1870s, or during the Samoa episode of the late 1880s. The concept did not come up during the Hawaiian crisis of the early 1890s.[55]

The charge that military troops became instrumental in nefarious activities on Hawaii did come up. Both the Blount report and like-minded writers such as James Schouler, believed that Queen Liliuokalani had been overthrown with the help of U.S. troops. However, these charges were qualified because the blame for these activities lay with the individual actions of U.S. Minister Stevens and did not have authorization to act from the President. What is more surprising is that Harrison's belief that the Hawaiian people should determine the issue of annexation did not receive a more thorough consideration.

The notion that the revolutionary provisional government did not represent the people was disqualified by its continued existence and the prosperity that reached its zenith in Hawaii in 1893. *The Nation* hinted at this when it stated:

Resistance to the Spanish-American and Philippine Wars

> The original conspiracy to overthrow the Hawaiian government and steal away the islands in which the American Minister participated does not now enter directly into the question. With the slate sponged clean because of the continued existence of the Provisional Government Mr. McKinley has undertaken to write on it a policy entirely new for the United States.[56]

Although the anti-imperialist meeting in Boston highly criticized the acquisition of the Philippine Islands, it did not denounce Hawaiian annexation. Such influential individuals as Andrew Carnegie believed that the cases between Hawaii and the Philippines differed on certain points. In comparing and contrasting the two, Carnegie contended that Hawaiian annexation did not represent a "measure of aggression" on the part of the United States, but only a "defensive" move aimed at strengthening U.S. security. The island had a small population, "so that in the case of Hawaii national aspirations are not to be encountered."[57]

The obscurity of the self-determination concept likely had something to do with its lack of application to the foreign policies of the United States. At its inception, the term self-determination related more to individuals than it did to global policies of nations. As an international legal concept, a precise definition is elusive. Such scholars as James Crawford have noted that "no one is very clear as to what it [the right to self-determination] means."[58]

That the moral implications of the self-determination argument never surfaced in the discussions during policy disagreements over Hawaii or Venezuela indicates that the term "imperialism" did not describe or apply to the concept of U.S. foreign expansionism. The word, as a policy concept, did not come into use until it was used to characterize Napoleon III's strategic policies. Senator Thomas F. Bayard of Delaware used the expression in a debate over the wisdom of annexing Santo Domingo in the early 1870s. Bayard suggested that annexing the territory would "embark the United States upon the vast and trackless sea of imperialism."[59]

However, in the following years the term rarely appeared in the U.S. political vernacular and when it did, its connection to U.S. foreign policy was minimal. One of the few references to the term came in an article by A. H. Thompson in 1879. Thompson used the term to criticize British repression of the Zulus, associating the term with the concept of a stronger nation subduing a weaker nation. He wanted to familiarize Americans with "what is now well known as 'imperialism,' that is to say

1. In the Shadow of the Past

a system under which the people are to submit to a course of secret policy directed to objects of conquest and aggrandizement few of them would approve."[60]

The use of imperialist policies by such European powers as Great Britain between the 1860s and 1890s illustrates that the word was not employed during this time period. Despite Napoleon III's lack of success and passion for debate, support for imperialist policies in Great Britain gained momentum up to the time of the Boer War. Disenchantment with the policy came from other countries following Jameson's raid on the Transvaal Boers during the first week of January 1896. The critical poem "The White Man's Burden" by Rudyard Kipling and many other articles published under the title *Imperialism: A Study* by British economist John A. Hobson helped facilitate the public's negative perceptions about imperialism.[61]

In the United States, the term imperialism was never advocated as a popular policy before the 1890s. Born of revolution against the tranny of colonialism, the United States had long harbored anti-militaristic sentiments. A strong Anglophobic streak in the U.S. fiber may have accounted for their failure to embrace imperialistic policies. A small group of expansionists in the 1890s, a list that included Theodore Roosevelt, were fervently Anglophiles who accepted imperialistic policies around the same time that these policies reached their zenith in Great Britain.

The anti-expansionists, although well aware of the European political term imperialism, did not use the expression during the policy debates over U.S. foreign relations during the late nineteenth century. One likely reason that anti-expansionists did not employ the word is that the term conjured up the image of conquest and aggrandizement of a foreign nation, as in the case with the Philippine Islands. Labeling such leading anti-expansionists as Carl Schurz as anti-imperialist prior to 1898 was somewhat of a misnomer. In essence, anti-expansionists did not use the term imperialism to characterize their arguments as they related to foreign policy issues, but rather saw U.S. foreign policy as one of over-expansionism, not imperialism.

In 1898, one U.S. leading anti-expansionist, William Graham Sumner, did not believe that the United States had undertaken a foreign policy of imperialism. Sumner, a nationally renowned Yale sociologist writing at the height of the 1896 presidential campaign and during a time when the Cuban crisis and the Hawaiian issue became pressing foreign-policy topics, expressed his views concerning U.S. overseas territorial expansion. His argument ran counter to those who believed "that gain of territory is gain of wealth and strength" for the United States. Given reasonable opportunities for commercial success, acquiring new territory would improve the financial status of only a certain segment in society, but in its totality, it meant the government would eventually be exposed to additional collateral expenses. Sumner noted that such colonial activities could only succeed in the old mercantile system of the past: "In the old colonial system, States conquered territories and founded colonies, in order to shut them out against all other States and to exploit them or principles of subjugation and monopoly. It is only under this system that the jurisdiction is anything but a burden."[62]

The influential Yale sociologist noted that the pressing foreign policy issues at hand proved his case in point. The annexation of Hawaii, for instance, would only become a financial burden to the United States because the country already enjoyed commercial advantages by trading with Hawaii without the additional responsibility of annexation. Contrary to the prevailing views of other anti-expansionists, Sumner opposed the annexation of Canada. He noted that foreign policy related to Canada and Hawaii should be the same: free trade but no annexation.[63]

Sumner considered the situation with Cuba an entirely different case. "Here is a case" he wrote, "which illustrates the fact that States are often forced to extend their jurisdiction whether they want to do so or not." If Cuba should fall into lawlessness and chaos, the world would "look to the United States to take jurisdiction and establish order and security there." Sumner remorsefully concluded that "it would, however, be a great burden, and possibly a fatal calamity to us."[64]

The most important point of Sumner's examination of the U.S. political system involves it relationship to the foreign policy of expansionism. The U.S. system of government did not contain a constitutional mechanism to govern colonies, and any effort to add Cuba to the U.S. domain would cause lasting problems. He emphatically noted that "this confederated State of ours was never planned for indefinite expansion or for an imperial policy." The most significant aspect of Sumner's analysis is that he distinguished between the policy of expansion, such as Hawaiian annexation, and the imperial policy of aggrandizement, such

1. In the Shadow of the Past

as the acquisition of Cuba. In the U.S. system, he observed, "it is the limitation of this scheme of the State that the State created under it must forego a great number of the grand functions of European States; especially that it contains no methods and apparatus of conquest, extension, domination, and imperialism."[65]

On its surface, Sumner's arguments revealed that as of 1896, the United States, while embroiled in a heated discussion concerning the benefits and drawbacks of annexing Hawaii, had not engaged in an imperial foreign policy or imperialism. Imperialism, by definition, involves expansion into territories with the goal of conquering and subjugating foreign populations. Finally, in view of the chorus of voices that rose against imperialism in 1898, Sumner's ominous predictions in 1896 concerning the future of the United States, should such a policy be embraced, is worth noting:

> Any extension will open questions; not close them. Any extension will not make us more secure where we are, but will force us to take new measures to secure new acquisitions. The preservation of acquisitions will force us to reorganize our internal resources, so as to make it possible to prepare them in advance and to mobilize them with promptitude. This will lessen liberty and require discipline. It will increase taxation and all the pressure of government. It will divert the national energy from the provision of self-maintenance and comfort for the people, and will necessitate stronger and more elaborate governmental machinery. All of this will be disastrous to republican institutions and to democracy. Moreover all extension puts a new strain on the internal cohesion of the preexisting mass, threatening a new cleavage within.

Surprisingly, very little attention is devoted to U.S. imperialism in the context of foreign policy by scholars of the late nineteenth century. In the work *The Transformation of American Foreign Relations*, Charles Campbell asserted that imperialism was used to facilitate and cultivate international markets for U.S. businesses. In George Herring's book *From Colony to Superpower*, imperialism was portrayed as a deliberate policy designed to help the United States take her place among global powers. The monograph *Empire by Default* by Ivan Musicant said virtually nothing on imperialism as an instrument that shaped the United States during the 1890s.[66]

During the years prior to 1898, the men who defined themselves as anti-expansionists did not use the expressions imperialism and expansionism interchangeably to describe U.S. foreign policy. To the U.S. anti-expansionists of the late nineteenth century, imperialism or imperialistic foreign policy moves involved conquest and a denial of self-government by a foreign power. Territorial expansion involved the beneficial developments that a global power brings to foreign inhabitants. Recognizing the inherent differences between the two concepts, anti-expansionists did not characterize foreign policy events prior to 1898 as imperialism, but promptly applied it with reference to the acquisition of the Philippines because they felt it conflicted with U.S. foreign policy actions of the past.

The difference between expansionism and imperialism was revealed in a letter written by a fierce opponent of the United States establishing an overseas empire. In a letter to Bourke Cochran, Canadian Goldwin Smith stated, "expansionism means extension without breach of continuity or loss of moral unity. Louisiana was expansion. Canada would be expansion. The Philippines clearly are not." Smith added that his fellow anti-imperialists allowed their opponents "an undue advantage in permitting them to use the term 'expansion' as they do."[67]

The responses of Fiske, Strong, Burgess, and Mahan to the acquisition of the Philippines were not incompatible with their beliefs. Their reactions indicated they favored some type of U.S. foreign expansion, but rejected imperialism in its totality; in other words they rejected the subjugating element associated with annexation by military force. In the case of Fiske and Strong, conquest related to the hearts and minds of men rather than physical domination. Strong expressed serious doubts about annexing the Philippines, whereas Fiske, a virulent anti-imperialist, outright opposed the taking of the Philippines. Burgess and Mahan felt that acquiring the Philippines was an unwise move.[68]

The attitude of these influential men toward the acquisition of the Philippines suggests that the label of imperialist did not apply to them. Their responses to the annexation of the Philippines indicated they differentiated between the abstract meaning of the term imperialism and the concept of expansionism. In the cases of Burgess and Fiske, their opposition to taking the Philippines is the most ironic. Each supported some type of U.S. foreign expansion that in many ways reflected the military subjugation associated with the imperialism they so despised.

Failure to properly establish a clear distinction between the concepts of expansionism and imperialism had a far-reaching negative impact on the message of caution that the anti-expansionists and anti-

1. In the Shadow of the Past

war groups attempted to implant in the minds of the American people. An ingrained awareness of U.S. exceptionalism coupled with the expansionist ideology of a sense of manifest destiny and security for the future of the nation, gave the American people a moral imperative that no amount of anti-expansionist propaganda could negate.

2

A Group of Many Shades: The Anti-Imperialists

At the end of the late nineteenth century, the United States was confronted with a major decision. Would it remain true to its isolationist heritage or become a colonial empire? The McKinley Administration chose the route of colonialism that eventually started a national debate between those who advocated expansionism and the anti-imperialists. Composed of a diverse group of Americans, the anti-imperialist main concerns centered on issues of national identity, economics, and race. Some believed expansionism violated the very principles upon which the nation rested. Some in the anti-imperialist camp suggested that such ideas as individual rights, political liberty, and the basic dignity of humanity formed the core of American principles and that imperialism repudiated these founding values. Others opposed U.S. expansionism because they believed that it would ultimately result in the unchecked powers of the national government. Many feared colonialism would trigger a confrontation with major European powers. Concern over economic protectionism became a mainstay in the belief system of anti-imperialists. The overtone of racism peppered the argument of others. Questions arose about the status of those who were compelled to live under the U.S. flag; causing many anti-imperialists to wonder if they would eventually become citizens.

Anti-imperialist sentiment was found in various groups. Some were Mugwumps whereas others were loyal Republicans. The Democratic Party, which opposed McKinley's foreign policies, had many in their ranks that shared these sentiments. The academic community had anti-imperialists in prominent places, with many becoming members of the Anti-imperialist League. The world of arts and letters were well represented in the anti-imperialist ranks, as well as labor unions and the

African American community. For the most part, the Christian community supported the foreign policy of the McKinley Administration but some in this group believed that expansionism was contradictory to the religious tenets upon which this country was founded. The political left also believed that McKinley's foreign policy was faulty, averring it would ultimately destroy the capitalist system of the United States.

Anti-Imperialism and the Mugwumps

The term Mugwump originated from individuals in the Republican Party that showed strong independence when it came to party loyalty. Some scholars argue that the political tradition of Mugwumpism started during the presidential election of 1884, though the origin of this tradition goes back to the antebellum period.[1] Strongly independent and unhappy with the course of the Republican Party when it came to the Grant Administration's malfeasance and the Reconstruction of the South, many Mugwumps left the ranks of the Republican Party. A deeply held ideological conviction rather than blind loyalty to the tenets of the Republican Party were key characteristics of Mugwumpism. A contemporary riddle likens the Mugwumps' constant changing of positions to a ferry that continually goes from one side to another.[2] Scholars commented that this independence led to opposition to McKinley's foreign policy and caused a division in Republican ranks.[3]

Carl Schurz was one of the most influential members of the Mugwumps. Born in Prussia in 1829 and eventually settling in Wisconsin in 1852, Schurz had been a major player in the Prussian Revolution of 1848.[4] After coming to the United States, Schurz became a leading figure in politics and became popular in the German community.[5] During the U.S. Civil War, Schurz served as the nation's Minister to Spain, then as a Brigadier General. After the Civil War ended, Schurz served the country in the U.S. Senate and as Secretary of the Interior under Rutherford B. Hayes.

Schurz had always displayed a certain degree of dissatisfaction with the expansionist foreign policies of the McKinley Administration. Over the years, he had gained a well-deserved reputation for opposing U.S. expansionism. While serving in Congress, Schurz opposed the Grant Administration's proposal to purchase Santo Domingo.[6] Schurz asserted that that the political apparatus of the U.S. system was not suited to take on the burden of colonialism. Schurz maintained that the United States should not (1) rule over other people without popular consent, because this was antithetical to the founding principles of the United States, (2) annex foreign territory without the consent of the population of that territory with the option of Statehood as a possibility, (3) assimilate tropical people into the U.S. body politic, and (4) annex such a foreign population.[7]

On its face, Schurz's objections to U.S. expansionism had a racist undercurrent that he made abundantly clear:

> Fancy ten or twelve tropical States added to the Southern States we already possess; fancy The Senators and Representatives of ten or twelve million of tropical people, people of the Latin race mixed with Indian and African blood; ... sitting in the Halls of Congress.... Throwing the weight of their passions and prejudices into the scale of the destinies of this Republic.[8]

Although Schurz was a loyal supporter of McKinley in the presidential election of 1896, he was disappointed when the United States became a signatory to the treaty that annexed the Hawaiian Islands in 1897. Two weeks after the convention was signed, Schurz chided McKinley for signing the treaty. Despite his personal feeling about expansionism, Schurz supported the U.S. venture during the Spanish-American War.[9] But later, Schurz vigorously opposed the subsequent decision to annex Puerto Rico and the Philippine Islands. In an August 1898 speech before the Civic Federation, Schurz asserted that annexing Puerto Rico was just the beginning. Soon, he argued, all the Caribbean, along with the Philippine Islands, will be a part of the U.S. empire. These moves would be detrimental to the United States because they would result in political corruption and foreign entanglements that bear similarities to the historical problems that plagued European nations.[10] In a *Century Magazine* article, Schurz argued that U.S. expansionists policies would cause great harm to the United States by allowing inferior people to descend on American society.[11] In a letter to the President, Schurz argued that Cuba should be organized into a semiautonomous confederation and that Puerto Rico and Cuba should be joined with Santo Domingo and Haiti to create a Confederation of the Antilles. Such a move would be compatible with U.S. founding principles and provide stability in the Caribbean region. This move would also satisfy the imperialists because one of their main arguments for annexation was the stability of the region.

Schurz did not oppose overseas U.S. investment and believed that U.S. businesses could own property abroad; however, developing irretrievable ties might undermine the power of the United States.[12] To the proponents of annexation who argued the economic and military advantages of adding the Philippines to the U.S. empire, Schurz suggested that an international conference be organized to ensure the independence and neutrality of the Philippine Islands. The surge of the Filipino insurrection compelled Schurz to rethink his position regarding independence of the Philippines and call for U.S. protection of the islands.[13] Although the independence of the Philippines would have been a more agreeable option, U.S. status as a protectorate would ensure the protection of the economic and security well-being of the United States.

Needless to say, Schurz's efforts were not successful. Although his efforts failed, the totality of Schurz's contribution as an anti-imperialist was influential. Having come to the United States from a troubled country, Schurz had good reason to attempt to stop the United States from descending down the same road as his homeland. As an influential founding member of Anti-Imperialist League, Schurz methodically organized the movement into a potential force of power. That the anti-imperialists did not stop the tide of U.S. expansion was not a reflection on the part that Schurz played in the movement.

Another influential anti-imperialist, Charles Francis Adams, brought a native touch to the anti-imperialist movement. A descendent of one of the founding families, Adams was educated at Harvard and served the Union Army in the capacity of commanding officer of a Black cavalry unit.[14] After the Civil War ended, he worked for the Union Pacific Railroad as its president. Although his views did not completely align with the standard views of Mugwumpism, he did support civil service and electoral reform, along with lowering the tariff.[15]

Like so many of his upper-class contemporaries, Adams was a staunch supporter of elitism. That is, he supported the notion that the government should be led by those who are best qualified by education and birth. Adams noted, "I believe in the equality of men before the law; but social equality, whether for man or child, is altogether another thing. My father, at least, didn't force that on us."[16] Adams' venture with Union Pacific Railroad did not work out and he lost his position with the company.[17]

To the extent that Adams' own personal failure in the private sector influenced his opposition to the war between Spain and the United States is pure conjuncture. But he did believe that war would negatively affect the United States economically. Ideologically, Adams believed that annexation of Cuba was inconsistent with the principles on which the nation was founded.[18]

Throughout the war between Spain and the United States, Adams remained quiet, but after the hostilities ended he began to speak out against the imperialist policies of the McKinley Administration. In a December 1898, speech at the Historical Society of Lexington, Massachusetts, Adams initiated a barrage against the imperialist direction of McKinley's foreign policy.[19] He scolded the core members of the Anti-Imperialist League (specifically Schurz) for naiveté and left the group. Adams felt that annexing the Philippines may have been a mistake; nevertheless nothing could be done about it. He even suggested a plan that would ensure the islands would be governed in an efficient manner. Still strongly opposing expansionism, Adams thought the nation could make do with the decision to annex the Philippines. In an article, Adams noted that "in this life we can rarely have our own way; but when the course of events has made it clear ... that our own way is no longer open, it is the course of wisdom to do what is in our power to eliminate ... the evil."[20] The leadership of the Anti-imperialist League was very upset by Adams' seeming abandonment of the tenets of the movement.[21]

Despite the defeat that was on the horizon, Adams once again renewed his fight against expansionism during the presidential election of 1900. He believed the expansionist policies of the McKinley Administration would cause great harm for America's future and began to seek ways to defeat McKinley's reelection efforts. As much as he was disenchanted with the policies of the Republican Party, Adams felt very little difference existed between the Republicans and Democrats when it came to expansionism. Although the anti-imperialists wanted immediate withdrawal from the Philippines, the Democrats supported limited occupation of the Philippine Islands. In essence, the Democrats' position lay between the ideology of the anti-imperialists and the Republicans.[22] For Adams, the Democratic position did not go far enough.

The selection of William Jennings Bryan as the Democratic nominee further complicated the matter. Adams believed that Bryan was personally corrupt and politically bankrupt, with interests aligned with other political operatives of the same stripe. He was particularly upset that many anti-imperialists considered voting for Bryan. As a solution to the coming problem, Adams suggested that the anti-imperialists work to secure the House of Representatives for the Democrats and the presidency for the Republicans. Adams believed that such a division would result in a reactionary Congress that would block any new imperialist policies the McKinley Administration tried to implement. However, Adams realized that such a plan was far-fetched and worked with Schurz to try to create a new party. In January of 1900, the Liberty Congress, comprised of a small group of anti-imperialists, met to discuss the chances a third-party would have in the coming election. Upon further review, many influential members of the Anti-Imperialist League either voted for the Democrats, McKinley, or not at all.

For the Democrats and the Republicans, the political topic of imperialism took a back seat to more pressing domestic economic concerns during the presidential election of 1900. McKinley's "full dinner pail" campaign slogan appealed more to the U.S. public than the directions of foreign policy. The feasibility of anti-imperialists stopping McKinley's reelection to the presidency is open to debate. But what is certain is that the internal division in the ranks of anti-imperialists impeded their efforts to further their cause.

Edwin Lawrence Godkin was another influential figure who opposed the expansionist leanings of U.S. foreign policy. Born on October 2, 1831, in Moyne, Ireland, Godkin migrated to the United States in November of 1856.[23] As a correspondent for the *London Daily News*, he covered the Crimean War. During his early thirties, Godkin became the editor of *The Nation*, a periodical that not only covered influential economic and political views, but also caught the attention of students and intellectuals.[24]

Godkin's acidic editorial commentary earned him more than a few adversaries among his readership. Theodore Roosevelt disliked him and called him "a malignant liar" and disloyal to the United States.[25] Godkin was patriotic, but he also was a Mugwump. His loyalty to the Republican Party was based on how similar Party values were to U.S. core principles. Godkin was upset about the rampant corruption that plague Washington at the end of the Civil War because he felt that the end of the war would usher in a new era, dedicated to the principles of the Constitution. By the late 1860s, however, Godkin believed that U.S. democracy was in its final stage of existence.[26]

Godkin, for years, had opposed U.S. foreign policy decisions. He was not comfortable with the Alaskan purchase in the 1860s and opposed U.S. efforts to infiltrate Latin America during the early years of the 1800s.[27] Godkin's opposition to U.S. foreign policy stemmed from his distrust of foreigners. Always critical of U.S. immigration policy, Godkin believed that commercial and political ventures with foreign peoples would be a dangerous road. The immigrants that had descended on the U.S. landscape in the mid- and late-nineteenth century had compromised the moral fiber of the nation. Incorporating millions of additional foreign peoples into the fabric of U.S. society would prove disastrous for the future of the United States. Godkin's views on immigration are ironic since he himself migrated to the United States from Ireland. Therefore, racism seems to be the mechanism that drove his views on immigration. In Godkin's mind, adding such foreigners as Latin Americans and Filipinos to U.S. society would depreciate the culture of the nation and facilitate its decline.[28]

Godkin attacked the role of yellow journalism in fanning the flames of war with Spain. In an effort to counter these efforts of yellow journalism, Godkin published an appraisal of public sentiment in the *North American Review*. He wrote that Americans were "a reckless people" who could be swayed by the yellow press.[29] At odds with the views of the majority of Americans and most anti-imperialists, Godkin praised Spain's efforts to keep control over Cuba. He felt that the founders' vision of U.S. democracy had taken a back seat to the avarice and corruption that facilitated an expansionist foreign policy. Using expansionist policies as a cover, Godkin believed the fundamental principles on which the nation was founded would be betrayed by covetous and unscrupulous men. Godkin continued to air this opinion on this issue. In *The Nation*, he lamented "the old American republic is in a bad way."[30] In essence, although Godkin believed in the core principles that made the United States great, in the end his confidence in the United States and her future waned.

A longtime friend of Godkin, Charles Eliot Norton, was also an influential member of the anti-imperialist movement. Born in 1827 in Cambridge, Massachusetts, Norton was a renowned traveler and spent extensive time studying and living in Europe.[31] While the North and South engaged in a war for the future of the United States, Norton worked abroad as a propagandist for the Union cause. He wrote and sometimes acted as editor of the *Atlantic Monthly*, *North American Review*, and *The Nation*.[32]

Like Godkin, the wholesale political malfeasance and immorality that followed the end of the Civil War embittered Norton. Godkin and Norton believed the growth of a market-focused economy, coupled with populism, facilitated the decline of the nation. In an 1884 speech at Cambridge University, Norton stated, "We are raising in the level of civilization in America the classes which have therefore been depressed. The natural result of that work is that the higher levels … the peaks of civilization sink, and the mass is raised to unexplained elevation."[33] Norton believed the Spanish-American War would be the end of U.S. exceptionalism.[34] He stated, "I have been too much of an idealist about America.... Never has a nation had such an opportunity, she was the hope of the world. Never again will any nation have her chance to raise the standard of civilization."[35]

Norton argued that expansion of the U.S. empire would create burdens that had plagued the great civilizations of the past.[36] The United States would lose her founding virtues and the government would mirror the tyrannical rule of European nations. Although he expressed grave doubts about U.S. prospects, Norton still held hope that the nation could change its direction. As he noted to a friend in a letter, "Humpty Dumpty had a great fall. Well we are defeated for the time; but the war is not ended, and we are enlisted for the war."[37]

Edward Atkinson was one of the alluring members of the anti-imperialist movement. Born near Boston in 1827, Atkinson never received a classical education; yet he believed he was knowledgeable on a wide range of subjects.[38] The *Boston Evening Transcript* wrote that Atkinson liked to spread himself "over fields too broad for a score of good men to cover effectively."[39] He considered himself a successful inventor and developed the Aladdin Oven, which he hoped would instruct wives on "how to get more appetizing food from the shinbone of beef … than workmen commonly get from the finer and better cuts when they can afford to buy them."[40] Atkinson was a proponent of hard currency and tariff reduction, and strongly opposed the Interstate Commerce Act of 1887. His contemporaries considered him the quintessential Mugwump.[41]

Although Atkinson opposed military expansionism, he actively supported using U.S. economic might to gain economic advantage on the world stage. He vigorously fought against the annexation of the Hawaiian Islands because he believed Hawaiians incapable of self-government.[42] What would be beneficial to the United States was access to global markets. Atkinson denounced the imperialist policies of Spain and Germany, but ironically admired the international policies of Britain. In the *North American Review* he wrote, "What a boon it would be to the world if systems corresponding to English law, English administration, and the English regard for personal rights could be extended over the continent of South America."[43] He believed that following the established British colonial system would be more beneficial to the world than creating an entirely new system.

As an influential member of the American Peace Society, Atkinson objected to the United States going to war with Spain. He tirelessly worked to get religious leaders across the United States to convince congressional leaders to avoid war with Spain. Atkinson advised the president to seek a peaceful means to the Cuban crisis and to organize an international conference to examine and find a solution to the Hawaii issue. He believed that Spain and the United States should attend this international conference, which would likely help ease the tension between the two nations. Atkinson also reiterated his belief that war would obstruct economic progress on the global stage. In a speech before the Atlanta Chamber of Commerce, he asserted that a peaceful world facilitated the growth of the U.S. cotton industry, which would open markets for cotton goods in such countries as China. Atkinson further noted, "Commerce is today the prime factor in the world's work. Its development is the chief object of nations." The destructive nature of war only impedes this economic progress.

When the United States finally went to war with Spain, Atkinson tried to find what little good he could in a bad situation. He reconciled himself to the notion that the United States would take control of Puerto Rico and Cuba while also annexing Hawaii.[44] Concerning the Philippine Islands, his attitude was guarded and mixed. He did not favor annexing the island but did believe that the Philippines would become a valuable trading route for the United States. Access to coaling stations, coupled with unlimited access to Chinese markets and ensuring political stability in the region, would aid the United States in foreign affairs.[45] Later, he amended this thought and revealed his true feelings about imperialism and the future of the United States. It a letter to the Textile Excelsior, he wrote that if the United States followed the path of imperialism, it would "bring itself down to the level of the semi-barbarous states and nations" of Europe.[46] Atkinson believed that the annexation of Cuba could not be supported in light of the Teller Amendment.

Atkinson developed a plan in which an international coalition would be formed to revitalize the Philippine Islands by maintaining peace. To secure support for this plan, nations would be allowed to have open trade in the Philippines.[47] He cautioned that U.S. occupation forces in the Philippines would encounter heavy casualties. In a letter to the president, Atkinson noted that "thousands of American boys, killed by dread Asian varieties of venereal disease, would never return to their families: additional thousands would return crippled and deformed, useless and disgraced for life."[48] Within a week of communicating his feeling to McKinley, Atkinson helped establish the Anti-Imperialist League and initiated a writing campaign in an attempt to compel the country's leaders to oppose ratification of the treaty with Spain.[49] Atkinson readership targets included congressional and religious leaders, along with state political leaders.[50]

After the treaty passed, Atkinson turned his campaign to rouse anti-imperialist sentiment toward the American people, warning them about the inherent personal and material cost of occupying the Philippines. He predicted that the U.S. military would fail in its mission and attempted to dissuade young men from across the nation from enlisting if it meant service in the Philippines.[51] Atkinson's propaganda campaign became so outlandish that the Anti-Imperialist League that he helped created sought to distance itself from him.[52] He contacted the War Department asking for the names and addresses of a half-million military personnel with the intent of causing discontent among service members. When the War Department ignored his request, Atkinson sent letters to high-ranking military officers, members of the U.S. Philippine Commission, as well as to Admiral Dewey and a journalist for *Harper's Weekly*.[53] Fed up with Atkinson's antics, Attorney General John W. Griggs threatened to bring charges of sedition against Atkinson. Charles Emory Smith, the Postmaster General, ordered that Atkinson's propaganda tracts be removed from the mail bags destined for Manila.[54] The government's campaign against Atkinson resulted in national celebrity.[55]

In reality, Atkinson's economic beliefs evolved over time. Previously, he had asserted that foreign markets were a viable outlet for U.S. surplus agricultural and manufactured goods. By 1900 he argued that domestic economic growth takes precedence over expanding economic opportunities in foreign markets.[56] Atkinson noted that the United States would derive very little economic benefit from the Philippines because of the minimal purchasing power of the Filipino population.[57] He believed the United States could only benefit economically if she traded only with nations such as Britain and other European nations, rather than having commercial intercourse with "primitive" people.[58] By the time of his death in 1905, the empire Atkinson had envisioned had developed into the empire he had fought so long against.

The Republicans and Anti-Imperialism

Although a great number of anti-imperialists embraced the doctrine of Mugwumpism, others remained loyal to the Republican Party. George F. Hoar was a prime representative of those who remained loyal to Republican values. A native of Massachusetts, Hoar attended Harvard University and established a law practice in Worcester. A proponent of abolition, he chaired the Free Soil Committee of Worcester County in the early 1850s. Hoar supported civil rights legislation and began his political career in earnest when he was elected to the U.S. House of Representatives. He helped pass the Sherman Anti-Trust Act of 1890 and supported civil service reform. Although Hoar favored protectionist tariffs, he also supported the doctrine of bimetallism.[59]

Disdainful of Mugwumps, Hoar believed that the principles espoused by the Republican Party far outweighed any deficiencies display by the GOP. He believed that individualism in public service was misguided and party loyalty took precedence over independence in the political system.[60] Interestingly, Hoar, while president of the American Historical Association, scolded historians for their lack of patriotism while he conducted a campaign against the Republican Party over the nation's imperialist policies.[61]

Although Hoar was not a pacifist in the truest sense of the word, he did oppose Grant's efforts to annex Santo Domingo in 1870.[62] He opposed the Chinese Exclusion Act of 1882 because he believed that the United States used undue influence to get China to sign the convention.[63] When it came to the issue of Hawaiian annexation, Hoar alternated

2. A Group of Many Shades

between supporting the treaty and opposing it. Although he eventually supported annexation, he had reservations about the imperialist direction of the country in foreign affairs.[64]

During the Cleveland Administration, Hoar had recommended that the United States remain neutral in the dispute between Spain and the Cuban rebels. He passively voted for war in 1898 and was disappointed when the details of the 1898 Treaty of Paris was revealed. Hoar thought U.S. interests did not go beyond the Hawaii Islands and any chance that the United States may add the Philippines to its empire was repugnant to him. To Hoar, expansionism represented the same threat to the U.S. future as the Civil War.[65] He firmly believed that the McKinley Administration wanted to purchase the sovereignty of a foreign people and argued against the annexation of the Philippines with the same vigor and language he had used against slavery. He cautioned Americans that they ran the danger of applying the slave-master model of the antebellum United States to the newly liberated peoples of the Philippines.[66] While highlighting the point that during a period of adjustment, the peoples of Cuba, the Philippines, and Puerto Rico would encounter problems in self-government. Hoar believed that this period would be of short duration. He believed the United States should be as disinterested in the internal affairs of the Philippines as she had been in the affairs of Latin America.[67]

When the United States ratified the Treaty of Paris in 1899, Hoar was one of two Republicans who voted no for ratification. To appease Hoar and his anti-imperialist colleagues, Senator McEnery proposed legislation that included a provision to eventually grant the Philippines their independence.[68] Hoar proposed an amendment that would require informed consent for the Filipinos before any government could be established in the region. This proposal, along with another one offered by Augustus O. Bacon of Georgia, was rejected. Eventually, McEnery's proposal passed with Hoar becoming the only Republican to vote no on the measure.

After the Treaty of Paris had been ratified, Hoar continued his fight against U.S. occupation of the Philippine Islands. In a speech before the Massachusetts Club of Boston, he compared the repression of the Filipinos to the lynching of Negroes in the U.S. south. He firmly believed the Filipinos could maintain self-government and drew wrath from his opponents concerning his attempts to sabotage U.S. efforts to suppress the Philippine insurrection. This did not stop Hoar from criticizing Supreme Court rulings in the "insular cases" that legalized U.S. imperial policy.[69]

Throughout this episode, Hoar remained loyal to the Republican Party. He believed his actions were justified because his fight was in defense of the principles on which the party was founded. In his autobiography he noted, "When I hear my party ... crushing out this people in their efforts to establish a Republic.... I feel very much as if I had learned that my father ... had been a slave trader."[70] When Hoar died in 1904, the United States still controlled the Philippines and would do so for the foreseeable future.

George S. Boutwell was another influential Republican with anti-imperialist sentiments. A sort of a political renaissance man who, at various times, served as Massachusetts governor, internal revenue commissioner, congressional member, and Secretary of the Treasury, Boutwell's political beliefs depended on the issues at hand.[71] He thought the purchase of Alaska was asinine and opposed the Grant Administration's proposed annexation of Santo Domingo. Boutwell thought it would be better for the future of the United States if the nation's interests remained inside its continental borders. The one exception to this principle was his support for reciprocal trade relations with Hawaii. Having served as counsel for the government of Hawaii in the 1880s, Boutwell believed the islands were vital to the security of U.S. trade in the Pacific. However, he still opposed the annexation of the islands in 1897.[72] Boutwell argued that annexation would involve absorbing a "Mongolian State in the Union."[73] He opposed the Treaty of Paris provisions that granted Spanish territory to the United States and became president of the Anti-imperialist League in 1898.[74]

Boutwell did not base his anti-imperialism on any sympathy for those who were compelled to be governed by the United States; instead he asserted that colonialism in general hurt the United States. His advanced age (eighty years old) and seeming refusal to compromise his positions made it easy for imperialists in the McKinley camp to disregard him. The most significant aspect of Boutwell's protests was that they highlighted the internal division that occurred in the Republican Party over the issue of expansionism. Many Republicans supported McKinley's decision to annex Spain's former colonies, but many saw U.S. colonialism as a dangerous charter into unfamiliar waters.

2. A Group of Many Shades

Two well-known Republicans, Senator John Sherman of Ohio and Representative Thomas Brackett Reed of Maine, also supported anti-imperialism. Sherman was a career politician who had served in the House of Representatives and in the Senate. He served in the Hayes Administration as Secretary of the Treasury and later under McKinley as the Secretary of State.[75]

Similar to Boutwell, Sherman fought against the Grant Administration's plan to annex Santo Domingo, but supported U.S. acquisition of Hawaii.[76] He also supported the liberation of Cuba even if it meant going to war with Spain. What Sherman did not support was the annexation of Cuba to the United States.[77] Later, the issue of Sherman's mental state was to blame for his changing positions during this period. Because of his mental instability, President McKinley was compelled to divide Sherman's Secretary of State duties among his subordinates.[78]

Although he was in prime position to exert influence during the months when the Treaty of Paris was being negotiated, Sherman's mental incapacities prevented him from influencing the fight between imperialists and the anti-imperialists. The case of Sherman highlights one of the glaring problems that the anti-imperialist movement encountered: many of the movement's leaders were men who were long past their prime and did not have the stamina to engage in a long drawn-out fight over the issue of colonialism.

Sherman's anti-imperialist colleague, Thomas Reed, served in the House of Representatives and as Speaker of the House during what turned out to be a distinguished political career. Known as "Czar Reed" among congressional members, Reed was loyal to the Republican Party but could be critical of its leadership. He once referred to Benjamin Harrison as "the ice man" and to President McKinley as the "Emperor of Expediency."[79] His mouth and the sobriquets that Reed bestowed upon individuals earned him the enmity of many.

Militarism was never a practical idea for Reed. He opposed the way President Cleveland handled the 1895 Venezuelan issue, believing that the mishandling of the dispute would lead the United States into war with Britain. Reed expressed his opinions about colonialism in an October 1896 article for the *North American Review*. In this article, Reed argued for the virtues of remaining a republic and abstaining from implementing policies that would lead to the nation becoming an empire.[80] As war with Spain drew closer, Reed used his influence to impede a naval build-up and in the spring of 1898, attempted to block passage of legislation that would incorporate Hawaii into the nation. Reed only gave up on both issues when it became evident that the number of those opposing him was too large to overcome.[81]

For Reed, the annexation of the Philippines represented a huge mistake and facilitated his dislike of William McKinley. He often expressed his displeasure with U.S. Philippine policy in such disparaging terms as "we have about 10,000,000 Malays at $2.00 a head unpicked, and nobody knows what it will cost to pick them."[82] In response to alleged atrocities committed by U.S. military forces in the Philippines, Reed proposed legislation that pardoned Spanish General Valeriano Weyler's crimes against the Cuban people.[83] Reed's opposition generally came in the form of reactionary responses to McKinley's proposed legislation in Congress. However, even after achieving some success in obstructing the administration's policy, Reed knew he could do very little to stop the tidal wave of imperialism.

Boutwell, Sherman, and Reed were the embodiment of the old guard of the Republican Party. They opposed imperialism because they believed a colonial policy betrayed the Party's core values and that an expansionist course would inevitably lead to confrontation with other global colonial powers.

Anti-Imperialism and the Democratic Party

The Democratic Party provided the most vigorous anti-imperialist opposition to the foreign expansionist policy of the McKinley Administration. The Democrats were not natural heirs to anti-imperialism and a large division emerged on the issue of the administration's colonial policy in the Democratic ranks during the Congressional and local elections of 1898. For the Democrats outside of the northeast, the elections seem to mirror the election of 1896. Although free silver remained the central issue at the Democratic National Convention, the gold Democrats of the northeast had a strong voice in the proceedings.

Although imperialism was not the central issue, the Democrats did not ignore it and were far from being united by it. Senator John Morgan of Alabama asked, "What shall we do with the conquered islands?"[84] The Senator did not know the exact answer to this question, but annex-

2. A Group of Many Shades

ation of Puerto Rico and the Philippines was a real possibility and the maintenance of military bases in the regions under any conditions was a certainty.[85] William Jennings Bryan gave his opinion in a speech at Omaha, Nebraska in which he benignly opposed the administration's colonial policy.[86]

Although the Democratic rank and file had a lively response to the issue of anti-imperialism, the leadership of the party did not particularly recognize the issue. Some Democratic congressional leaders, specifically those who had opposed the annexation of Hawaii, opposed the concept of further annexation. However, this sentiment was not representative of the majority of the Democratic congressional delegation. The *Democratic Campaign* Book for the 1898 Congressional elections did not have a stand on the issue of annexation or anti-imperialism.[87] The issue of free silver was the central focus of the campaign book. The secondary issue of the campaign book involved the role Democrats would play in pushing for recognition of Cuban belligerency and that "democracy has indeed taken a noble share in the expulsion of Spain from the western hemisphere."[88] The central motive put forth by the Democrats for supporting the war with Spain involved the liberation of Cuba. Despite loud support for Cuba's liberation before hostilities started, after the war ended, Democrats did not show much concern regarding Cuba's independence.

The platforms adopted at the state conventions of the Democratic Party reflected no widespread concern about anti-imperialism. The *Literary Digest* surveyed the political platforms of the Democrats in twenty-five of the forty-six states. Twelve of the twenty-five platforms did not indicate a stand on the annexation of the Philippines, five were opposed to the annexation of the Philippines, and two platforms supported using the Philippines as coaling stations.[89] The remaining platforms either generally condemned imperialism or favored retaining a portion of the Philippines.[90]

Newspapers that promoted the Democratic Party and its agenda were outspoken on anti-imperialism, but this group had no consensus on this subject. The Democratic newspapers of the Midwest displayed anti-imperialist sentiments, but in the South and East were divided over the issue of anti-expansionism.[91] The *New York Times* supported annexation of Cuba and the Philippines.[92] The editor of the *Louisville Courier Journal*, a Democratic power-broker named Henry Watterson, believed that abandoning the territories the United States acquired through war "would be a wanton and cowardly abandonment of obligations and opportunities literally heaven sent."[93] William Randolph Hearst proposed a five-point expansionist plan in the *New York Journal*, which he called a national program; not an "imperial policy." When the campaign ended, Hearst criticized the Democratic leadership because they "brought on the war, refused to share the honors of war" or ensure the lasting benefits of war.[94]

The Democrats in New York, who wanted to make the free silver issue of 1896 a thing of the past, did not adopt anti-imperialism as a political platform. Instead, they focused their attention on local issues. The Chair of the State Convention anticipated that "by November 8 the voters will get over the war flurry, and be in a right mood to pass on practical instead of sentimental issues."[95] In New York City, as the campaign was drawing to a close, the subject of anti-imperialism was not the central focus of discussions on national issues. The New York State boss, David Hill, spoke in Brooklyn about an array of national questions pertinent to the Democratic Party's ideology. He used this opportunity to gather the same support for imperialism and annexation that the Democrats of the past had given, out of fear that the Republicans would use these issues as political capital. Hill noted, "American valor has easily triumphed on both sea and land" and that the American flag that flies over conquered territory should never be lowered.[96]

Although the issue of expansionism was a major subject among the American people during the campaign of 1898, it is hard to say that imperialism was a principle political issue among the Democrats. In general, the Democrats were consumed with the issue of free silver except in the Northeast where they wanted the fight over this 1896 issue completely forgotten. The various segments of the Democratic Party were divided when the issue of annexation was broached. Although anti-imperialist proponents more or less dominated the Party, specifically among the rank and file, the Party's leadership did not have imperialist sentiment. However, the issue was not considered politically important enough to make it a central point for dispute.

Between the years 1898 and 1900, imperialism evolved into a political issue that caught the attention of the U.S. public and national leaders. The leadership of the Republican Party pushed the nation toward an imperialist policy. The Philippines were acquired almost as an afterthought, Puerto Rico was annexed, and these majestic achievements associated with an imperialist policy were glorified in newspapers across the nation.

The anti-imperialists confronted these majestic achievements with their own brand of reasonable arguments. The central point of these arguments was a genuine concern about whether the United States would embark on a policy of colonialism and whether the status quo would endure. These arguments grew out of the fear of a growing monopolistic power that would threaten the very existence of the nation. The failure of the anti-imperialist movement to confront and come to terms with the role of monopoly and its own limitations in annexing foreign countries limited the influence of the anti-imperialist movement.

The Democrats did little more than the anti-imperialists in approaching the issue of expansionism. Bryan, who had presidential aspirations, supported the signing of the Treaty of Paris whereby the United States acquired the Philippines. Bryan made his first public utterances on this policy in December of 1898 in the South where there was a strong pro-imperialist sentiment among the population.[97] Bryan asserted that the treaty should be ratified so neither the Spanish nor any other foreign nation could gain control over the Islands. He thought the United States would be in a better position to settle the issue of independence. Privately, Bryan supported the notion of independence for the Philippines, but in the public sphere he was equivocal of this issue and came out against coercive annexation.[98]

Bryan, ever the political opportunist, changed his position on the question of imperialism as a political issue two months before the Senate would debate the ratification of the Treaty of Paris. At first, he addressed this issue with caution because he likely wanted to pacify southern Democrats. Whatever the reason, it is certain that Bryan wanted to steer clear of the issue of imperialism as a major plank for the Democratic Party at this time. Andrew Carnegie, an influential anti-imperialist Republican, informed Bryan that "there are hundreds in our party who will vote for the American as against the Imperialist. I am one of these." Carnegie also made it a point to encourage Bryan to drop the silver issue, but Bryan balked at this suggestion, rejected a coalition with the anti-imperialist Republicans, and felt that imperialism as an political issue would not last long.

But, for reasons unknown, Bryan changed his position on January 12, 1899, deciding to make expansionism a political issue that would be solved by the American people. Although Bryan took a more active stand against imperialist policies, he still supported the treaty that annexed the Philippines. He felt that supporting the treaty was a good way to get the issue out in public for the American people to decide.[99] In essence, Bryan would make the issue of expansionism a political issue. His actions could only be considered a calculated political move in preparation for the 1900 presidential election.

Many reasons have been given concerning Bryan's motives for urging ratification of the treaty. Bryan stated he did so because it was a moral choice that should be in the hands of the American people, who would more likely grant independence to the Filipinos than the European powers. To achieve this goal, he supported the Bacon Amendment to the ratification of the Treaty of Paris.[100] The amendment would have granted independence to the Philippines but failed to pass when it came to a Senatorial vote. The Senators who left written records on this issue asserted that Bryan's chief reason for supporting the treaty lay in that he wanted to make a campaign issue of imperialism.[101] He also took this course of action because it would put him in good standing with pro-imperialist elements of the Democratic Party. Regardless, Bryan, by his own admission, had the next election in mind and did not want the Democratic Party to take the blame for extending the war to see the Filipinos gain their independence. It is very difficult to ascertain Bryan's stand on the issue. The inconsistency of Bryan's position was epitomized by Senator Pettigrew: "He [Bryan] was seeking political capital and he was willing to take it where he found it, without paying too much attention to nice questions of principles." When the treaty passed, Bryan started his campaign with an anti-imperialist plank that would gather him support from those who had opposed him on the silver issue and in those areas that held a negative view of anti-imperialism.

With the U.S. Army's continued suppression of the military forces of the Philippines, the Anti-Imperialist League grew in strength. Surrogate leagues were established in dozens of cities and literally hundreds of thousands of leaflets and pamphlets flooded the nation. At the start of this propaganda campaign, the approach was a nonpartisan one. In Chicago, April 30, 1899, the first major anti-imperialist meeting, members gave speeches that castigated the McKinley Administration for

2. A Group of Many Shades

pushing a foreign policy of occupation and annexation, but no political plan was proposed to counter McKinley's action.[102] By October, enough local Leagues had sprung up that they bolstered the strength of the national American Anti-Imperialist League. A conference was held in Chicago on the 17th and 18th of October with 10,000 people in attendance. This was very much in line with the plans of the New England Anti-Imperialist leadership who wanted to initiate a campaign that would defeat McKinley and the congressmen who supported his policies. The anti-imperialists were willing to support a candidate in the 1900 elections who would only support the independence of the Philippines. Despite a more favorable view of the Democrats by the anti-imperialists, there definitely was not a willingness to enter into a political coalition with them.[103]

Some of the more passionate anti-imperialists looked toward the third-party option to advance their agenda. On January 6, 1900, the New Anti-Imperialist League held a meeting to discuss a third-party candidate to compel the Republicans and Democrats to come out in favor of independence for the Philippines and against tropical colonialism. These anti-imperialists included Andrew Carnegie, Senator Pettigrew, and other influential members of the anti-imperialist movement. Carnegie agreed to provide the financial backing, but pressure from the leadership of the steel trust forced him to reconsider his involvement in the plan. Despite this unfortunate development, the Anti-Imperiasts held their own convention, organized under the banner of the Liberty Party.

The feasibility of a third party was recognized, and the anti-imperialist Gold Democrats asserted that the Democratic Party was the vehicle through which the annexation of the Philippines should be opposed. They believe that the issue of anti-imperialism could be used to deflect attention from the issue of free silver. Bourke Cochran, a leading Gold Democrat from New York, argued in a speech in Boston in February of 1900, "It is self-evident that opposition to imperialism must be made through the Democratic Party." He promised that anti-imperialism and the silver issue would be two separate political issues.[104] Later on, virtually all of Cleveland's cabinet members supported Bryan's stand on the issue of anti-imperialism, although Cleveland remained adamant that Bryan would have to renounce the free silver issue if he wanted the former president's support.[105]

Some elements of the independent Republicans expressed third-

Resistance to the Spanish-American and Philippine Wars

party sentiments even after Bryan got the Democratic nomination. They were uneasy with Bryan's views on free silver and felt that Bryan was a vacillating ally against expansionism. However, influential members in the anti-imperialist movement, notably George S. Boutwell and Erving Winslow, were against the notion of a third-party candidacy and all talk about such a run eventually died out. Some of these men backed Bryan while others supported President McKinley.[106] The strong anti-imperialist sentiment in the Democratic Party neutralized another chances for an anti-imperialist third-party run.

The Democratic nomination was Bryan's to lose before the convention assembled. He had worked tirelessly to mend the divisions in the party that resulted from the campaign of 1896. Bryan, who already had the support of the majority of Populists and free silver elements, moved to gain the support of the New York Democrats and the Gold Democrats. The Gold Democrats were comfortable supporting the issue of anti-imperialism, whereas the New York Democrats would support any issue as long as it was not the free silver issue. William Randolph Hearst, a devoted imperialist, who had designs on the vice-presidency, seems to have been instrumental in bringing the New York Democrats around to Bryan.[107] In return for Hearst's help, Bryan installed Hearst as the president of the National Association of Democratic Clubs. James Creelman, a Hearst agent, informed Bryan before the convention: "I have also cabled to England to get signed statements from England princes and nobleman thanking McKinley for his friendly attitude to Great Britain during the Boer War. These I will publish in contrast to expressions of sympathy for the Boers."[108]

This correspondence was part of a plan to woo German American voters for Bryan. To supplement this plan, Hearst created another paper in Chicago, *The American*, to help bolster support for Bryan in the Midwest. Creelman suggested this move was the brainchild of Bryan and other Democratic leaders. As the campaign progressed, Hearst's *New York Journal* showed signs of anti-imperialism, but after Bryan's defeat in November, asserted that free silver and the abandonment of the Philippines became two main issues "needlessly dragged into the campaign."

While preparing for the 1900 Democratic Party's convention, Bryan also fortified the strategy of highlighting anti-expansionism while minimizing the issue of free silver. The question of anti-imperialism was a preeminent position that pleased the Gold element of the Democratic Party. Bryan instructed the leadership of the platform committee to strengthen the anti-imperialist plank in the platform. Simultaneously, Bryan made an adamant stand against the inclusion of the free silver question in the plank. This represented his campaign strategy in Populist areas.

The convention itself painstakingly made anti-imperialism a featured issue of the gathering. The keynote speaker, the Governor of Colorado, mocked the Republican Party's expansionist policy: "We have kept faith with Puerto Rico by substituting the sugar baron for the Castillian duke, and confirmed the Philippine estimate of the white man by prolonging the Spaniard's method of colonial government in those islands of the far-off seas."[109] The convention high point came when Senator Tillman of South Carolina read the Democratic Party's platform to the attendees. Tillman stated,

> The importance of other questions now pending before the American people is in no wise diminished and the Democratic Party takes no backward steps from its position on them, but the burning issue of imperialism growing out of the Spanish war involves the very existence of the Republic and the destruction of our free institutions. We regard it as the paramount issue of the campaign.[110]

As if on cue, a large U.S. flag was displayed behind the speaker's podium. Written on the unfurled flag were the slogans "The Constitution and the Flag, one and inseparable, now and forever" and "A Republic can have no colonies." An eighteen-minute demonstration followed, which was the final coronation to the event.[111]

The seminal moment and point of reconciliation of the Convention came when former Senator David Bennett Hill, leader of the upstate New York Democrats and former candidate of the Gold Democrats at the 1896 Convention, endorsed the nomination of Bryan. Although he explicitly stated he would not support the 16 to 1 silver plank, Hill, who had previously given a rousing imperialist speech in Brooklyn during the 1898 campaign, also clarified his position on the question of anti-imperialism: "It is believed that some portion of this country the 'paramount issue' is going to carry, and carry strongly."[112] The emphasis placed on the question of expansionism can be seen in the *Democratic Campaign Textbook*. Of more than 340 pages in the book, 140 pages were devoted to the section "The Republic or Empire," whereas only fifty pages were dedicated to the free silver question.¹¹³ The money question was only given third place after the trust issue.

The position taken regarding the independence of the Philippines was not as straightforward as many anti-imperialists would have liked, because the proposals would have left room for the maintenance and control of the Philippines by the United States for an extended period of time. The proposal was "first, a stable form of government; second, independence; and third, protection from outside interference such as has been given for nearly a century to the republic of Central and South America."¹¹⁴ No specific guidelines were given to determine exactly when a stable government had been put in place.

The campaign speeches of Bryan began to make imperialism a central political issue. But his acceptance speech at the Populists' Convention in Topeka on August 23rd indicated that in the areas of their strength, he was going to wage yet another battle over free silver and added (seemingly as an afterthought) that imperialism was also an important issue.¹¹⁵ In New York, Bryan highlighted the question of trusts and imperialism, completely ignoring the silver issue. After Bryan lost the election, he regarded the importance of anti-imperialism as a political impediment that "discouraged many of our active voters" and had caused him to lose vital support in the South, Midwest, and West while giving him substantial gains in the Northwest.¹¹⁶

Concurrently, the anti-imperialists at the Liberty Party Convention gave their support to Bryan. They overlooked questions associated with domestic policies, encouraged members to support congressional candidates who opposed imperialism, and advised "direct support for Mr. Bryan as the most effective means of crushing imperialism."¹¹⁷ A fight over the creation of a third party had developed, but the vast majority supported the policy that was adopted.¹¹⁸ The Democrats recognized this support and used it as propaganda in political leaflets and pamphlets.¹¹⁹

McKinley defeated Bryan by a larger margin than he had in 1896, but because of the confusion surrounding the questions of anti-imperialism, free silver, and trusts, it is hard to discern whether the election was a referendum for colonial expansionism.¹²⁰ The reaction of the anti-imperialists after McKinley's victory was to repudiate their loyalty to any political party and call for a formation of a national party "pledged to defend the Republic against the Empire."¹²¹ However, shortly after this proclamation, they turned their attention away from direct political participation and toward provincial cases on which the Supreme Court would rule.[122] By the time of the 1902 Congressional elections, the anti-imperialists had established close ties with the Democrats, in large part due to congressional hearings on the Philippine issue. The anti-imperialists made a great effort to get congressional candidates committed to anti-expansionism. In Massachusetts, which was the only state where anti-imperialism was energetic, the gubernatorial election was won by a Democrat who supported the independence of the Philippines, but this was far from being the perfect coalition the anti-imperialists had in mind.

The Democratic Party still supported the issue of anti-imperialism, but did so mildly. According to the contents of the campaign book for 1902, imperialism was no longer the vital issue over which to wage a political war. The issues of tariffs and trusts became just as important as the question of Philippine independence.[123] Although other political issues became just important as anti-imperialism for the Democrats, prominent Democratic leaders voiced their opinions on expansionism. Adlai Stevenson's "A Republic Can Have No Subjects" pointed out the economic and political hazards of imperialism. Stevenson wrote,

> Is it too much to say that the enforcement of the proposed policy of the expansionists in a large measure involves the question of a change in our form of government? Shall the closing hours of the century witness the American people abandoning the pathway in which past generations have found prosperity and happiness?[124]

Stevenson referred to the Teller amendment, asserting that annexation of foreign colonies ran counter to the principles outlined in that document: "It was this solemn disclaimer by the American Congress that justified the war at the bar of our own conscience and that of the world. To say now that our disclaimer applied only to Cuba ... would be only to palter with words in a double sense"[125]

George G. Vest, an influential Senator, used legal arguments to oppose annexation. Vest argued that the effort to annex colonies was unconstitutional. In "From A Legal Point of View" he noted, "What is the colonial system against which our fathers protested? It is based upon the fundamental idea that the people of immense areas of territory can be held as subjects, never to become citizens?"[126] Vest argued that the Fifteenth Amendment would grant the Filipinos the right to vote in U.S.

elections. In essence, Vest believed that a culturally inferior people would have access to the full privileges of U.S. democracy. Although he put his arguments in legal terms, they were also couched in racial fears.

Academia, the Literary World and Anti-Imperialism

The anti-imperials were well represented in the world of arts and letters and the academic community. The president of Stanford became a member of the Anti-Imperialist League and authored many articles opposing U.S. expansionist foreign policy.[127] The president of Cornell University, a former supporter of expansionism, opposed U.S. occupation of the Philippines in 1902.[128] Charles Eliot Norton and William Graham Sumner, form Harvard and Yale, respectively, represented the anti-imperialist among their colleagues at their institutions. Felix Adler of the University of Chicago, J. Neal Steere of the University of Michigan, and Melville B. Anderson of Stanford University played similar roles at their respective institutions of higher education. Harvard, Stanford, and the University of Chicago were the institutions that were most vocal in their support of anti-imperialism.[129] Arguments put forth by the academic world generally had a morality tint to them. Regarding the Philippines, William James noted that the United States was guilty of destroying "the one sacred thing in the world, the spontaneous budding of national life."[130] Felix Adler believed that those who sought to protect the country from doing wrong were those who loved the country best. Signing petitions and attending anti-imperialist rallies seems to be the major avenue of protests against expansionism. The protests generally consisted of small groups and seemed to flourish among college students. However, no major movement against McKinley's decision to annex the Philippines emerged from these college youths. Although the leadership of college campuses articulated opposition to expansionism very well, their protests did not seem to influence students to any degree. It seems their arguments against imperialism did not provide the intellectual fuel for others in the anti-imperialist movement who struggled to grasp the imagination of the public on this issue.

William James was the most well-known intellectual to oppose imperialism. Born in 1842, James was exposed to communism, spiritualism, and homeopathy through his father's experimentation with these subjects.

2. A Group of Many Shades

James' father was also an early supporter of women's rights and abolitionism. These exposures to various philosophies greatly influenced James and perhaps explain his willingness to entertain different perspectives.

During the height of the war fever that engulfed the nation in 1898, James believed the country displayed an aggressive trait that had long been hidden. He thought the combativeness of the jingoes was not so much due to rabid nationalism, but rather a longing to go to war. The entire affair with Spain was reminiscent of a high-stakes sporting event rather than an altruistic need to free an oppressed people. In reflecting on the readiness of U.S. naval forces' ability to confront the Spanish fleet in Cuba, James wrote, "Now let baseball and prize fights hang their heads. For really exciting sport there is nothing like such a naval battle as now seems to be imminent."[131] James did not believe that imperialism centered on the notion that it helped uplift an inferior people. Rather, it was a display of power and suppression that really motivated imperialists.[132]

Although James was caught up in the excitement of going to war with Spain, like his fellow Americans, he opposed McKinley's decision to annex the Philippines. His philosophical background seemed to play a role in James' rejection of expansionism. For James, imperialism represented an ideology that was not open to debate. James believed in viewing events in the abstract, and imperialism rejected this type of observation. James felt that the way that the U.S. government treated Filipinos epitomized this concept. Although reasons to colonize the island involved bringing civilization to the Philippine population, in reality the practice oppressed fellow human beings. He noted that the maltreatment of the Filipinos was the result of the United States' viewing their conditions in hypothetical terms.[133]

Mark Twain, Ambrose Bierce, and Finly Peter Dunne headed the list of famous prose writers who espoused anti-imperialist sentiments. Twain joined the ranks of the anti-imperialists after he had initially supported America's war with Spain. Not until the McKinley Administration had made the annexation of the Philippines a primary objective did Twain reevaluate his position. In 1901, Twain published an article entitled "To the Person Sitting in Darkness" in the *North American Review*. In this article, he exposed the duplicity of imperialists' arguments concerning colonialism. Twain wrote:

> There have been lies; yes, but they were told in good cause. We have been treacherous; but that was only in order that real good might come out of appar-

ent evil. True, we crushed a deceived and confiding people; we have turned against the weak and the friendless who trusted us ... we have stamped out a just and intelligent and well-ordered republic; ... we have invited our clean young men to shoulder a discredited musket and a bandit's work under our flag ... but each detail was for the best.[134]

Twain also published another article entitled "A Defense of General Funston" in 1902 that editorialized Funston's capture of the insurgent leader Emilio Aguinaldo.[135] This opinionated piece drew criticism from different sectors, though *The Nation* gave Twain credit for his courage. However, *Puck* editorialized that the work could not be the work of Twain but rather from "a certain peevish, dyspeptic Mr. Clemens with a bad case of in-growing ethics."[136]

Other prominent men of letters also supported the anti-imperialist movement. In the novel *Captain Jinks, Hero*, Ernest Crosby spoofed Rudyard Kipling's famous poem "The White Man's Burden":

> Take up the White Man's Burden;
> Send firth your study sons.
> And load they down with whisky
> And testaments and guns.
> Throw in a few diseases
> To spread in tropic climes
> For there the healthy niggers
> Are quite behind the times.[137]

William Vaughn Moody gave a poet's voice to the chorus when he wrote:

> For manifest in that disaster light
> We shall discern the right
> And do it, tardily, —O ye who lead
> Take heed!
> Blindness we may forgive, but baseness we will smite.[138]

In "On a Soldier Fallen In the Philippines," Moody wrote:

> Toll! Let him never guess
> What work set him to.
> Laurel, laurel, yes;
> He did what we bade him to.
> Praise, and never a whispered hint but the
> Fight he fought was good;
> Never a word that the blood on his sword
> Was his country's own heart's blood.[139]

Those who supported and opposed imperialism were well represented in academia and the literary field. The academic and literary worlds supported U.S. war with Spain but had trouble accepting annexation as a viable foreign policy. Like their anti-imperialist colleagues, they felt annexation abandoned the principles on which the nation was founded and would ultimately lead the country down a dangerous path. In the end, these influential anti-imperialist did very little to impact public opinion. Their most important contributions lay in the fact that they were able to articulate reasons for the nation to stay away from colonialism.

Left and Anti-Imperialist Sentiments

Although America's socialists expressed support for anti-imperialism, some of this group's leading advocates, such as Eugene Debs, were somewhat silent on the question of imperialism. Influential members of the socialists, such as Morrison I. Swift, let their opinion be known concerning U.S. expansionism. On this issue Swift wrote, "I declare that it is treason to support the army" in the Philippine–American War.[140] He wanted U.S. soldiers fighting in the war to abandon their weapons and cease all fighting.[141] A representative for the Socialist Labor Party, Daniel De Leon, editor of *The People*, cautioned against colonial tendencies he saw emerging as the United States drifted toward war with Spain. He noted that the real reason for going to war was not the altruistic freeing a people from tranny, but rather a move to take advantage of Cuba's resources.[142] Some socialists had sensed this aggressive side of U.S. foreign policy since the early 1890s. The *Weekly People* harshly criticized the Cleveland Administration's management of the Venezuelan controversy: "Those fiery old war horses snuff the battle from afar, and burn to rush to the defense of our endangered country. Of course, it is not endangered yet, but they hope it will be in order to show their patriotism."[143]

The editors of *The People* echoed the same sentiments regarding a U.S. war with Spain. An editorial piece shortly before the commencement of hostilities noted, "The Government of the United States represents, not our people, but a small minority thereof."[144] In the view of U.S. socialists, capitalists intensified the already bad relations with Spain to facilitate the economic expansion of U.S. corporations.[145] Although one of the main reasons behind the Teller Amendment was to appease these who saw the war as a front for expansionism, this failed to placate the editors of *The People*. The editors asserted that U.S. business magnates would seek ways to circumvent the guidelines of the Teller Amendment: "This won't suit our American capitalists at all; and already it is considered necessary for us to interfere with a strong hand, and make the Cubans submit to our will."[146]

Regarding the Philippines, the Socialist Labor Party considered the McKinley Administration's annexation of the Island a ruse to corner the Chinese market:

> Hence, the Spanish-American War, whereby, while fighting Spain in the Antilles, the color of plausibility could be given to the seizure of the Philippines as belonging to the same power. Observe, that Manila, so absolutely disconnected from the Cuban question that it lies almost directly straight through the earth from us and Cuba, 8,000 miles beneath our feet, was where the first battle was fought! Cuba was simply the fulcrum of the lever used by the capitalists in prying the "Open Door" of China.[147]

The Social Democrats even went so far to say that there was a mysterious relationship between the Boer War and the Philippine War.[148]

Although the McKinley Administration, Congress, and the capitalists received the brunt of the Socialist Labor Party's attacks, the Party did not launch an attack on the military forces fighting in the Philippines. The Socialist Labor Party's diatribe centered on the economic dynamics of class struggles and aimed their attacks at the capitalist system.

Anti-Imperialism and the African American Community

In many ways, U.S. imperialism of the late nineteenth century seemed to rest on a type of social Darwinism sense of progress. In other words, human beings could be classified according to race and that in the competition for valuable resources, some races will win and others lose. Moreover, imperialist actions were animated by the belief that Anglo-Saxons were at the top of the human food chain. However, these assumptions could easily be assigned to those who opposed expansionism as it can to those who supported it. The unique position of African

2. A Group of Many Shades

Americans as former slaves and targets of oppression suited this community well when it came to assessing the effects of colonization on those who are colonized.

The opinions of African Americans concerning expansionism can be garnered, in most instances, from examining the Black press of the era. In general, the Black press opposed U.S. expansionism. Despite the social conditions associated with discrimination faced by the African American community, they were patriotic and served in the war with Spain and in the war in the Philippines. But, fighting for one's country was very different from subjugating a foreign people. Many African Americans saw a parallel between the exploitation of alien people and their personal experiences of oppression. In an editorial entitled "Why Colored Troops Were Not Sent Earlier," *The Richmond Planet* wrote that Blacks would be "too close to the smoldering volcano of brutal oppression, and consequently of revolutionary discontent ... this is why Afro-American troops ... were not promptly thrown into Cuba at the outbreak of war."[149]

The McKinley Administration was soundly criticized by the *Planet*, the *Defender*, and the *Broad Axe* concerning the annexation of the Philippines. African Americans who expressed anti-imperialist sentiments believed the racial oppression that characterized the culture of U.S. society would be transplanted to the new colonial acquisitions. The editor of the *Defender*, H. C. Astwood, stated that U.S. actions in the Philippines were immoral.[150] *The Richmond Planet* believed the annexation of Cuba was contemptible.[151] In August of 1898, the *Washington Bee* asserted that subduing the Cubans would not be only immoral, but unwise: "The moment an attempt is made to establish American prejudice on the Island of Cuba, that moment there will be trouble. The negro will not tolerate it."[152]

When reports of causalities reached the shores of the United States, many in the African American press noted similarities between the oppression of minorities in the United States and the resistance put forth by Filipino rebels:

> The report of the loss of several Americans by Filipino insurgents last week renews the saying that nothing is settled unless settled right. This is true of the race question. In proof of it our nation needs no evidence, if it did, such would be superabundantly furnished by the Indian, Negro, and Chinese problem of long standing.[153]

Resistance to the Spanish-American and Philippine Wars

The *Broad Axe* asserted that U.S. imperialism was diametrically the opposite of the principal on which the nation was founded: "Thomas Jefferson exclaimed before expiring, 'If there be one principal more deeply written than any other in the mind of every American, it is that we should have nothing to do with conquest.'"[154] By eliciting Jefferson's thoughts on colonialism, the *Broad Axe* attempted make the public more aware of the founding principles of the nation. The editors opined that the McKinley Administration had dishonored this principle.[155]

The McKinley Administration argued that colonizing the Philippines would bring order and civilization to an otherwise unstable region. John Edward Burke challenged this view of imperialism given by the McKinley Administration in *The Colored American*:

> The Filipinos have much good in them, and General Aguinaldo's government seems to have been fairly successful in preserving order, so that there is ... no reason why they should not be entrusted with a large share in their own government. From present appearance ... before the Americans are comfortably settled in their new possessions, they are likely to be tempted to feel much more sympathy for the automatic Spaniard than for the people they went to war to assist.[156]

African American writers made practically the same arguments that the anti-imperialists made in the labor movement. In May of 1899, *The Colored American* wrote, "The Filipino war continues and the American laborer is footing the lion's share of the bills."[157] Bruce Grit suggested that any economic gain made by annexing the Philippines would only benefit others: "There will be nothing in the new possessions for the Negroes except those things which are of no possible use or benefit to the whites."[158]

During the presidential elections of 1900, Blacks made a concerted effort to defeat the reelection of McKinley. *The Colored American* reported that the African American community attempted to organize an Anti-Imperialist and Anti-Trust League. The leadership of this group included members from the *Globe* and the *Negro World*. The leadership of this group came from every region of the country.[159] They had a plan to create a national party, the National Afro-American Party, whose platform called for the independence of the Philippines.[160] Other African Americans threw their support to Bryan's candidacy for the presidency. The *Broad Axe* reported that the Negro National Democratic League championed Bryan's bid for the White House.[161]

2. A Group of Many Shades

Some members of the African American community endorsed the President's position on expansionism. *The Recorder*, reporting on the activities of the Afro-American Press Association, included the observation of leading representatives of the Black Press who supported McKinley's foreign policies and supported the Republican Party's presidential ticket of 1900:

> The undersigned members of the association, who constitute more than five-sixths of the membership present ... endorse the foreign and domestic policy of the national Republican administration, and believe that the best interests of ... the Afro-Americans people ... will be served by a consistent support of McKinley and Roosevelt in the coming election.[162]

The Black newspapers that supported McKinley's reelection bid included *The Appeal, The Age, The Freeman, A.M.E. Zion Review, The Afro-American, The Forum,* and *The Bee*.[163] However, the vast majority of the Black press opposed McKinley and colonialism. It is easy to understand why. African Americans displayed patriotism at a high level and wanted to give all their support to their country. However, unlike their fellow White citizens, Blacks found it hard to accept the arguments for expansionism, specifically those based on racial Darwinism. From the perspective of African Americans, the color of Emilio Aguinaldo's skin did not bar him from successfully running a government nor did it impede him from building a republic. In analyzing the Black press of the period, most African Americans opposed expansionism. However, societal racism of the era prevented their opposition from becoming a major force in the debate between imperialists and anti-imperialists. The Anti-Imperialist League did very little to gain support for its cause from the Black community. How much influence African American anti-imperialists could have effected, in light of the institutional racism of the times, is hard to assess.

Anti-Imperialist Sentiments Among the Religious Community

A large majority of the religious community supported the expansionist policies of the McKinley Administration. Despite this, the McKinley Administration was concerned that rumors of U.S. military personnel stealing crucifixes and other religious artifacts from Filipino churches might cause dissent among the religious faithful.¹⁶⁴ These rumors, coupled with the military-imposed censorship on the press in the war zone made the situation worse. The Catholic press became suspicious and saw General Elwell Otis, the originator of the press censorship, as a coconspirator with the Protestant missionaries in curtailing Catholic activities in the region. The Metropolitan Truth Society and the Catholic Young Men's National Union made their displeasure known to the McKinley Administration.¹⁶⁵ A photograph displayed in *Collier's Weekly* showing the extent of the Luzon Catholic church's damaged interior further enflamed passions. The editors of the *Monitor* and the *Freeman's Journal* wanted the administration to provide an explanation for this desecration.¹⁶⁶

In an attempt to calm the fears of U.S. Catholics, the War Department issued an official statement vowing that the rights of the Catholic Church in the Philippines would be honored.¹⁶⁷ U.S. Catholics had others reasons for not letting their concerns get blown out of proportion. U.S. Catholics were concerned that their protests would be seen as unpatriotic and would worsen the relationship between U.S. Catholics and U.S. Protestants. This was one reason that Catholics were encouraged to stay clear of those who supported the Anti-Imperialist League. Despite this, some Catholics did let their feelings be known. Bishop John L. Spalding delivered a speech before an anti-imperialist gathering.¹⁶⁸ He also published an essay denouncing U.S. policy in the Philippines, noting, "Unlike other nations, we began as a civilized people."¹⁶⁹ Directly challenging expansionism he wrote, "Conquest and forcible annexation and military rule are in opposition alike to our traditions and our fundamental principles of government."¹⁷⁰

Although a large majority of U.S. Catholics seemed to have supported U.S. policy in the Philippines, anti-imperialist sentiments among the U.S. Protestants was also rare. However, such voices of opposition could be found among such religious leaders as Charles G. Ames, Isaac M. Atwood, E. Winchester Donald, William H. P. Faunce, Scott F. Hersey, Frank O'Hall, and Charles H. Parkhurst.¹⁷¹ Two influential papers that shared anti-imperialists sentiments were *The Friends Intelligencier and Journal* and *The Observer*. Many clerics who supported anti-imperialism were of the Unitarian faith. The Unitarian Church of New England was particularly close to the anti-imperialist movement.¹⁷²

Many religious leaders published essays that highlighted their support for anti-imperialism. Robert E. Bisbee published an article denouncing

U.S. foreign policy in the Philippines.[173] Henry Van Dyke, who celebrated the U.S. victory over Spain, raised two important questions:

> Are the United States to continue as a peaceful republic, or are they to become a conquering empire? Is the result of the war with Spain to be the banishment of European tyranny from the western hemisphere, or is it to be entanglement of the western republic in the rivalries of European kingdoms?[174]

Van Dyke also noted that expansionism desecrated the principles that the Founders inscribed in the Constitution.[175] To those who use the annexation of Puerto Rico and Hawaii as a template for the colonization of the Philippines, Van Dyke answered, "The legal government of Hawaii has asked for annexation; Puerto Rico is a small island, close at hand, and inhabited principally by white people who have received us willingly."[176] Those two examples could not be applied to the situation in the Philippines. In essence, Van Dyke believed that the litmus test for annexation included geographical location, race, and the willingness of the people to assimilate into the U.S. system.

The Reverend George C. Lorimer published an essay disparaging the peace treaty between the United States and Spain that was formally adopted by the Anti–Imperialist League. In the essay, Lorimer suggested that the U.S. government orchestrated the Philippine rebellion by luring Emilio Aguinaldo out of exile and helping him organize the rebel movement. He stated, "Any right we assert to ownership in the Philippines must rest, therefore, upon conquest or upon purchase from their Spanish oppressors, or both, and in any case it is ... inconsistent with the principles of this Republic."[177]

The leader of the American Board of Missions, Reverend James L. Barton, noted in a letter to the *Boston Herald*, "I do not know anyone who is in favor of an imperialist policy."[178] Barton argued that for his church board, "we should be most loath to ask the extension of the American protectorate over any non–Christian country."[179] Of course, Barton made an error in his commentary. The Philippines were Christians. Maybe he meant to say Catholic? Despite this error, Barton opposed expansionism on the grounds that it would make the work of Christian missionaries much more difficult. Henry C. Potter made the same argument when he stated:

> The things that this ... nation ... supremely need [is] not more territory, more avenues of trade, more places for place-hunters, more pensions for idlers, more subject races to prey on, but a dawning consciousness of what ... are a people's

Resistance to the Spanish-American and Philippine Wars

indispensable moral foundations—those great spiritual forces on which alone men and nations are built.[180]

All evidence suggests that although most U.S. churches supported the U.S. war with Spain and the McKinley Administration's policy toward the Philippines, voices of dissent did exist. Although these voices were scattered, they were enthusiastic. Could those who opposed U.S. expansionism have used religious-community opposition to imperialism better? Probably. Would it have made any material difference? Likely not. One major flaw of the leadership of the anti-imperialist movement was their lack of willingness to unify and coordinate their activities with other groups that shared their sentiments about U.S. imperialism.

U.S. anti-imperialists encompassed various groups that included political independents, alienated Republicans, academic and literary elites, the business community, and the socialists. African Americans and religious sects also opposed expansionism. The anti-imperialists opposed imperialism for many reasons, but four specific reasons seem to have a common thread.

A majority of anti-imperialists believed the United States would violate the core principles of the U.S. Constitution if it became an imperial power. The United States was found on the belief that liberty and self-government were the cornerstone of a successful government and that these principles set the United States apart from the oppressive policies of European nations. Using coercive measures to incorporate foreign people into the U.S. system betrayed the principles on which the nation was founded. For this reason, the anti-imperialists, as a group, were generally repulsed by the policy of colonialism.

Others in the movement asserted that colonialism would inevitably lead the United States into conflict with other world powers. For these anti-imperialists, national security demands dictated that the United States remain a continental power. Although some were willing to accept the annexation of Spanish possessions in the Caribbean, the possibility annexing the Philippines was unacceptable. Still other anti-imperialists suggested that imperialism was not an economically viable plan. U.S. products, specifically agricultural products, would not be able to compete with the cheaper goods of the colonies. Outsourcing labor became a major concern for U.S. workers. Still other dissenters argued that the colonies would not be able to purchase U.S. products, which would indirectly lead to a national deficit.

2. A Group of Many Shades

The issue of race played a major role in anti-imperialist arguments. The running theme through these arguments is the problems that may arise from incorporating a foreign culture into the national body. What would be the status of the colonists? Would they be eligible for full citizenship? Would they have the right to return to their homeland? Many in the anti-imperialist movement believed the United States already had its share of immigrants. To incorporate uncivilized people into the U.S. system would destroy the moral fiber of the nation. Others saw the racial component in a different light. They believed Filipinos could govern themselves. Had not the Cubans been struggling for their independence when the United States and Spain went to war? The point of the war was the liberation of the Cuban people. A similar situation had been playing out in the Philippines. Since the United States had backed activities in the Philippines, how could the country now claim these people were incapable of self-government?

To the anti-imperialists, the expansionists' arguments seemed illogical. Where the imperialists saw the United States developing into a world power, the anti-imperialists saw the nation losing its core identity. Where the imperialists argued that colonization and a strong naval force would bolster national security, the anti-imperialists claimed that the projection of U.S. power on the global stage threatened the security of the United States. Where the imperialists saw the economic benefits in an expansionist foreign policy, the anti-imperialists saw threats to the U.S. economic infrastructure. Finally, where imperialists insisted that the United States was morally bound to uplift backward peoples, anti-imperialists believed expansionism undermined the vitality of the White race and that the United States had no moral obligation to oversee the development of foreign nations.

3

The Cuban Rebellion and American Politics, 1895–1896

Both the interest of the United States in the affairs of Cuba and the consequences of the Cuban revolt of 1895 brought the Cuban crisis to the forefront of U.S. politics. President Grover Cleveland and the nation's congressional leaders were challenged by international problems that resulted from naval incidents, filibustering excursions, illegal imprisonments, and the destruction of U.S. property that demanded action. Although the response from Congress temperamentally supported the Cubans' cause, the President of the United States took a more cautionary approach in drafting and implementing a policy of neutrality. Cleveland supported U.S. claims against Spain for the collateral damage that resulted from the rebellion, but had little sympathy for the insurrectionists, believing Spain might seek the financial and military aid of major European powers if the Cuban rebels' victory became imminent.[1]

One chief cause of the naval incidents centered on the dilemma that resulted from the filibustering expeditions. The Spanish government had good reason to be concerned about the filibustering activities in the United States because these expeditions facilitated the insurrection by supplying Cuban rebels with war materials and by encouraging hostile activities in the United States and abroad. U.S. filibustering contingents gained their strength from the activities of Cuban-Americans who used their resources to aid the insurgents' cause in Cuba. Some even became members of the Cuban Junta and gave direct support to the Cuba *Libre*, whereas others supported the liberation materially through financial donations and by personally transporting munitions to military camps of Cuban rebels.[2]

Spain's determination to impede the efforts of the U.S. filibustering expeditions resulted in the first incident that caught the attention of the

3. The Cuban Rebellion and American Politics, 1895–1896

United States. In early March of 1895, the Spanish warship *Conde de Venadito* fired on the U.S. mail ship, the *Alliance*, in the Florida Straits. After investigating and concluding that the *Alliance* was on routine business in the area, Secretary of State Walter Q. Gresham asked Spain to explain the unprovoked action. The captain of the Spanish warship claimed the U.S. ship had violated international law by coming within the three-mile limit of Cuba's coastline and refused to hoist her flag for identification. After receiving the assurance of the U.S. captain that the ship was flying the U.S. flag and was well beyond the three-mile limit of the Cuban coastline, Gresham asked the Spanish government to repudiate the actions of the *Conde de Venadito* and to give orders that no such actions would occur in the future.[3]

At the height of the rebellion, the U.S. and Spanish governments collaboratively attempted to stop the actions of the filibustering. To uphold U.S. neutrality, President Cleveland issued an executive decree on June 12, 1895, that clarified U.S. international obligations. Cleveland stated that any citizens engaged in any military-oriented aid that aimed to help the Cuban revolt would face prosecution. The Spanish government strategically placed agents in U.S. cities and ports, and required these agents to report any shipment of military supplies to the insurgents to U.S. State Department officials.[4]

However, the efforts to stop the filibustering expeditions by the Spanish and U.S. governments had very little effect on the activities of the filibusterers. During the peak of the Cuban insurrection, the number of expeditions organized in the United States steadily rose. In all, filibusterers organized seventy-one expeditions, with forty-six established during the Cleveland Administration. Filibusterers became successful at maintaining a high level of organization centered on the shallow waters along the coastline, had numerous small outlets that impeded Spanish and U.S. ships from adequately patrolling the coastline.[5]

The Spanish government also encountered problems with a U.S. judicial system that failed to fully support neutrality legislation aimed at stopping the filibustering activities. From the thirty-three failed filibustering expeditions, the U.S. Judicial system only imprisoned five men and levied fines on the others. During the early stages of the rebellion, the legal interpretation generally favored Cuban-Americans. The U.S. courts ruled that the legality of the filibuster expedition was valid unless the government proved it had military aspirations, established in the

Resistance to the Spanish-American and Philippine Wars

United States to aid in the fight against Spain, and supplied immediate and direct help to the rebellion by providing insurgents with officers and equipment.[6]

The U.S. Supreme court vacillated between the illegitimacy and legitimacy of the filibustering expeditions. In practically all early court cases involving the validity of the filibustering expeditions, at least one key requirement of the treasury department was missing. More than a year after the revolt started, the Supreme Court strengthened U.S. neutrality laws by ruling that the filibustering expeditions might not be legal if they were disorganized and lacked essential elements that made up a military force. President Cleveland attempted to use this interpretation of the neutrality laws as a key component in a revised neutrality proclamation, but a ruling by a federal judge on the limits of U.S. jurisdiction and the international law requirement of a coastal three-mile limit defeated any changes to the neutrality policies Cleveland had in mind.

This ruling by the federal judge also had a direct effect on the activities of the filibusterers' expeditions. From the very instance that the ruling became known, the majority of filibusterers made sure they organized their forces well out of range of U.S. territorial waters. However, these elusive practices became illegal a little more than a year later when a federal judge ruled that any individual who knowingly gave aid to the expeditions violated the neutrality laws of the United States. Although the ruling came a little too late to materially affect the insurrection, it did indicate that if the neutrality laws were strictly enforced, U.S. neutrality laws could stop the activities of the filibusterers.[7]

Another problem that arose concerned the imprisonment of U.S. citizens in Cuba during the rebellion. The jailed Americans, for the most part, were Cuban-Americans who gained naturalization as a protective measure against being imprisoned by the Spanish government. As a precautionary measure, the Spanish government jailed known rebels and ultimately placed U.S. citizens in confinement. The imprisonment of Americans continued as the insurrection developed, and the number of Americans who Spain caught in a dragnet reached to seventy-three over the course of two years.[8]

The issue of imprisoning Americans crystalized when Spain jailed a former insurgent General Julio Sanguily. Sanguily, who had applied for U.S. citizenship in 1878, came under arrest for inciting a rebellion.

3. The Cuban Rebellion and American Politics, 1895–1896

During imprisonment, the former General faced a civilian and a military court for alleged crimes. Both courts sentenced him to life imprisonment. The State Department vigorously protested the arbitrary methods used by the courts to convict Sanguily, but to no avail.

The issue of Sanguily's imprisonment caught the attention of influential Americans. One of the General's leading supporters in Congress, Democratic Senator Wilkinson, called for Sanguily's immediate release. Prominent press outlets also championed Sanguily's cause. Eventually, after over two years of high-level pressure from U.S. political leaders and newspapers, Spain released Sanguily from jail.[9]

The capture of the *Compeditor* while it was performing operations in support of filibustering initiated another issue concerning imprisonment. After landing men and military supplies to help the rebels, the *Compeditor* and its passengers (which included Captain Alfredo Laborde, the British citizen mate William Gildea, and U.S. newspaperman Ona Melton from the *Florida Times-Union*) were captured, arrested, tried, and sentenced to death by a military tribunal. Prompt action by the U.S. government saved the crew from certain execution. Gildea gained protection only because he held the Captain's chair of a ship flying the U.S. flag. A little over a month after the capture of the *Compeditor* two sailors who had escaped the Spanish, one an American and the other an Englishman, came forward and surrendered to the Spanish authorities. Only vigorous action on the part of the U.S. government prevented another sentenced execution.

In spite of international tensions created by collateral issues, including the imprisonment of Americans, the status of the Cuban rebellion became a minor focus of President Cleveland in the December 1895 annual message to Congress. Cleveland especially noted the *Alliance* incident and the arrest of U.S. citizens and stated that the U.S. government gave full support to these situations. Using the guidelines of international law as a reference point, Cleveland refused to recognize the insurgents and vowed to continue a policy of strict neutrality, regardless of the material losses or atrocities that occurred in Cuba.[10]

Shortly after Cleveland delivered the annual message to Congress, a new problem arose that threatened Spanish-American relations: the wholesale destruction of U.S. property. The month of December marked the beginning of the sugarcane harvesting season in Cuba and the insurgents, aligned with Gomez's orders, began a campaign of destruction that included cane fields and grinding machinery. The high point of this destruction came when the insurgents, working under the cover of darkness, started enormous fires in the cane fields that could not be extinguished before the flames had consumed a vast amount of the valued crops. By late April, the sugarcane crop production of 1896 had dropped precipitously from the sugarcane crop production of 1895.[11]

Damage to U.S. property became clearer in this wholesale destruction of the sugarcane crops. Leading U.S. businessman used this destruction of U.S. property as a catalyst to facilitate U.S. intervention in the Cuban crisis. Officials from the Juragua Iron Company sent the State Department letters condemning the actions of the insurgents and requesting diplomatic aid to protect their property. Considering the value of the property destruction, the complaints the Juragua Iron Company conveyed to the State Department seemed justifiable.[12]

Letters of protest, registered claims, and general inquiries helped show the extent of the damage done to U.S. property. The January 1897 reports on the Cuban crisis indicated that claims resulting from property losses, imprisonment, personal injuries, and death reached an aggregated loss estimate of $9,742,146.73.[13]

The damage to U.S. property not only caught the attention of U.S. businessmen, but also the attention of Congress. The introduction of legislation favoring recognition of Cuban belligerent rights by Senator John T. Morgan of Alabama found kindred support among members of Congress. The major reasons for advocating recognition of Cuban belligerency involved geography, the expropriation of property, illegal imprisonment, preservation of the Monroe Doctrine, and the financial consequences of patrolling U.S. coastlines to prevent filibustering activities. However, the foremost reason for advocating recognition was that war in Cuba required international recognition.[14]

The introduction of legislation favoring recognition raised two major questions: what impact would the passage of such legislation have on the U.S. relationship with Spain, and did Congress or the executive have the constitutional authority to recognize Cuban belligerency? In one of the most significant speeches of the debate, Senator Morgan analyzed and answered both questions. Morgan assured the senators that recognition of Cuban belligerency would not lead the United States into war with Spain nor would Spain view the recognition as a hostile act. On the constitutionality of the problem, Morgan argued that Congress

3. The Cuban Rebellion and American Politics, 1895–1896

alone is invested with the power to recognize Cuban belligerency; a point that raised doubts among his most ardent supporters.[15]

The introduction of legislation to recognize the Cuban belligerency did not go unopposed. Senators who led the opposition to this legislation included Democrat Stephen M. White from California and Republicans George F. Hoar from Massachusetts and Eugene Hale from Maine. Using the precision of legal reasoning, this congressional trio attacked the constitutionality of the belligerency legislation as violating the tenets of international law and favoring the Spanish government over the insurgents. Using excepts from leading experts of international law to bolster their argument that a recognizable state should have a stable and functioning government, as well as the infrastructure to support seafaring commerce, they asked the Senate what evidence it had that indicated the revolutionist government had these essential elements.

The senatorial opposition to the legislation also questioned the newspaper coverage of the events in Cuba. The senators contemptuously questioned the newspapers' atrocity stories and *Junta* proclamations that some senators introduced as evidence, recommending that no action be taken until the Senate receive some type of tangible evidence concerning the events in Cuba. The senatorial opposition stated that even if the evidence supported the pro-belligerency side, recognition of the Cuba belligerency belonged to the Executive branch, not the legislative branch of the government. The opposition also opposed the notion that the Executive branch should give recognition to the Cuban belligerency, because they believed it would negatively affect the interests of the United States.[16]

Senator Hoar of Massachusetts became adamant in arguments concerning the collateral affect that recognition of Cuban belligerency would have on the United States and on Spain. The Massachusetts Senator believed that if the insurgents were granted recognition, the responsibility for property damage could not be blamed on Spain nor could the United States be compensated for damages done to U.S. property. Recognition of the Cuban belligerency would facilitate the Spanish cause by giving them the authority to inspect all seafaring vessels for contraband, which would ultimately result in a more encompassing blockade of Cuba. By allowing Spain unrestricted access to search ships, the pro-belligerency legislation could result in war when Spain searched U.S. ships for prohibited materials on the high seas.[17]

Resistance to the Spanish-American and Philippine Wars

The opposition against recognition of Cuban belligerency spread and attracted the attention of many influential members of Congress. The chairman of the Foreign Relations Committee, John Sherman, opined about the issue. In an anti-Spanish speech, Sherman noted that the United States must, at some point, intercede in the Cuban crisis and stop the atrocities. Sherman also suggested that the solutions to the crimes committed on the island might be solved through Cuban independence.[18]

To support his argument concerning Spanish crimes, Sherman used a book published by the *New York Journal*. According to Sherman, the book revealed the appalling details of Spain's barbarousness toward civilians in Cuba. The Senator bolstered this source of information by referring to the *New York Journal* as the best news informant in the United States. In final remarks, Sherman predicted that if the United States followed the unlawful events in Cuba as reported by the newspapers, nothing on earth would prevent the American people from physically ousting the "barbarous robber" from the Cuban island.[19]

The voting on the issue of recognition showed that Sherman had wide support for these views. In all, the Senate took three votes: two for previously submitted alternative resolutions and the third on the resolutions that Senator Morgan submitted. Senator White submitted one substitute measure that included a statement of sympathy for the Cubans and supported the argument that the President alone had the authority to grant belligerent rights. This measure failed to get approved by a margin of fifty-seven to twelve, with twenty Senators refusing to cast their votes.[20]

Senator William V. Allen, a populist from Nebraska and faithful supporter of the Cuban cause, introduced a second measure aimed at recognizing Cuban independence. This substitute resolution ultimately failed by a vote of fifty-two to seventeen. However, this defeat turned out to be more of a blessing than a curse because it indicated that the Senators who actively supported government action to achieve Cuban independence had a strong foundation to achieve its goals. Thirteen votes for the Allen measure came from the trans-Mississippi West and reflected the strong support of western Republicans and Populists.[21]

After settling the issue of the substitute measures, on February 28 the Senate voted on the Morgan resolution, which passed by an overwhelming vote of sixty-four to six. The Republicans gave the Morgan measure the most support with thirty-five votes, whereas the Democrats

3. The Cuban Rebellion and American Politics, 1895–1896

supported the measure with twenty-five votes. The six votes that opposed the Morgan measure came from three Northeastern Republicans and three Democrats from the South. The vote on the Morgan resolution showed that the Cuban crisis had become a national issue that cut across both geographical and political lines.

While the Cuban issue became national in scope, it did not translate into political harmony when the issue arose in congressional debates. Senator Hale, from Maine, vehemently attacked Sherman for presenting false information in the Senate. Hale introduced evidence that Sherman misquoted the *New York Journal* and proved that the material contained in the *Journal* was faulty at best. Hale seriously questioned the patriotism of the Cuban rebels and their objectives, concluding that since the information that Sherman presented before the Senate lacked veracity and the Cuban rebels' crimes rivaled those of Spain, the Senate did not have enough reliable information to take action.[22] Senator Sherman defended these actions by introducing a new list of Cuban barbarities and reiterated strong faith in the validity of the *Journal*'s reports. But Sherman's defense revealed a weakness in the resolutions: it showed that Sherman did not actively support the interventionist clause contained in the resolution.[23]

In the ensuing debates, many congressional speakers expressed unhappiness with the third section of the House measure and the overall logic of the entire House resolution. After much haggling, Orville H. Platt, Republican Senator from Connecticut, and a senatorial colleague who opposed the measure, bluntly stated that the debates were prolonged because only five members of the Senate approved the resolution in its entirety. Platt suggested that a senatorial conference take place to craft a measure that the Senate would readily accept. Sherman agreed and the debate concerning the Cuban issue fizzled out in the galleys of the Senate.[24]

During the second conference meeting, the House voted on the two Senate resolutions. These votes awakened an entirely new line of opposition and exposed how much public opinion influenced the issue. Illinois Representative Robert R. Hitt gave a vivid picture of the attention generated by the resolutions. Hitt noted that the committee was flooded with petitions from the American people demanding action; however, these petitions were balanced against the onslaught of business petitions that opposed the resolutions.[25]

Charles A. Boutelle, Representative from Maine, took the floor and challenged Hitt's statements on the resolutions. In an adversarial rebuttal, Boutelle stated that public clamor for the resolutions did not contain the intensity portrayed, and the fever of jingoism negatively influenced the mood in the House of Representatives. Representative Adams objected and testified that the committee did indeed receive literally hundreds of messages from the public on the resolutions, and that no foreign issue had resulted in so much interest from the American public. Representatives William Baker of Kansas and Andrew R. Kiefer of Minnesota both stated that public opinion overwhelmingly favored passage of the resolutions.[26]

Other Congressional Representatives introduced new arguments to the debates concerning the resolutions. Frederick H. Gillett, Republican from Massachusetts, and Tazewell Ellett, Democrat from Virginia, vehemently criticized the resolutions because they wrenched attention from vital domestic issues. Representative Gillette denounced the Senate for taking action on domestic legislation and using the Cuban resolutions as a diversion from its inability to act. Ellett chimed in, stating that Congress should pay more attention to the needs of the American people and not get bogged down in foreign affairs.[27]

The view held by Gillett and Ellett had support among their congressional colleagues. Rowland B. Mahany, Republican from New York, charged the Senate with forcing the original resolution through the House without regard to the guidelines established by international law and spreading the fever of jingoism throughout the halls of Congress. Representative Henry G. Turner from Georgia added a dimension to the arguments that seemed to elicit memories of post–Civil War politics. Turner, who opposed the resolutions, argued that Cuba, with its large Black population, would be unable to govern itself and if Spain left, the island nation would need some type of foreign help to prop up the government.[28]

Although opposition in the House of Representatives had more intensity and developed along new lines, the balloting indicated little change. On April 6, the House of Representatives overwhelmingly approved the Senate's resolutions with 247 votes supporting it and twenty-seven votes against it. The huge vote differential supporting the resolutions came from a partisan vote of 186 Republicans, fifty-six Democrats, four Populists, and one Silverite. Those Representatives who

3. The Cuban Rebellion and American Politics, 1895–1896

cast a no vote for the resolutions showed a much clearer sectional bias. Over half of the votes against the resolutions came from Massachusetts and New York, with eight and six votes, respectively.[29]

The strong geographical bias against the resolutions represented fear, real and imagined, in the minds of Representatives from those states that cast negative votes. The coastal States feared that if war broke out, bombardment of their coastal cities and ensuring commercial loss through Spanish privateering represented reality. The heavy voting against the Senate resolutions in New York and Massachusetts likely reflected the worries of conservative financial interests about losing property if the Cubans gained belligerent rights. The sentiments of those who opposed the resolutions was just as strong as those who supported the measures.

Any analysis of the congressional debates involving the resolutions must consider the election year and the acute awareness of public opinion. During this time of partisan conflict, the Republicans and Populists challenged President Cleveland's leadership, although their political rhetoric never reveals this motive. Some congressional members delivered speeches they printed and circulated throughout their districts to show their constituents their hardline stance against Spain's actions and their support for the oppressed Cubans. Although the circulated speeches included a taint of political partisanship, the majority of them contained deep sincerity.

Although the resolutions passed with a resounding majority vote, they achieved very little because the President had to take action to make them effective; Cleveland refused to work with a hostile Congress. Although Cleveland refused to let congressional advice influence action, the administration did take action through diplomatic channels. A couple of days before the House took its final vote, Secretary of State Richard Olney completed and presented the Spanish Minister, Enrique Dupuy de Lôme, with the administration's most important communiqué concerning the Cuba crisis. The detailed document covered the Cleveland Administration's assessment of the Cuban revolt and what it hoped Spain would do to bring the crisis to an end.

The communiqué also detailed the U.S. role in the Cuban crisis. In the note, Olney assured Spain that the United States did not, in any way, want to annex Cuba; it only wanted to see lasting peace on the island. But humanitarian, geographic, commercial, and financial reasons compelled the United States to act and the United States would not allow an indefinite war to take place in the western hemisphere. The document highlighted the serious consequences of the Cuban rebellion and concluded that Spain's military intervention did very little to quell the revolt.

The note focused on collateral issues that inherently affected the Cuban crisis and the best way to confront these issues. Olney stated that the Cuban rebels had no centralized government to control their activities and that Cuba's future looked much brighter under Spanish rule. The Secretary of State suggested that Spain give Cuba its independence, because the longer the rebellion continued, the longer it would take to reconcile. Olney left it up to Spain to initiate a viable solution to the crisis, and if the United States accepted the plan, the Cleveland Administration would fully support it.

In spite of the widespread anti–Spanish sentiment that flowed from the U.S. public, Dupuy de Lôme considered the Cleveland Administration's overtures a move in the right direction. In a letter to the Duque de Tetuán, Spain's Minister of State, he wrote about the "very satisfactory" note he received from Olney concerning "explicit recognition of the sovereignty of Spain" and its honest appraisal of the Cuban rebels.[30]

Although Spain regarded the Olney communiqué favorably, the Spanish ministry used the note as a defense of Spain's response to the Cuban crisis. The Duque de Tetuán rebutted the assertion that Cubans suffered at the hands of Spain and declared that Cuba had one of the most democratic political systems in the world. The Duque acknowledged U.S. property losses, but added that Spain's losses far exceeded those of the United States and asserted that foreign interests would incur additional losses if Spain abdicated its role in Cuba. In essence, the note reaffirmed Spain's theory that the only way to induce a lasting peace was by military force.

The confidence that Spain displayed in its communications led her to gauge the sentiment of her European neighbors regarding the Cuban crisis and the possibility of U.S. involvement. The Duque de Tetuán secretly contacted the six major European powers to determine what action they would take against Spain if the United States intervened in the Cuban crisis. With the exception of Russia and England, the majority of European nations expressed sympathy with Spain's actions in Cuba. Notably, the English considered any hostile joint military actions involv-

3. The Cuban Rebellion and American Politics, 1895–1896

ing European nations wrong, a sentiment that ultimately brought Spain's efforts to seek kindred spirits among the European nations to an end.[31]

Although Spain attempted to gain European support for its Cuba policies, the United States tried to obtain factual information about the crisis in Cuba to determine if the Cuban Republic should be recognized. To achieve this goal, President Cleveland ordered the consul-general, Fitzhugh Lee, to Havana to gather information on the stability of the Cuban Army and government. If Cleveland sought an objective opinion in assessing the conditions in Cuba, he selected the wrong individual for the mission. Three weeks after arriving on the island of Cuba, Fitzhugh Lee who sympathized with the Cubans, informed the State Department that only U.S. intervention could end the carnage and atrocities in Cuba and requested that a U.S. warship be dispatched to Havana harbor to protect the interests of the United States.[32]

The report that Lee gave Cleveland bewildered the President. In a letter to Richard Olney, Cleveland wrote that Lee "seems to have fallen into the style of rolling intervention like a sweet morsel under his tongue." Although the president favored protecting Americans and U.S. interests, he did not want the United States to go down the slippery slope of war with Spain by projecting an image of military insult.[33]

As the U.S. political scene of 1896 developed, the Cuban crisis slowly lost centrality as a major issue. At the nominating conventions, foreign affairs still caught the attention of political leaders, especially in the ranks of the Republican Party, which called for a "firm and vigorous" foreign policy that would protect U.S. interests and lives in all parts of the world. The Republican platform announced its faith in the Monroe Doctrine and called for a policy of expansion in the western hemisphere that consisted of acquiring the Danish West Indies, controlling the Hawaiian Islands, and constructing a Nicaraguan canal that came under U.S. authority. The Republican platform did not support the idea of protecting Americans with financial interests in the Cuban sugar industry because the tariff portion of the platform assured U.S. farmers that all sugar consumed in the United States would come from domestic sugar farms.

Although interest in the Cuban crisis slowly receded in the minds of political leaders, it still played an important part in the political planks of the major political parties. In the Republican Party's platform, the plank read,

Resistance to the Spanish-American and Philippine Wars

> From the hour of achieving their own independence, the people of the United States have regarded with sympathy the struggles of other American peoples to free themselves from European domination. We watch with deep and abiding interest the heroic battle of the Cuban patriots against cruelty and oppression, and our best hopes goes out for the full success of their determined contest for liberty.[34]

The campaign platform of the Democratic Party contained a foreign policy initiative that complimented the Monroe Doctrine and supported the Cuban people in their struggle to win liberty and independence.[35]

The elaborate platform phrases concerning the Cuban crisis eventually took a backseat to such issues as free silver, which ultimately engulfed the nation and stirred public sentiment away from the events in Cuba. William McKinley's political speeches never covered the foreign policy issues of annexing Hawaii, formulating a foreign policy comparative with the Monroe Doctrine, or problems arising out of the Cuban crisis. Instead, McKinley's campaign rhetoric focused on the various aspects of tariff protection and the intricate problems related to the money question.[36]

Like most U.S. presidential contests, the campaign of 1896 was a temporary break in U.S. political life during a time when foreign problems simply would not go away. When the presidential election had passed, the Cuban issue reemerged as strongly as ever, but on an entirely different political level. A new President took office after the 1896 elections and assumed the duties of the presidency. In a little over a year, this new President, William McKinley, would lead the U.S. people into war with Spain.

4

A Critical Dilemma in Spanish-American Relations

After a period of relative harmony during the final months of 1897, the relationship between Spain and the United States shifted toward the murky waters of hostility in the early months of 1898. The failure of Spanish reforms to improve Cuban conditions, coupled with the concentration of U.S. naval forces in Cuba's territorial waters, facilitated this spirit of antagonism between the two nations. The tension between Spain and the United States intensified due to the influence of anti-autonomy riots in Havana, the ordering of the *Maine* to Cuba, and the disclosure of de Lôme's letter. As the diplomatic situation worsened and war seemed imminent, the United States and Spain prepared their military forces for the coming hostilities.

The anti-autonomy riots that took place in Havana became the critical moment in Spanish-American relations. Although the riots did not pose a direct threat to U.S. interests, it did indicate that the policy of Cuban autonomy had failed. The main participants in the riots descended to the street, destroying property and offices belonging to pro-autonomy opponents, proclaiming allegiance to Weyler, and calling for the immediate execution of Ramón Blanco. Fitzhugh Lee later reported that although some rioters urged the mob to destroy the U.S. consulate, the riot itself decidedly lacked an anti–U.S. atmosphere.[1]

Because the riots indicated that the policy of autonomy had serious opposition from the military and civilian populace, the result of the riots became more important than the rioting itself. With Blanco acknowledging the failure of the autonomy policy, Americans who supported sending naval forces to Havana used the riots to bolster arguments favoring military intervention in the Cuban crisis. During the initial stages of the riots, Lee asked that a ship be put on notice for possible deployment to Havana if the rioting situation deteriorated. Lee informed the State Department that the ship would not be so conspicuous if it was sent under the guise of a coal-supply vessel during the last week of January, when German ships would also visit the port of Havana.[2]

After analyzing the riot situation and the internal activities of Cuban politics for three days, Lee decided a ship did not need to be deployed to Havana, largely because the Spanish factions in Cuba were essentially fighting each other. Lee felt this worked to U.S. advantage. Lee had confidence that if the fighting continued, Spain would become weaker and the powerful Cuban and Spaniard leaders would turn to the United States for intervention out of the necessity to ensure peace.[3]

The riots had enormous impact on Washington's perception of the success of Spanish reforms. In public utterances, McKinley stated that the new system of reform must be given the opportunity to succeed and the riots did not indicate the overall failure of autonomy. However, in private, the President believed the riots represented a bad omen for the success of Spanish political reforms. The essence of McKinley's public persona concerning the riots was demonstrated when McKinley, plagued by news about the riots, calmed inquirers, stating that no new information had come to him from Cuba and people who do not have access to the information on the Cuban disturbances could take it upon themselves to make an informed decision about the crisis.[4]

At the height of the rioting, Spanish officials questioned McKinley's actions concerning the disturbances. Dupuy de Lome noted that the administration showed an "abrupt" change in its perception of the riots that strengthened the enemies of Spain; de Lome believed McKinley agreed with Lee's assessment on autonomy because he was informed privately that the President had declared autonomy an unmitigated failure. de Lome advised the Spanish government that preventing any new rioting in Cuba could ultimately result in dire consequences in the United States. de Lome believed that Washington's loss of faith in Spanish political reforms necessitated this move.[5]

The riots also effected the actions of Congress. In the months leading up to the riots, Congress had attempted to force a vote on the Cuban crisis. Senator Frank J. Cannon, Republican from Utah, introduced a bill that indicated the importance of the Cuban riots. In the January 13 resolution, Cannon called on the president to show what protective

4. A Critical Dilemma in Spanish-American Relations

measures McKinley was putting in place to ensure the safety of U.S. citizens in Cuba.[6]

The House of Representatives showed more discontent with the administration's policy in Cuba and decided to take legislative action that posed a direct threat to presidential leadership. On January 17, Representative Robert Hitt introduced the consular and diplomatic appropriation bill that acted as a filibuster tactic to compel Republicans to take constructive action on the Cuban crisis. Democratic Missouri Representative David A. de Armond opened the obstructionist maneuver by attempting to insert an amendment that recognized the existence of war between Cuba and Spain. Hitt declared the amendment out of order, a move that gave the Democrats the opportunity to debate the finer points of the bill.[7]

The introduction of the consular and diplomatic appropriation bill in the House became a focal point of the democratic strategy. After the introduction of the bill, five Democratic members of the House interrupted the reading of the measure to offer amendments, increasing the number of debates on the Cuban crisis. During the course of speeches on the bill, Democratic Representative William Sulzer maintained,

> The Democrats in this House are in favor of passing the joint resolution granting belligerent rights to the Cubans. The Republicans have persistently refused to permit a vote on the question. The people of this country will hold the Republican Party responsible for that action at the coming election. We will meet you on the stump all over this country, and we will tell your recreancy on this important question, and the people will condemn you.[8]

After the introduction of the bill, Hitt used his floor time to point out the finer points of the bill, highlighting McKinley's sterling leadership. Hitt criticized Cleveland's actions on the Cuban issue and pointed out McKinley's positive results through such actions as the release of U.S. prisoners, Spain's autonomy recommendations, and the recall of Weyler. Hitt punctuated the speech by noting that because the president had succeeded in getting the Spanish to formulate a plan for political reforms, it became vital to the Cuban crisis to give them adequate time to ensure these measures worked. However, the military activities of the insurgents, coupled with rioting on the Cuban island, limited the success of the political reforms and put the Cuban crisis on the path of uncertainty.[9]

The speech Hitt gave painted a dire picture of an increasingly bad situation. Hitt noted that the unsteadiness of Spain's sovereignty became noticeable and McKinley needed to act to protect U.S. lives and property. Hitt highlighted pertinent parts of McKinley's annual message concerning intervention to congressional colleagues and asked them to consider supporting the President if circumstances compelled the United States to intervene. Although other members of the House debated the issue long after Hitt spoke, the analysis Hitt gave concerning the Cuban crisis effectively sent the House of Representatives into a state of sober reflection.[10]

Within a week of the House debate on the imminent crisis in Cuba, McKinley ordered the *Maine* to Havana harbor. On the surface, the President ordering of the *Maine* to Cuba seemed like a gesture of approval concerning Spain's success on the island nation, but the visit by the *Maine* fulfilled other important needs for the McKinley Administration. The *Maine*'s presence offered protection to U.S. citizens in the event the riots turned violent toward Americans. Sending the *Maine* to Havana also ended the risky arrangement between Fitzhugh Lee and Captain Charles Sigsbee, which could had caused a major maritime incident that led the United States and Spain into war.[11]

Lee's arrangement with U.S. naval forces was precarious to say the least. Before January 24, Lee had the authority to order the *Maine* to Havana at any time, and if the communication contact between Key West and Havana failed, the ship would immediately go to Havana's harbor. Under these circumstances the arrival of the *Maine* would likely involve less than perfect timing that could have resulted in aggravating an already tense situation in Spanish-American relations. During the tense times of the Cuban crisis, the last thing McKinley wanted or needed was an international incident that would propel an unprepared nation toward war.

The ordering of the *Maine* to Havana also gave McKinley much needed political help. The *Maine*'s voyage to Havana helped unite congressional Republicans behind the President's leadership and facilitated Republican efforts to nullify Democratic attempts to force the House to take action on the Cuban issue. Although Republicans in the Senate and the House supported McKinley's decision to send the *Maine* to Havana, all members of the Senate Foreign Relations Committee believed the President should have ordered the entire naval fleet to the Cuban island.[12]

Once McKinley had resolved that some type of action must be

4. A Critical Dilemma in Spanish-American Relations

taken, the President acted quickly. Undeterred by Lee's suggestion that the ordering of a ship be postponed for at least a week, the Department of the Navy ordered Charles Sigsbee, Captain of the *Maine*, to Havana harbor the morning of January 25, 1898. Once the *Maine* arrived in Havana harbor, Cuban officials gave it a proper but reserved acknowledgment. The arrival of the *Maine* did not set off any significant objections from the native Cuban population.[13]

Shortly after sending the *Maine* to Havana harbor, McKinley confronted the problem of removing, or at least replacing the ship. Because the Cuban harbor environment had a reputation for unsanitary conditions that supported the growth of yellow fever, many in the administration believed the ship should withdraw from Cuba as soon as possible. Lee maintained that the issue of any ill effect from disease was highly overblown and if the President ordered the removal of the *Maine*, the United States would lose control of the Cuban situation. Captain Sigsbee concurred with Lee's assessment and added that the ship should only be removed if a much larger naval force replaced it.[14]

The arrival of the *Maine* did not sit well with Spanish officials. A majority of Spanish officials regarded the ship's presence as a menace to peace. They believed that, rather than encouraging peacefulness on the Cuban island, the presence of the *Maine* encouraged Cuban rebels to continue their fight and facilitated hostile feelings toward Madrid. In Madrid, Segismundo Bermejo, the Minister of Marine, believed the presence of the *Maine* revealed something more threatening: the naval superiority of the United States.[15]

As the *Maine* anchored in Havana harbor, reports from Cuba highlighted the lack of success of the Spanish reforms on Cuba, proven by the onslaught of starvation and the intensity of the rebellion. The most disturbing report on the Cuba situation came from Commander of the *Montgomery* George A. Converse, whom the Navy department had ordered to Cuba as part of a good-will gesture and to investigate conditions on the island. For Converse to get an overall picture of the conditions in Cuba, the Commander visited Matanzas and Santiago de Cuba. After visiting Matanzas, Converse reported to Washington that some 59,000 people, of a population of 253,616 in Matanzas Province, had died from starvation since December 1897, whereas another 98,000 had suffered the ill effects caused by the lack of food.[16]

The reach of the starvation epidemic spread and affected many on the Cuba island. In the city of Matanzas, 14,000 *reconcentrados* stayed, with 11,000 of this number becoming homeless and another 3,000 living in poor housing. The Spanish officials attempted to alleviate the situation by supplying the 14,000 starving people with 900 individual serving of rice a day, which ultimately became inadequate to quell the level of suffering among the populace. Even the citizens of the United States became victims to the dangers of the famine, when funds appropriated for food rations became exhausted.[17]

The appalling conditions that existed in Matanzas and occurred in other parts of the Cuba island required a quick resolution to the Cuban rebellion, but the first month and a half that autonomy was in practice did not result in the quick settlement the Cuban crisis required. Blanco's military actions seemed successful, but efforts to quickly end the rebellion through diplomatic channels with the insurgents failed because a majority of the rebels did not accept the policy of autonomy. The fate of one of Blanco's chief negotiator, Joaquin Ruiz, demonstrated the level of hopelessness in negotiating for peace. When Ruiz arrived at the rebel camp to discuss a peaceful way to end the hostilities, the insurgents court-martialed and executed him on Gomez's orders to kill anyone who supported surrender under the guise of peacemaking.[18]

The financial and commercial risks associated with the Cuban crisis came to the forefront in the first weeks of February. The State Department received constant claims and authorized Woodford to present Spain with a list of U.S. claims Spain must act upon. Many U.S. businesses pleaded with the administration to seek a peaceful resolution to the Cuban crisis. The petition to take action to make peace recapitulated business and financial losses brought about by the Cuban rebellion and asked McKinley for relief through peace.[19]

The disheartening news that came from Cuba concerning starvation, loss of property, and the failure of Spain's political reforms did not stop the administration from asking Spain to enter into a new reciprocal trade treaty with Cuba. Spain and Cuba had both shown interest in entering a new reciprocity trade agreement in 1897 that would adhere to the guidelines established by the Dingley tariff, but no action was taken until the United States brought up the subject in January in Madrid. For Spanish officials, creating a new trade agreement came with qualifications. Spain only agreed to establish a new agreement if the negotiations took place in Washington so Americans would see that the

4. A Critical Dilemma in Spanish-American Relations

Cubans had the right to establish treaty terms that best suited their interests.[20]

The negotiations of a new reciprocal trade agreement between Spain and Cuba coincided with Congress attempting to pressure McKinley into ending the Cuban crisis. William E. Mason, Democrat from Illinois, introduced a resolution that requested the President to bring the Cuba crisis to an end, while "Uncle" Joe Cannon presented one that called for the United States to recognize Cuban belligerent rights by March 4 and recognize Cuban independence by June 4. In the House's counterpart, the Senate introduced a measure that tied funding for the diplomatic corps into a resolution that sought to compel the President to end the Cuba war. The bill was soundly defeated before it came up for vote.[21]

The release of the de Lome letter overshadowed the introduction of congressional resolutions. Published by the *New York Journal* on February 9, de Lome's letter was written to an influential Spanish newspaper editor and politician, José Canalejas, who oversaw the progress of Spain's colonial reforms. The publication of the letters cause a diplomatic crisis because an excerpt from the letter placed McKinley's action in a negative light, indicating that the President felt Spain was deceitful in its dealings with the United States. In the letter, de Lome depicted McKinley as a weak politician who sought admiration from the public and "tries to leave a door open behind himself while keeping on good terms with the jingoes of his party."[22]

The letter de Lome sent to Canalejas revealed much about Spain's sentiments concerning Cuba's autonomy. Dupuy de Lome implied insincerity of the part of Madrid by acknowledging that the autonomist government's only purpose involved taking U.S. pressure off Spain by giving the Cubans a large share of the responsibility for the Cuba situation, and by suggesting that autonomy would not bring a lasting peace because only military action could achieve an end to the rebellion. The Spanish Minister further noted that trade negotiations between Spain and Cuba could become advantageous to Spain, even if they were just for show. de Lome added that Spain needed to send "a man of some prominence ... in order that I may make use of him here to carry on a propaganda among the Senators and others in opposition to the junta and to try to win over the refuges."[23]

The President did not know of de Lome's letter until he received information that the *New York Journal*, which had gotten the document from the Cuban junta, planned to publish the contents of the letter on February 9. On the morning of February 9, Horatio S. Rubens, legal counsel working on behalf of the junta, gave the letter to Day. Day had the letter translated by Alvey Adee. Because the administration could not authenticate the document, Day took the letter to de Lome, who verified its authorship.[24]

McKinley and Day took immediate action to ensure Spain was held accountable for the contents of de Lome's letter by asking for an official apology from Madrid and a retraction of the statements that de Lome expressed in the letter. Satisfied that the recall of the Spain Minister would serve as repudiation of the sentiments of the letter, McKinley and Day directed Woodford to present a request to the Spanish government calling for de Lome's removal from the ministry post. When Woodford presented the request for de Lome's dismissal, Spain's Minister of Foreign Affairs Gullon informed him that the Spanish ministry had already asked for and received de Lome's resignation. Shortly thereafter, Woodford discovered that Gullon had only told him part of the truth; de Lome, after learning that the *Journal* published one of his letters, had presented his resignation to Madrid on February 9, but the Spanish government had accepted it without taking action on it.[25]

To U.S. officials, acknowledgment of de Lome's resignation did not represent an apology. On February 14, Woodford informed Gullon that the administration needed "a formal indication that his Majesty's government" regretted the sentiments that de Lome expressed in his letters. To bolster Spain's self-esteem, Woodford suggested the reason Madrid did not disavow the language earlier was because the contents of the letter were unknown at the time, so he delivered only the most offensive parts of the letters to the Spanish ministry. Woodford also informed Segismundo y Moret Prendergast that if Spain did not comply with his request for an apology, he would resign his position because could not work with a government that he did not trust.[26]

Woodford justified his action in giving the Spanish government an ultimatum from the President of the United States:

> You may think I was possibly too positive and possibly too severe, but I know my decision was right. ... I believe that what I said gives us the only present chance of avoiding present war. You can hardly realize at Washington how tense is the situation here and the scratch of only one match may explode the dynamite.[27]

4. A Critical Dilemma in Spanish-American Relations

The Spanish government became divided over the recent demands from the United States. A normally optimistic Sagasta was ambivalent, whereas Gullon and governmental allies believed Spain should go to war rather than cave to U.S. demands. Between these two groups, a Moret-led faction fought for peace. By supporting the Moret group call for peace, the Queen Regent broke the gridlock on February 15 by formally repudiating the contents of de Lome's letter and by announcing that Spain is committed to commercial negotiations and autonomy in Cuba.[28]

Although the McKinley Administration accepted Spain's apology, the de Lome letter created a great deal of press commentary concerning the Cuban crisis and the direction of the McKinley Administration's foreign policy. The yellow journalism of certain newspapers, particularly the *New York Journal* that first published the letter, led the press in its determination to expel the Spanish minister. Virtually all news outlets believed the Spanish minister's usefulness had ended, but they cloaked their opinions in different ways; the Republican and independent newspapers hinted that the publication of the letter was very unfortunate. The Republican *Boston Transcript* reminded readers that for the last ninety years, the United States had dismissed three Spanish diplomatic representatives, three British, two French, and one Russian, because these representatives disrespected the U.S. government.[29]

Although the de Lôme letter drew the interest of the U.S. press, it drummed up very little excitement from Congress. In the House of Representatives one Democratic congressman, William Sulzer from New York, offered legislation that would give the Spanish minister his passports, but Congressman James Lewis, Democrat from Washington, seemed to agree with the contents of the letter when he offered a measure to retain de Lôme as minister. The de Lôme incident caused minor excitement in the Senate, when Senator Morgan introduced a measure requesting all consular information on the state of war and the conditions in Cuba be made available for congressional debate. Influential Senators William E. Mason and Joe Cannon gave incendiary speeches in behalf of the resolutions they had offered earlier.[30]

The magnitude of the de Lôme letter lay in its long-term effects. The incident strengthened the events that led to war, such as reports generated by yellow journalism and the negative feelings the United States held toward Spain. The most conspicuous aspect of the letter is that it showed the American people and President McKinley the insincerity on the part of Spain concerning its actions in Cuba. It presented tangible evidence to the administration of the veracity of Lee's reports and showed that regardless of Spain's denials, Madrid had firm doubts concerning McKinley's policy toward Cuba.

The State Department's consular correspondence arrangement for publication indicates that McKinley's views toward Spanish-American relations had changed. During the second week of February, Republican Representative Lemuel E. Quigg introduced a resolution requesting all pertinent information concerning the *reconcentrados*. The specifics of the measure asked whether Spain authorized the *reconcentrados* to resettle on their property, described how effective zones of cultivation were, recounted what Spain was doing to ensure the commercial success of the sugar mills, and outlined the policies Madrid implemented to make autonomy a success. Because the legislation originated from the Foreign Affairs Committee with unanimous consent, it indicated the President support the measure.[31]

The introduction of the resolution served as an informative bridge between Congress and the U.S. public. Presenting the measure served as a way to inform the American people about the Cuban crisis and to determine what, if anything, the United States could do to mitigate the situation in Cuba. Introducing the measure also had other collateral goals. Because the evidence contained in the State Department's consular reports was methodical in its denunciation of Spain, the measure served as a way for McKinley to prepare for a confrontation with Spain.[32]

Thus, the Spanish and U.S. road to war seemed to be assured. Both countries prepared naval forces for the coming hostilities, with McKinley using the umbrella issue of Spanish inhumanity as a war cry, while Spain blamed the U.S. government's violation of international law as a facilitator of the coming conflict. But before McKinley could release the State Department's reports, one single event occurred that surpassed the de Lome incident in importance: the explosion of the *Maine*.

5

Sliding Toward War

On March 4, 1897, William McKinley took the oath of office for the presidency of the United States. Campaigning on the theme of harmony and prosperity, McKinley embodied the slogan "agent of peace and prosperity." The election itself became known for being one of the bitterest presidential elections in American history. The tension surrounding campaign issues symbolized the nation's inner turmoil with international issues and domestic duties.

Enlightened to the increasingly belligerent circumstances associated with the Cuba crisis, the newly elected McKinley initiated an extensive program of military preparedness. While he prepared the country for military action, McKinley sought peace through diplomatic channels, but the sinking of the *Maine* altered any diplomatic moves the President had in mind. With the destruction of the *Maine*, McKinley decided not to make any preemptory moves, diplomatic or otherwise, until the naval report surrounding the *Maine*'s incident came to a conclusion. However, a current more forceful than the *Maine* explosion compelled the president to take action.

While the naval court deliberated on the events surrounding the destruction of the *Maine*, two competing issues developed that changed the nation's course in international affairs: the changes in public opinion and their effect on the administration's complacency in foreign relations. Ironically, the dramatic shifts in public opinion concerning the Cuba crisis strengthened McKinley's ability to respond to growing foreign relations problems. While the administration's diplomatic policy became a policy of wait and see, public opinion, attuned to the unofficial reports that drifted out of Cuba, moved perceptibly toward the need for direct U.S. intervention in the Cuba crisis.

The most significant action McKinley took from the time of the *Maine* explosion until the naval court's finalized report of the events involved the decision to increase the country's preparations for war. Firmly believing Spain would not settle the underlying problems of the Cuban crisis, and reassured by Woodford that the Spanish government would not implement much needed reforms, McKinley's only option involved direct intervention that ultimately translated into preparation for war.

Preparation for war meant the rising of funds to sustain the U.S. war effort. On March 6, 1898, McKinley summoned the chair of the House Appropriation Committee, "Uncle Joe" Cannon, to the White House to talk about raising money for U.S. military action. When Cannon entered the meeting with the President, McKinley wasted very little time informing the influential congressman of the details of the meeting. McKinley bluntly told Cannon that although he had worked tirelessly for a peaceful resolution to the Cuba crisis, war seemed imminent and he need "money to get ready for war."[1]

On a personal level, Cannon opposed war with Spain. In a hotly disputed debate on the House floor concerning the benefits and drawbacks of waging war with Spain, Cannon severely criticized the war hawks that sought to shed U.S. blood on the altar of business profits. But in spite of his earlier anti-war sentiments, Cannon eventually believed war with Spain was inevitable and the nation must prepare for war. Prior to meeting with McKinley, Cannon reviewed the Treasury accounts and informed the President that withdrawing $50 million for the war effort was reasonable and could be accomplished without levying additional taxes or raising money through government bonds.[2]

During the meeting with McKinley, Cannon suggested that the requested funds come from a presidential directive. However, McKinley informed Cannon that such a move would give the Spanish the impression that he wanted war during the delicate time of diplomatic negotiations. The President informed Cannon that to avoid the appearance of duplicity, another way must be found for the funds to become available.

McKinley suggested a way for Cannon to secure the funds without leaving a paper trail back to the White House. The President proposed that the House Appropriations Committee introduce a bill calling for the raising of the $50 million. Cannon agreed with this suggestion, but his agreement was qualified. The Illinois congressman would introduce the bill to raise the funds, but the President must draft the language of the motion.[3]

5. Sliding Toward War

The measure Cannon introduced materialized into the Cannon Emergence Bill. The intricate details of the resolution involved appropriating $50 million "for the national defense" of the country and all collateral expenses associated with this purpose. After seventy-three speeches in the House supporting the measure, the bill passed by 311 votes. The Senate passed the bill by a resounding seventy-six yeas and zero nays. This tremendous welcome of the bill indicated to McKinley that fervent patriotism had gripped Congress and the nation.

Upon passage of the Cannon Emergence Bill, President McKinley put the newly appropriated funds to use. McKinley first act involved sending a naval officer to Europe to make a bid on any available ships. The President ordered the improvement of the infrastructure of the armed forces that facilitated the nation's move toward military preparation. Within a week of the passing of the appropriation measure, naval and expeditionary-forces capabilities vastly improved, after years of lying dormant.

With preparations for war well on their way, the President knew that such dire situations as the starvation of the Cuban rebels had to be addressed. McKinley learned, through reports supplied by Fitzhugh Lee, that U.S. relief efforts greatly aided Cubans in the ports and mainland, but the rebels needed much more relief than the administration gave. Spanish civil officers made a concerted effort to cooperate with the U.S. distribution of relief items in Cuba, but Spanish military personnel attempted to impede the relief operation in many ways. Although Lee reported that relief supplies were not wasted, Stephen Barton, Chair of the Central Cuban Relief Committee, informed William Rufus Day that wholesale wastage, corruption, and overall poor management hindered much-needed food items from reaching their destination.[4]

The most disruptive news that threatened Spanish–U.S. relations centered on the investigation of the *Maine* explosion. Lee informed McKinley that the Spanish investigation into the destructive events surrounding the *Maine* explosion bordered on the ridiculous, with their divers only going underwater as a matter of policy and with Spain using their reports to conclude that the *Maine* explosion resulted from internal and accidental mishaps. At the same time, U.S. news outlets reported that the U.S. court believed the *Maine*'s destruction came from external sources and that naval experts accepted the theory that external forces caused the explosion. The two conflicting accounts threatened any peace efforts in the negotiations between Spain and the United States.[5]

Resistance to the Spanish-American and Philippine Wars

Regardless of these troubling signs, President McKinley, during the latter part of March, decided to strengthen his diplomatic position on the leading issues while also seeking a common peaceful avenue on which the U.S. and Spain could agree. He discussed the possibility of the United States recognizing Cuban independence through naval intervention with Whitelaw Reid, but ultimately the President decided the idea was not feasible. Cognizant of the dangers inherent in the conflicting naval reports, McKinley decided that whatever the American court concluded, the U.S. government would support these conclusions and that any variations in the reports given by the Spanish and American governments would not be liable to arbitration. McKinley added that if the American naval court concluded that Spain had a hand in the destruction of the *Maine*, he would ask the Spanish government to pay the United States an indemnity for the damages to the *Maine*.[6]

McKinley became well aware of the future of Cuba. Confident of Cuba's imminent independence, he decided to ask Spain to recognize the island country's independence. If Spain refused to honor the request of payment for the *Maine*'s destruction or official recognition of Cuba, McKinley felt that noncompliance translated into a cause for war. Concerning these requests, McKinley did not view his requests as improper or offensive.[7]

Seeking a new means of a peaceful settlement, McKinley examined a plan suggested by Oscar S. Straus that involved giving suzerainty to Cuba. Straus, a former U.S. minister to Turkey, informed McKinley that this plan might satisfy both Cuba and Spain since it had been used as a working model for Egypt and Turkey to settle their crisis. The intricate details of the arrangement would give Spain titular sovereignty and Cuba tangible independence. Straus also believed that the powerful nations of Europe would accept such a plan since they had experiences with a similar situation involving the Ottoman Empire, and that Spain should accept the arrangement as a means of upholding its national pride.[8]

McKinley heard about the feasibility of the plan from its two leading proponents. Both Straus and John McCook went to the White House to analyze the merits of the arrangement with the President. After discussing the suzerainty in detail, it became apparent that the Cubans would not accept the plan because Spain had previously granted similar rights to the island nation. Thus, the plan in which McKinley had put much faith in did not come to fruition.[9]

5. Sliding Toward War

In mid-March of 1898, gossip appeared around Washington that the President wanted to adjourn Congress in order to take further diplomatic action without the interference of Congress. Several disclosures facilitated the adjournment rumors. In private, McKinley stated that the war fever "agitation in congress," coupled with the "storming for war" by the U.S. press, tried to force his hand. The President also privately admitted that once the naval report came to its conclusions, "nothing could hold back Congress and the press" from calling for drastic actions.[10]

These rumors of congressional adjournment originated from some of the President's chief allies. Various conservative senators and at least one friendly newspaper editor suggested that early adjournment of Congress would make McKinley's diplomatic efforts so much easier. Taking advantage of the adjournment information, the Democrats acted swiftly to avert any congressional adjournment when Bailey convinced a Democratic House conclave to remain in session all summer in order to obtain a vote on the Cuban crisis. However, two days after this maneuver by the Democrats, McKinley publicly stated that he wanted Congress to stay in session because only Congress could declare war and receive information on the Cuban crisis.[11]

During the month of March, the Spanish navy's actions threatened to push Spanish–U.S. relations over the edge and toward war. Spain, taking precautionary steps toward a possible war with the U.S., ordered a naval-combat fleet consisting of three torpedo boats, three destroyers, and a cruiser, to cross the Atlantic with Cuba as the final destination point. The naval armada's movement indicated that Spain desired a naval concentration in the Caribbean that justly caused U.S. senior naval leaders much concern. Senior naval fleet officers informed Secretary of the Navy John D. Long that ordering the flotilla to Cuba represented a hostile act on the part of Madrid and urged him to issue a stern warning to Spain about its naval activities.[12]

William Rufus Day took up the issue with Polo de Bernabe, sternly questioning the military intentions of Spain. Announcing that Spain's naval actions compelled the U.S. to prepare for war, Day attributed Spain's desire for war as a way of extricating itself from the quagmire that the Cuban crisis presented. The Spanish minister denied Day's allegations and asserted that the ships sailing to Cuba were there to fight the rebels. But Day refused to believe that any type of naval activities on the part of Spain could defeat the insurgents who lived and fought inland.[13]

Ambassador Woodford notified Washington about other naval activities on the part of Spain that threatened peaceful relations with the United States. The U.S. minister confirmed that Spain had assembled a new fleet that consisted of an additional three torpedo boats and three destroyers. Although events seemed dire to U.S. leaders, Woodford still believed that peace could be achieved. The ambassador firmly believed that autonomy would not work and the Cubans could not sustain self-government; thus, the only option for peace between the United States and Spain centered on U.S. acquisition of the island.[14]

Because of his belief that ultimate peace lay in the acquisition of Cuba by the United States, Woodford, without the consent of the President, engaged in talks with Spain about the sale of Cuba. The ambassador met Moret and mentioned the possibility of the United States purchasing Cuba, explaining why Spain should sell the island. Woodford built his argument on the theory that the United States and Spain could resolve their problems by creating a commission to mediate their outstanding debts, with Queen Victoria as arbiter for any points of difference that may arise in the discussions. Woodford suggested that this arbitration meeting would include a secret understanding that the Queen would allow the United States to purchase Cuba for a large amount of money.[15]

On March 19, the day after Woodford revealed his plan to Moret, the ambassador recommended that the President demand Spain settle its problems in Cuba. Woodford surmised that if McKinley applied enough pressure to Spain, Madrid would readily seek a solution for its Cuba problems that would satisfy "both nations." He suggested McKinley set a final deadline for Spain to meet, giving the Spanish the details of the terms that must be met, and allowing them much leeway in accomplishing these terms.[16] Woodford further argued:

> But I do regard it as very essential that they [Spain] should see that the United States mean business and mean it *now*. The Spanish mind is so ingrained with "mananaism" that few Spaniards over act until they have to act. When at San Sebastian I told the Duke de Tetuan of November and when he found that you meant this, his Cabinet resigned and Weyler left Cuba. It has been the same in several instances, some small—some important. It was so in the de Lome incident. I believe it will be so now if you give me the authority to say it. I shall not have to threaten it officially. That might humiliate Spain. The indication, informal, pleasant but discreetly positive, will now (in all reasonable certainty) be sufficient.[17]

5. Sliding Toward War

The plan in which Woodford had so much faith did not sit well with Maria Cristina, the Queen Regent. The same day that Woodford laid out his plan to President McKinley, Moret informed the ambassador that the Queen Regent stated she would rather give up her crown than relinquish command over Cuba. In spite of this troubling news, Woodford remained optimistic that Moret would exchange the loss of Cuba if it resulted in lasting peace, and that Spain would agree with the plan if McKinley established a deadline for the Spanish to meet. Later in the same week, Woodford reported that Spanish faith in autonomy had eroded and that the government could only correct the situation by granting Cuba a greater degree of independence.[18]

Although the President simultaneously sought a peaceful solution to the Cuban crisis and prepared the nation for war, circumstances concerning public opinion took a dramatic turn. Analyzing U.S. public opinion during March of 1898, Jules Cambon, the French Ambassador representing Spain, concluded that Spain must give Cuba its independence because the island nation fell within the confines of U.S. foreign policy, as expressed by the Monroe Doctrine. But American public opinion became divided over whether the United States should go to war with Spain over Cuba. During the early part of March, McKinley received numerous letters from across the country that indicated vast support for his policy toward Spain, however the President received almost the same amount of correspondence from U.S. people who were skeptical about his Cuban policy.[19]

During this time period, a dramatic shift in the conservatives' attitudes concerning the intervention in the Cuban crisis took place. Initially, conservative Republicans wanted to peacefully end the crisis with Spain, but a speech given by Republican Senator Redfield Proctor from Vermont concerning the deteriorating conditions in Cuba seemed to change the course of the conservatives' thinking. Proctor's speech evolved from a personal two-week trip he had taken to Cuba in late February and early March of 1898. Although Proctor had always displayed an active interest in the events surrounding the Cuba crisis, many in the press speculated that the Senator's trip came as a request from McKinley, and the President used Proctor's speech as a way to mold public opinion.[20]

The speech that Senator Proctor made treaded along familiar territory and startled the senses of his congressional colleagues. The speech gave much credence to the newspaper reports on Cuba that saturated the U.S. public. Proctor publicly and privately supported U.S. intervention in the Cuban crisis, and his unabashed demeanor in giving the speech projected an air of truthfulness.[21]

On March 17, Proctor stood confidently before a filled chamber of Senators and representatives to deliver his speech. Surveying his congressional colleagues, Proctor started his speech by describing the conditions in Cuba. After giving the congressional chamber a geographical depiction of the island, the Senator declared the war had little effect on Havana, but the outlying areas of Havana were greatly "changed." Proctor gave a vivid picture of entire towns uninhabited because the people who formerly occupied these towns were forced to fortify trenches and create other man-made impediments to keep the insurgents out and the *pacificos* in.[22]

The most disturbing aspect of Proctor's speech concerned the horrific effects that starvation had in Cuba. He noted that *reconcentrados* first numbered about 400,000 and that after coming to the villages, many families lived in shacks that measured ten by fifteen feet in diameter with inhumane unsanitary conditions. Graphically descripting the conditions of these people to Congress, Proctor related that these people were

> turned from their homes, with foul earth, foul air, foul water, and foul food or no food at all. What wonder that one-half have died and that one-quarter of the living are so diseased that they cannot be saved? Little children are still walking about with arms and chests terribly emaciated, eyes swollen, and abdomen bloated to three times the natural size. The physicians say these cases are hopeless.[23]

According to Proctor, public death in the streets was a common occurrence and many starving people die within walking distance of their only food source: the market. Proctor added:

> I went to Cuba with a strong conviction that the picture had been overdrawn; that a few cases of starvation and suffering had inspired and stimulated the press correspondents, and that they had given free play to a strong, natural, and highly cultivated imagination. But what I saw I cannot tell so others can see it. It must be seen with one's own eyes to be realized.[24]

The Senator from Vermont also used this occasion to lay to rest any racial fears that may have caused a serious barrier to Cuban–U.S. cooperation. White people in the United States during the late nineteenth century were all but unanimous in their belief in Black inferiority and the need to keep the races separated. During his speech, Proctor set out to negate the "negrophobia" that permeated the minds of White Americans. Proctor assured his colleagues and the country that three of four Cubans were "like the Spaniards, dark in complexion, but oftener light or blond."[25]

The Proctor speech achieved its goal of convincing many that war with Spain seem inevitable, although a large segment of U.S. society seem convinced that peace could be established. In spite of the peace wave that spread throughout U.S. society in the spring of 1898, public and congressional pressure that compelled intervention on behalf of the Cuban insurgents continued to mount. Only one major event was needed to push the United States toward the path of war, and that push came from the official report of the Naval Court of Inquiry concerning the destruction of the *Maine*.

6

Naval Capabilities

When the Cuban crisis erupted during the late nineteenth century, the United States was at economic, social, and political crossroads. As the Presidential elections of 1896 approached, many conservatives firmly believed that the Democratic Party would slowly destroy the United States' social infrastructure. The Democratic Party, noted these conservatives, had become hostage to the disciples of William Jennings Bryan who fervently supported the free coinage of Silver. But Bryan and his free-silver message lost at the polls and the United States saw vast improvement in an economy that had known economic depression since the early 1890s.

While the conservatives rejoiced over the vast improvement in America's economy, they knew that the economic recovery stood on fragile ground. The final six months of 1897 saw the United States' budget deficit grow to well over $50 million. This deficit influenced Congress' overall view of foreign relations. As noted by the *New York Chronicle*, if the nation were compelled to act in an international crisis the military expenses to support such a venture could swell the federal deficit.[1]

Since the most important foreign policy issue facing the United States in 1898 centered upon the Cuban crisis, many pro-war advocates and press outlets noted how easy victory would come to the United States in a war with Spain. The *Chicago Tribune* editorialized that Spain represented imbecility in both her domestic and international relations when compared to the other European nations. Other high-profile newspapers wrote that Spain "is a bankrupt and broken down" nation that had encountered problems putting down a rebellion in a colony as small as Cuba.[2] In short, the pro-war advocates along with their newspaper counterparts, believed war with Spain would involve little or no effort to achieve a military victory.

The anti-war newspapers presented a diametrically opposite view,

6. Naval Capabilities

noting the overall strength of the Spanish navy in comparison to other national navies. They wrote extensively on the hazards associated with a land war in Cuba. The anti-war press also drew attention to the risk of foreign intervention on Spain's behalf.

During the 1890s, the most powerful nations in the world measured their naval strength in terms of battleships and armored cruisers. Although armored cruisers represented less fire power than the battleships, they made up for this lack of power with speed. At the height of the late-nineteenth-century naval-armament race amongst global leaders, the creation of two small crafts revolutionized naval warfare: destroyers and torpedo boats. While destroyers employed numerous gun-armaments to offset the advantages of speedy armored cruisers and torpedo boats, their effectiveness in naval warfare came under scrutiny during the late 1890s.[3]

Prophetically, the United States and Spain both began to "modernize" their naval forces in the 1880s. During this naval rehabilitation period, the United States built their modernization around battleships whereas Spain focused on torpedo boats and armored cruisers. At the time of this naval rejuvenation, neither nation's naval forces could compete with the naval powers of the late nineteenth century. However, their naval architecture became the envy of other more powerful countries.[4]

The small stature of the United States and Spain's naval forces masked intimidating forces that other nations underestimated at their peril. The naval forces of Spain consisted of a homogeneous and formidable fleet that could challenge most naval global powers of the late nineteenth century.[5] The United States had four battleships and numerous light armored cruisers with the ability to adapt to any concerted naval action. Thus, both nations had small but admirably effective navies.

On the surface, both the Spanish and the U.S. navies seemed formidable enough to give pause to the great naval powers of the world. The superficial analysis of these naval forces by the press masked a more sinister flaw in the naval forces of both nations. In reality, the Spanish warships had questionable abilities to fight a concerted naval war and consisted mostly of a fleet deprived of the primal necessities of war: inadequate guns, little coal, and no knowledgeable naval engineers.[6] While the naval forces of the United States appeared better equipped than the naval forces of Spain, the flaws that lay within the U.S. naval forces seemed to come from a lack of information on the part of American naval experts.

The naval experts of the United States did not clearly understand the true plight of the Spanish navy. Many naval experts in the United States considered the Spanish naval forces a powerful match for American naval forces.[7] Most American naval experts also believed that Spain's indifferent crew members and inadequate fleet maintenance had a negative effect upon the overall performance of Spanish naval vessels. At the first strategic conference held in April 1898, American naval planners expressed the belief that the Spanish navy could only win a naval confrontation with America if the United States' naval forces committed a grave mistake or if the Spanish fleet were extremely lucky.

The naval experts and leadership of the United States became susceptible to faulty reporting by the pro-war press as much as to their own poor judgment. The pro-war American press focused more on the power of U.S. battleships and the superiority of its crew rather than the pathetic state of the Spanish naval forces. In a roaring editorial, the *Chicago Inter-Ocean* explained that naval conflict between the United States and Spain cannot simply be determined by naval equipment, but only could be determined by the "bravery and skill of the men, from the commander on down," of each nation's respective naval forces.[8] The *Chicago Tribune* echoed this rousing sentiment by noting that the United States' navy had "the best fighting boys" in the world and it would only take "twenty-four hours" to banish the naval forces of Spain.

While the pro-war press boasted about the prowess and superiority that characterized the men of America's naval forces, they did so without giving a true assessment of the manpower within the U.S. naval forces. During the late nineteenth century, the United States' navy found it very difficult to adequately staff its naval forces. A great majority of the resourceful men behind the American naval guns had foreign backgrounds. The *Washington Post* noted that although Spain "is a nation infinitely inferior" to the United States in every aspect, the difficulties of providing native-born competent seamen made Spain superior to the United States when it came to naval manpower.[9]

The same doubtful sentiments that the American press raised about the manpower of the U.S. naval forces also applied to the practical ability of the United States' battleships. During the months prior to the Spanish-American War many of the leading newspapers lamented the nation's

6. Naval Capabilities

battleships' lack of practical experience and noted that there existed no recent example of how well the battleship would perform under wartime conditions. No major battleship fleet engagement had taken place between two Western powers since the Austrians' naval forces squared off against the Italians naval forces at Lissa in 1866. The unproven status of the U.S. battleships, coupled with the successive emergence of a series of naval offensive crafts (torpedo boats, cruisers, and torpedo boat destroyers) made it unclear whether the U.S. battleships could succeed in naval combat.

The Sino–Japanese War of the mid–1890s casted further doubt on the viability of the battleship as a useful naval weapon. During the naval engagement at Yalu in September 1894, the Japanese armored cruisers battered the Chinese fleet including its two battleships. Five months later, Japanese torpedo boats sank two additional battleships in the harbor of Weihaiwei. In a highly charged debate on naval appropriations in the House of Representatives during the month of April 1898, some members argued that the Sino–Japanese War indicated that Japan's light cruisers proved the battleship's susceptibility to speedy naval craft.

The press played upon the vulnerability of battleships to lighter naval crafts. The *San Francisco Chronicle* noted that the torpedo boats and armored cruisers had a lot in common with the English cruisers and gunboats that caused the Spanish armada so much trouble in the sixteenth century. Like these sixteenth-century English light craft, the torpedo boats and armored cruisers of the 1890s became a "terror of the sea ... both silent and deadly."[10] The editor of the *San Francisco Chronicle* further noted that the big weakness of the battleship lay in its inability to detect or prevent small craft such as torpedo boats from getting within striking distance of its enormous hulk.

Many contemporary newspapers proclaimed the effectiveness of the torpedo boats and light cruisers as the United States' Achilles' heel if she went to war with Spain. The *Seattle Post-Intelligencer* wrote that the U.S. naval forces lacked a war craft comparable to the torpedo boat. The *Chicago Times–Herald* warned that, properly and effectively deployed, the torpedo boat was "better than any battleship constructed."[11] Even the jingoistic *Chicago Tribune* noted that the U.S. Navy would make short work of the Spanish fleet if it did not employ the most formidable naval engines of war: the torpedo boats.

As war between the United States and Spain drew near many anti-war newspapers took Spain's naval capabilities seriously. The *Washington Post* believed that the overall strength of the Spanish fleet equaled that of the United States, but the superior character of the U.S. sailor would make the difference. The *New York Times* agreed, writing that on the surface the naval forces of the United States "is not distinctly superior to Spain's as a fighting force" and is inferior to it when it came to the high speed torpedo boats.[12] Even the Assistant Secretary of the Navy, Theodore Roosevelt, who had only contempt for the Spanish forces, wrote in a letter to Elihu Root that "the Spaniards have assembled a fleet of seagoing armorclads" equal in strength to the United States and augmented by the very effective torpedo boats.

Similarly, the anti-war newspapers displayed a grim assessment when it came to naval confrontation between the United States and Spain. The *Boston Journal of Commerce* reasoned that naval warfare between Spanish and American ships would not likely result in unconditional surrender from either nation nor would it result in the total destruction of either country's naval forces.[13] The Boston newspaper concluded that Spain's powerful armored cruisers would resort to a form of naval "guerrilla warfare," possibly drawing the war out. In other words, the Spanish fleet might prove inadequate to win the war at sea, but guerrilla attacks on the seas could cause the U.S. naval forces great misery.

Acknowledgment that Spain's insolvent government might spur the nation to victory out of desperation became a running theme throughout the anti-war American press. The *Omaha Bee* noted that, in the event of war, the Spanish people would, without a doubt, create a solid financial infrastructure to sustain a government teetering on bankruptcy.[14] The *New York Chronicle* agreed with the *Omaha Bee* when it wrote that Spain had a history of "preparing to make sacrifices" during a time of war, and that history demonstrated Spain's capacity to weather the most severe crisis. The anti-war press believed that a vindictive and desperate Spanish people might continue to fight after victory had long escaped their grasp.

7

Land Warfare

During the mid–1890s, over 200,000 Spanish troops occupied the island of Cuba. The ranks of these troops became diluted more by disease than by the Cuban rebels' fire power. Although the ranks of the Spanish troops had significantly dropped, Spain still had about ninety thousand troops fit for duty. During the height of the Cuban crisis, the United States army consisted of only about 28,000 troops who had never fought a foreign war.[1]

While the majority of the American press treated the Spanish land forces with the same contempt that they held for the Spanish naval forces, this contempt for the Spanish army had a cautionary bent to it. The *Chicago Chronicle* reported that the Spanish army consisted of undisciplined youths who could not shoot their antiquated weapons straight; therefore, it would behoove the American army not to take the Spanish army lightly.[2] After all, the *Chronicle* further noted, the North held the same contempt for the South during the Civil War and woke up to the realization that the rebel forces fought ferociously. While Spain projected the image of an incompetent military force, some members of the U.S. press believed that reality would overshadow illusion when the war actually materialized.

The views by the cautionary newspapers countered the jingoistic presses' views that American troops would encounter very little trouble from the Spanish army. The nationalistic newspapers built their positive outlook on war with Spain around the concept of enhancing the military capabilities of the Cuban rebels through direct military aid. The *Chicago Tribune* informed its readers that as soon as war broke out between the United States and Spain, the United States would aid the rebels by sending them arms, provisions, and munitions. The theory behind this aid being that a better equipped Cuban rebellion force would enable the insurgents to take the offensive and devastate the Spanish army.

Resistance to the Spanish-American and Philippine Wars

This new offensive capability on the part of the Cuban rebels would become an important part of the U.S. military strategy. Once the Cuban rebels successfully assumed the offense, noted the *Chicago Tribune*, the U.S. fleet would establish a naval blockade of Cuba. Cornered by an aggressive Cuban rebel force and cutoff from key military and food supplies by the U.S. naval forces, the Spanish army would surrender and the war would come to an end. The *Chicago Inter-Ocean* echoed similar sentiments when its editor wrote that such a plan would end the hostilities "within two weeks."

The anti-war press had a much less cheerful outlook on war with Spain. As a whole, the anti-war press had little confidence in the fighting abilities of the Cuban rebels. The *New York Herald* editorialized that the chief military achievement of the Cuban insurgents during their clash with Spanish troops involved "the destruction of sugar, tobacco plantations, and the island forests." The *Chicago Chronicle* noted that the insurgents refused to fight, while the *New York Journal of Commerce* wrote that the rebels sought to "avoid all encounters" with the Spanish forces and confined their military operations to destroying Cuba's rail and agricultural systems.[3]

The potential effectiveness of a U.S. naval blockade also came under intense scrutiny. The keenly observant *London Times* cautioned that the Spanish soldiers can manage very well on "what seems like an inadequate amount of supplies" that would ultimately negate any real effect of a naval blockade by the United States. On the contrary, noted the *Times*, the naval blockade establish by the United States would hurt America's military capabilities rather than Spain's. The *London Times* theorized that a naval blockade compels any military organization to deal with a war over a large geographical area, and the United States lacked the experience and the ability to improvise to succeed in such a military operation.

Other members of the press questioned America's ability to even raise an army to fight such a distance war. The *Saturday Review* rhetorically asked it readers, "Where are the munitions and the officers to lead the men?"[4] The *Review* further wrote that while the U.S. Congress could approve resolutions associated with preparing for war, these resolutions could not create an army nor could they transport the military across hundreds of miles of sea lined with mines and constantly patrolled by Spanish torpedo boats. The editor of the *Saturday Review* also noted that even if the United States militarily negotiated these obstacles, they still faced the prospect of a battle hardened Spanish army whose numbers reached over 100,000.

7. Land Warfare

The reality of fighting a distance war became a constant theme in other American newspapers. The *Baltimore American* wrote that patriotic "exhilaration" complete with marching bands may raise the spirit of the American people and the American troops, but this exhilaration would soon dissipate when the reality of swamps and constant fire power from an elusive enemy comes into focus.[5] The *New York Herald* concurred when it noted that the most critical stage of any war is when the invading army confronts an occupying army that has obtained a firm and secure foothold on the base of operations. In essence, the United States' army would face two enemies: the natural environment of the Cuban island and the entrenched Spanish forces.

Many American leaders also lamented the difficulties facing the American army in Cuba. Senator Joseph Foraker from Ohio informed his congressional colleagues that since the Spanish army had occupied Cuba, their ranks had dwindled from 250,000 to a mere sixty thousand due to the island's various diseases. The esteemed Senator from Ohio further noted that such "raw and unacclimatized troops" as the American army can expect a similar fate. In complete agreement with Senator Foraker's assertions, the *New York Herald* wrote that thousands of American troops would fall prey to "the deadly scourge" of Cuba's climate.

While both the press and national leaders voiced concerns about American troops facing the destructive powers of yellow fever native to the Cuban island, the military's communication logistics also came into question. The editor of the *Emporia Gazette* cautioned that exposure to the yellow fever were not the only difficulties the American military force would face. The *Gazette* noted that inherent problems related to intercommunications between the United States and Cuban insurgents concerning the rules of quarantine needed addressing.[6] Without establishing a protocol for quarantine, the United States risked spreading the dreaded yellow fever to mainland America.

Without a doubt, the spread of yellow fever to the United States became a hot topic among the anti-war press of late-nineteenth-century America, but the overall numerical strength of the United States army also occupied vast space in the anti-war presses' many pages. *Harper's Weekly* posted a running commentary on the need for America to send an army to Cuba that outnumbered the occupying forces of Spain. The *Weekly* wrote that in order for the United States military venture to succeed at least seventy-five thousand men should descend on Cuba. The editor of *Harper's Weekly* further noted that the regular army strength of fifteen thousand troops would not succeed in a major clash with the sixty-thousand-plus strength of the Spanish forces.

The U.S. officials knew little about the true strength of the Spanish forces in Cuba. Major Howard Bliss and other U.S. military attachés relied on press clippings from the Spanish press for information concerning the Spanish troop levels in Cuba. The only information that Bliss and other attachés received concerning the Spanish occupation forces centered upon the number of Spanish troops fit for combat duties and the poor equipment and low morale of these troops. The information the U.S. military attachés relayed to their civilian superiors did not paint a true picture of the Spanish forces in Cuba, but it did raise the specter of U.S. troops facing a battle-tested Spanish army acclimated to Cuba's natural environment.

8

The Sentiments of the European Press

At the height of the Cuban crisis, the real possibility of a Spanish-American War caught the attention of the European nations. Most European nations sympathized with Spain. However, this sympathy did not materialize in active support because the governments of Europe had to contend with the deep hostilities that divided them. In addition to this, Britain, the only European nation capable of leading a European coalition in favor of Spain, sympathized with the United States in the name of Anglo–American solidarity.

Many of the newspapers on the European continent displayed pro–Spanish sentiments or at least anti–American bias while Britain newspapers openly supported the American cause. The views of the British press played a large part in the editorials of the American press particularly in the anti-war presses. For instance, the *Westminster Gazette* concluded that war between the United States and Spain would invariably lead to an American victory, but the struggle would be so sever and the costs so high that most of the American people would implore the President to seek a peace initiative.[1] The *Gazette*'s counterpart, the *London Engineer*, asserted that American ingenuity would give way to Spain's genius of "copying and purchasing the best naval guns" of the world, which would ultimately force U.S. leaders to avoid a confrontation with Spain.

The European assessment of the outcome of a Spanish-American confrontation included an analysis of American naval manpower. The *Engineer* believed that the present contingent of hired foreign manpower within the ranks of the U.S. Navy might prove successful if these foreigners were fighting to defend their own homeland. But the editor of the *Engineer* noted that no hired hand from an alien state would fight as ferociously for the United States. Due to this point, concluded the *London Times*, the United States would find a military victory in Cuba entailed "great difficulties" and would likely dissolve into an inconclusive naval guerrilla war that favored Spain.

Many British naval experts agreed with the British press' assertion concerning Spain's success with naval guerrilla warfare. In the *Fortnightly Review*, British naval expert Fred Jane stressed that Spain's torpedo boats and armored cruisers complemented the tactics of guerrilla warfare and would inflict heavy damage on the U.S. forces by impeding U.S. shipping routes, attacking larger U.S. warships, and striking the coastal area of the United States.[2] Jane believed that patriotic U.S. citizens would realize that the United States had picked a fight with a "tenacious" opponent. The editor of the *Westminster Gazette* agreed, reasoning that America would take the bull by the horns and start a war of aggression with Spain out of the mistaken belief that victory would come easily.

Newspapers across Europe came to similar conclusions. The *Nieuws van den Dag* of Amsterdam declared that in a war with the United States, Spain would undoubtedly lose but not until "she has inflicted" considerable damage upon the United States.[3] From the pages of the *Journal des Débat* in Paris, the editors noted that the United States would need to incur enormous sacrifices in order to break the Spanish troops' spirit. Thus, the news media of continental Europe generally believed that American jingoists underestimated the substantial harm associated with a war with Spain.

The citizens of the United States knew that public opinion across Europe contained anti–American sentiments when it came to the Cuban crisis. The *New York Times* wrote that many American citizens who kept abreast of the editorial comments coming from Europe's press were shocked and saddened at learning "of the unanimity" amongst the continental Europe press favoring Spain in the Cuban crisis.[4] While the internal conflicts between the European nations caused many of Europe's powerhouses to come to the brink of war, the American press noted that their unity in supporting Spain in the Cuban crisis suspended their hostility toward one another. The *Boston Herald* dryly remarked that the European countries' united "hostility" toward the United States is the one thing that they agree upon.

The pro-war newspapers of the United States either ignored the favoritism the European press showed Spain or they simply lied about

8. The Sentiments of the European Press

the support that these newspapers gave to the United States. The *Chicago Tribune* informed its readers that the most powerful European countries had become disillusioned with Spain's action in Cuba and looked forward to the day the United States "puts Spain in her place."[5] Some of the pro-war American newspapers simply relied on irrelevancy rather than lies when it came to reporting on the sentiments of the European press. These American newspapers wrote that European nations had their own problems to figure out rather than try to solve the problems associated with the Cuban crisis.

The American anti-war press vehemently disagreed with the notion of European nations focusing more on their internal problems than the problems of the Cuban crisis. The *San Francisco Chronicle* warned that "Spain has powerful friends in Europe," and these powerful friends might intervene on Spain's behalf in a war with the United States. The *New York Chronicle* noted that since Spain had incurred heavy debts, her European creditors "may feel compelled" to help her just to keep from losing their investments.[6] The *Chicago Chronicle* asserted that sympathetic European leaders, fearing a powerful American menace if Spain lost in a war with the United States, might intervene in a common cause to keep the United States from conquering the world.

As the eve of the Spanish-American War approached, clear evidence that the European powers would not get involve in a war between the United States and Spain coupled with rising British sympathy for the American cause dissipated fears of a European intervention. The *New York Herald* wrote that the great powers of Europe "had an undue preoccupation" with their own internal matters and would not give their full attention to the Cuban crisis. The European nation's "preoccupation" with internal problems still did not completely convince the American anti-war press that European intervention remained an impossibility. The *New York Herald* noted that if the European countries saw a U.S. victory over Spain as inevitable, they (especially Germany and France) would likely side with Spain in order to cripple America's manufacturing and commerce capabilities.

The anti-war presses' assessment of Spain's ability to resist U.S. military actions had its origin in the anti-war advocates' belief that a war with Spain would prove expensive and would compromise America's gold standard. The *New York Herald* wrote that a war with Spain would cost the United States approximately $500 million during the initial stages of the conflict and such a war-related cost would accelerate inflation.[7] *Herald*'s cross-town rival, the *New York Chronicle*, cautioned that a war with Spain would weaken America's "hold on the gold standard" and would eventually lead the country to accept the unstable free-silver standard. These same anti-war newspapers stressed the fact that engaging in a prolonged offensive war against Spain will cause the United States to incur war expenses greater than those it incurred during the Civil War.

The anti-war press also noted that the call for war by the pro-war advocates involved more political maneuvering than humanitarian action. Many editors across the United States noted that the political warmongers did not really care for Cuba or the Cuban rebels; they only wanted to get the country off the gold-standard and onto the free-silver standard through the means of war.[8] The *Chicago Times–Herald* wrote that "the jingoes'" desire for war with Spain involves their deeply held belief that a war would force the nation onto a free-silver standard. The *New York Tribune* concluded that "the most impatient patriots and the nosiest advocates of unconditional and uncompromising war are the money power advocates" who desire to put the nation on the free-silver standard at the expense of U.S. soldiers.

The pro-war newspapers also believed that voices for war contained a large free-silver streak. The *New York Journal of Commerce* argued that the silverites' chief desire was to force the country into bankruptcy by breaking down the gold standard through a so-called humanitarian war against Spain.[9] The *Journal of Commerce* further noted "the Populists and the Bryanites" in Congress would do whatever necessary to aid Spain by destroying the credit of the United States and depreciating her currency. The silverites, noted the *New York Journal of Commerce*, would force the United States to fight two wars; the Spanish on the front and the cheap money advocates in the rear.

While the pro-war newspapers focused on the cost of the United States giving aid to the Cuban rebels, the anti-war press emphasized that war with Spain would hamper economic recovery. *Bankers' Magazine* wrote that the prolonged Cuban insurrection had already inflicted great losses upon the commerce of the United States and a war between the United States and Spain would "incalculably increase" the losses of business investments.[10] Both the *Boston Transcript* and the *New York Chronicle* warned the country that war would not only affect the quality of life

8. The Sentiments of the European Press

in America, but also could cause a great financial setback that would leave the country's financial infrastructure vulnerable to collapse. The anti-war press firmly believed that the prospect of serious damage to America's financial system exceeded any advantage that the United States might gain through a victory over Spain.

9

Voices of Concern: The Business Community and the Spanish-American War

Throughout the years since the Spanish-American War, scholars have entertained two diametrically competing theses concerning the business community and its relationship with the Spanish-American War. Contemporary writers of the late-nineteenth century wrote that "the financial and business interests of the country were opposed to the war." This assumption develops from the belief that the war resulted from a combination of humanitarian compassion for the plight of the Cubans and the popular excitement skillfully generated by yellow journalism. On the other side of the argument, historians contended that U.S. industrial and financial expansion facilitated the war between Spain and the United States.[1]

That business sentiment, specifically in the east, contained a strong anti-war fervor during late 1897 and early 1898 is not open to debate. Wall Street stocks precipitously dove whenever the news indicated that war seemed on the horizon and rose just as quickly when the news presaged peace. Bulls and bears on the market were those who became apprehensive, respectively, about a peaceful and a hostile solution to the Cuban crisis. The "jingoes" in the press and in Congress became the target of antagonism from the editors of financial and business publications because they sought to defeat the anti-war editorials that flooded the business columns.[2]

The financial and business journals had their allies in the fight against the jingoes. Boards of trade and chambers of commerce added their call for peace to those of the financial and business publications. So intense was the solidarity of the business interests and their spokesmen that the jingoes started a campaign of slander that questioned the patriotism of Wall Street. Wall Street announced the pro-war publication the Sacramento *Evening Bee* represented a colossal "and aggregate Benedict Arnold of the union, and the syndicated Judas Iscariot of humanity."[3]

Congressional members also vented their frustration with the anti-war business press. Senator Thurston from Nebraska accused the anti-war press of being a safe haven for "money-changers." This charge brought a quick and blunt reply from the editor of the *American Banker*. The editor replied, "there is not an intelligent, self-respecting and civilized American citizen anywhere who would not prefer to have the existing crisis culminate" into a peaceful settlement.[4]

This anti-war sentiment on the part of the business journals continued up to the start of war between the U.S. and Spain. On February 28, the *New York Journal of Commerce and Commercial Bulletin* asserted that war could only be justified if (1) the naval board investigating the Maine disaster concluded that the destruction of the ship resulted from an official act of the Spanish government or (2) if Spain refused to compensate the United States if the board should hold that Madrid failed to exercise due diligence in safeguarding the vessel. On March 12, the *Commercial and Financial Chronicle* editorialized that the opposition of financial interests would stop the nation from going to war; and on April 2 labeled "monstrous" the proposition to settle the Cuban crisis by war while the slightest chance remained for a peaceful resolution. And on April 16, after the House of Representatives passed the Cuban resolutions, the Boston *Journal of Commerce* noted that "sober second thoughts had but little to do with the deliberations.... The members were carried off their feet by the war fever that had been so persistently worked up since the Maine explosion."[5]

The economic climate of the early 1890s is the main reason business interests held such sentiments. Since the panic of 1893, American businesses had experienced a severe economic depression. Efforts to revive the sagging economy faced an impediment brought on by the Venezuela controversy in December 1895 and again by the free silver campaign in 1896. However, in 1897 a real economic recovery seemed on the horizon and before the end of the year, signs of prosperity looked quite promising.[6]

Financial journals kept a keen eye on the improving economic conditions. The *New York Commercial* surveyed the business climate in various trades and industries and concluded that "after three years of waiting and false starts, the groundswell of demand has at last began to rise with a steadiness which leaves little doubt that an era of prosperity has appeared." In January of 1898, the *Commercial* noted "a supreme moment in the period of transition from depression to comparative prosperity." This optimism seems to represent the changing attitude of the financial and business worlds.[7]

This optimism also seems to have affected the sentiments of traditional conservative business journals. As early as July 1897, the *Commercial and Financial Chronicle* declared, "We appear to be on the eve of a revival in business" and in December remarked that "in brief, no one can study the industrial condition of today in America without a feeling of elation," after it had conducted a financial survey on the condition of the railroad and iron industries. The *Wall Street Journal* found only two negative "spots" in the entire country: Boston, because of the depressed demand for cotton goods, and New York, because the rate cutting created nervousness among the railroads. The *Wall Street Journal* celebrated that "throughout the west, southwest, and on the Pacific Coast business has never been better, nor the people more hopeful."[8]

The expansion of the American export trade facilitated the optimism of financial interests. A volume of exports that far exceeded the one of the previous year, and a notable increase in exports in manufactures of iron, steel, and copper, convinced business experts that the United States was on the verge of becoming the financial capital of the world. The editors of *Banker and Tradesman* noted, "there is no question that the world, generally, is looking more and more to the United States as the source of its supply for very many of the staple commodities of life." These sentiments must have brought elation to leaders in the iron and steel industries.[9]

The expansion of the U.S. export trade also had international implications. Cheaper materials and improved methods of creating the materials permitted U.S. manufacturers to undersell their European counterparts. Leading U.S. producers, such as iron magnate Andrew Carnegie, spoke constantly of taking advantage of these low costs. The business journal *The Iron Age* predicted the complete elimination of the business cycle through an improved planned economy, consolidation of the railroads and major industries, and higher wages and lower prices for U.S. consumers.[10]

9. Voices of Concern

The dark clouds of war threatened to dampen this great business revival. An editorial by the *Commercial and Financial Chronicle* in October of 1897 noted that international problems would ruin "the trade prosperity which all are enjoying." In April of 1898, the *Commercial* commented on the effect that the war rumors had on Wall Street: "Every influence has been, and even now is, tending strongly towards a term of decided prosperity, and that the Cuban disturbance, and it alone, has arrested the movement and checked enterprise." The *Banker and Tradesman* saw in the foreign complication the threat of "a material setback to the prosperous conditions which had just set in after five years of economic upheaval."[11]

The business news journals of the period generally shared the same sentiment about the effects of foreign problems on the stock market. The *Banker and Tradesman* summarized a calculation made by the Boston *Transcript* concerning the threat of war and the fluctuation of stocks. The *Banker and Tradesman* noted that the wave of prosperity had carried the average price of leading stocks to within five and a half points of the all-time high for the preceding decade and the Cuban crisis had, in less than two months, caused a ten percent loss in leading stocks. The New Jersey *Trade Review* roared that "war would impede the march of prosperity and put the country back many years."[12]

Other business news editors commented about the improving economy. The *Railway Age* noted that the country was coming out of a severe economic cloud and needed peace to complete the process of recovery. The *Railway* editorialized "from a commercial and mercenary standpoint it seems peculiarly bitter that this war should have come when the country had already suffered so much and so needed rest and peace."[13]

Business journals publicized the disadvantages that would result from war with Spain. The *Commercial and Financial Chronicle* editorialized that war would endanger the value of the dollar, interrupt foreign trading, and threaten the coastline and the commerce cycle. The *Banker's Magazine* piped that it would "incalculably increase the loss to business interests." The *United States Investor* joined this chorus, noting that war never materially benefitted a country.[14]

The transportation industry chimed in, offering perceptions about how war would affect their industrial cycle. The *Railroad Gazette* prophesied that war would disrupt "the business enterprise of every kind, stopping new projects and diminution of the output of existing businesses and contraction of trade everywhere." In essence, railroads stood to lose more than they could gain if war materialized between the United States and Spain. Even the one business segment that would benefit from war, the arms manufacturers, were not all in agreement about the profitability of war. The iron and steel news editors roared that war "would injure the iron and steel makers ten times as much as they would be benefitted by the prevailing spurt in the manufacture of small arms, projectiles, and steel plates for war ships."[15]

Many conservative business journals feared war would irreversibly devalue the currency and reanimate the long dead free silver debate. The abatement of the free silver agitation and the prospect of currency reform became the centerpiece of hopeful goals during the political season of 1897. During this time, "jingoes" had been accused of animating the expectations of war in the hope of inflating paper currency or silver. In an article entitled "The Breeding Grounds of Jingoism," the *New York Journal of Commerce* called attention to jingoistic groups that contained a large number of silverites whose ranks included "the financiers who desire to force bankruptcy on the country as a means of breaking down the gold standard," and collaterally pointed out that the chief ally of the Cuban insurgents, Senator Morgan, had schemed to place the United States on the silver standard.[16]

Other leading business journals endorsed this view. The *Commercial and Financial Chronicle* noted that many Cuban agitators "are only interested in the establishment of a free-silver standard, a plan which they think war would advance." Similar views peppered the editorial columns of such leading financial journals as the *American Banker* of New York, the *United States Investor* of Boston, and the *Rand-McNally Bankers' Monthly* of Chicago. The *Rand-McNally Bankers' Monthly* highlighted a speech by Secretary of the Treasury Gage: "It would be scarcely possibly for this nation to engage in war in its present condition ... without a suspension of specie payments and a resort to further issues of government notes."[17]

Many editorials in the business sector supported the Cuban rebels and their quest for independence. *The Financial Record*, in November of 1897, condemned "the cowardice of our Administration in refusing the phenomenally brave Cubans the commonest rights of belligerency" as disgraceful to the United States and commented that war with Spain, far from devaluing securities or injuring business, "would vastly increase the net earning power of every security sold on our market today." The mystery of the *Record*'s jingoistic attitude became clear when it considered unilateral free coinage of silver and clearly became the exception to the rule.[18]

Opposition to war and the results it would bring seemed less prominent in the west than it did on the Atlantic Coast. The Kanas City Board of Trade recommended that Cuban independence be recognized. On March 29, 1898, the Cincinnati Chamber of Commerce passed a resolution condemning Spain for its cruelties to the rebels and the destruction of the *Maine*, and called for a "firm and vigorous policy which will have for its purpose—peacefully if we can, but with force if we must—the redress of past wrongs, and the complete and unqualified independence of Cuba." The Chicago *Economist* did not support the notion that war would seriously hurt business or jeopardize the gold standard, and argued that liberation of Cuba, by peace or war, would produce "results of the highest value to mankind."[19]

Many leading financial journals also leaned toward the notion that war was not as bad as it was portrayed. The *Rand-McNally Bankers' Monthly* of Chicago, while hesitant about going to war with Spain, called attention to war mongering in the demoralized the stock market: meanwhile, "general business activity apparently received an impetus." Sharing the same sentiments, the *Age of Steel* in St. Louis noted it preferred peace but not peace "at the price of national honor." A leading St. Louis banker believed war would "cause a boom in many lines of business in this country ... and give employment to a large number of persons who are now out of work."[20]

Other like-minded financial journals highlighted the potential for economic growth that comes during a time when war is a great possibility. The Chattanooga *Tradesman* noted that a "small prospect" of war had already stimulated the iron trade and benefited the railroads by causing grain and other commodities shipments to increase in anticipation of future war prices. The *Mining and Scientific Press*, a San Francisco-based business journal that believed, in general, that war brings "havoc and waste and entails destructive expense," conceded that "to nearly everything related to the mining industry that war [with Spain] will be a stimulus."[21]

Even in the bastion of pessimism, New York, businessmen believed they saw beams of light among the thickening war clouds. According to the *Wall Street Journal*, after the *Maine* explosion, many stock market analysts "did not look for any great break in the market, because actual war with Spain would be a very small affair compared with the Venezuela complication with Great Britain." These analysts expected a sharp drop in stocks during the initial stages of hostilities, followed by a resumption of recent stock advances. In fact, these financial experts firmly believed that after the initial shock to the stock market brought on by war, a financial boom would occur.[22]

Other leading financial outlets joined the chorus of optimism in the face of impending war. On March 5, *Dun's Review* proclaimed "the nation looks for peace, but knows that its sources of prosperity are quite beyond the reach of any attack that is possible." *Bradstreet* contrasted the nervousness of Wall Street over war news with "the calm way in which general business interests have regarded the current foreign complications," and on March 12 *Dun's Review* noted that no industry or branch of business showed any restriction, and that the rapid gains in the financial sector indicated a growing demand for all products associated with the nation's leading industries.[23]

With war between the United States and Spain on the horizon, an examination of the attitude of U.S. business and industries that had a direct stake in Cuba must come under consideration. A large percentage of U.S. capital was invested in the Cuba sugar industry. The civil war in Cuba had devastating effects on this industry, not only by cutting off profits on capital that had been invested, but also by stifling valuable trade commodities between Cuba and the United States. As a matter of protecting their financial interests, many firms that suffered under these conditions desired to see the United States put an end to the conflict, although such intervention would drag the United States into war with Spain.

In May 1897, a group of concerned U.S. businessmen sought to take action. This group of businessmen presented Secretary of State John Sherman with a memorandum bearing over 300 signatures. The petitioners described themselves as

> citizens of the United States, doing business as bankers, merchants, manufacturers, steamship owners, and agents in the cities of Boston, New York, Philadelphia, Baltimore, Savannah, Charleston, Jacksonville, New Orleans, and other places, and also other citizens of the United States, who have been for many years engaged in the export and import trade with the island of Cuba.

9. Voices of Concern

The signers of the memorandum called attention to the significant losses that their businesses had incurred as a result of the ongoing hostilities in Cuba and expressed deep hope that to re-stabilize U.S. commerce and prevent additional serious losses, the United States needed to secure "the blessings of peace for one and a half millions of residents of the Island of Cuba" who suffered untold atrocities and to take the necessary steps to bring an honorable reconciliation between the parties involved in the civil conflict.[24]

On February 9, another group of businessmen delivered a memorandum to President McKinley that contained similar concerns. The memorandum straightforwardly informed the president that the Cuban war has directly cost the loss of $100,000,000 a year to the import and export trade market between the United States and Cuba during the three years of hostilities. The committee of businessmen further bolstered their case by adding to this loss:

> The heavy sums irretrievably lost by the destruction of American property, or properties supported by American capital in the island itself, such as sugar factories, railways, tobacco plantations, mines, and other industrial enterprises; the loss of the United States in trade and capital by means of this war being probably far greater and more serious than that of all the other parties concerned, not excepting Spain herself.

The foreboding memorandum that the businessmen presented to President McKinley went a step further in casting a dark shadow over the prospects of future import and export trade if the Cuban crisis continued. The memorandum informed the President that unless some type of peace accord could be established before May or June of the current year, the crops of the 1898–1899 season would be lost due to the inclement weather associated with the rainy season of late summer and early fall that would ultimately compel businessmen "to prepare for" the coming winter's crop "by repairing damaged fields, machinery," and lines of railways. Highlighting the importance of the Cuban trade to the United States and of U.S. participation "in the ownership or management of Cuban" sugar refineries, transportation, "and other enterprises," the committee of businessmen displayed optimism that the events in Cuba would help the president see that the situation on the island "was of sufficient importance as to warrant prompt and efficient measures by our government, with the sole object of restoring peace … and with it restoring to us a most valuable commercial field." Although it is clear

Resistance to the Spanish-American and Philippine Wars

that such business lobbyists made their voices and concerns known, it is difficult to measure the effect of their efforts on the decision-making process of the McKinley Administration.[25]

Although some business enterprises, such as the sugar plantations, felt the negative effects associated with the war in Cuba, other businesses thrived financially in spite of it. The U.S.-owned iron mines in Cuba continued to run smoothly during the height of the Cuban insurrection. Three U.S. iron entities in the single province of Santiago announced they had a large investment (some $6,000,000) of U.S. capital in the region that could easily be lost financially due to the direct or collateral effects of war. "We are fully advised as to our status in case of war," noted an official from one of the company to the assistant secretary of state, "and that this property might be subject to confiscation or destruction by the Spanish government."

Expropriation of their property was not the only concern of these businessmen. War between the United States and Spain, lamented a representative from another company, "will very likely mean the destruction of our valuable plant and in any event untold loss to our company and its American stockholders." A U.S. cork company with large interests in Spain; a New York exporter with trade in the Mediterranean and Black Sea; and a timber firm located in Mobile are samples of business enterprises that saw the clouds of war as a direct threat to their business interests. C. R. Fowles, a businessman from Norfolk concerned by the potential loss of profits, wanted the U.S. government to help businessmen protect themselves financially by granting them a letter of marque that would "enable" the businessmen "to lawfully capture Spanish merchant vessels and torpedo boats" in order to negate the impact that hostilities may have on the U.S. business community.[26]

The vocal output of the U.S. business community gives a clear picture of those who clamored for intervention and those who supported it. The business interests who supported it, either directly or indirectly, came from those with large interests in the Cuban sugar industry. Those business entities that opposed intervention included businesses that faced direct financial injury from the war. Although some conservative factions came to think of intervention on humanitarian grounds as inevitable, many influential business news outlets opposed U.S. intervention in the Cuban crisis to the end.[27]

In looking at the sentiments of the U.S. business community during

9. Voices of Concern

the Cuban crisis, an examination of that community's imperialistic motives is important. In assessing these motives, a number of questions arise. For instance, did U.S. business opinion favor schemes to acquire foreign territory to help supply U.S. markets for capital investment? Did U.S. businesses support or want a commercial base in distant lands in order to compete with its European counterparts?

As noted previously, the rising tide of prosperity became closely connected with the increase in U.S. exports; specifically the exports of manufactured goods. That the future well-being of the U.S. business community relied on the command of foreign markets became a universal opinion among many business journalists. The *New York Journal of Commerce* commented that U.S. industrial plants had expanded beyond the needs of domestic consumption. In the nail wire industry, the production of nails increased at such a high rate that it outpaced demand.

The production rate affected the wire nail manufacturers' mirrored production in other industries that resulted in an effort to expand the foreign trade export–import ratio. At a January 1898 annual meeting of the National Association of Manufacturers, "the discussion of ways and means for extending this country's trade, and more particularly its export business, was, in fact, almost the single theme of the speakers," reported the editor of *Bradstreet*. This same editor further noted, "nothing is more significant of the changed attitude toward this country's foreign trade, manifested by the American manufacturer today as compared with a few years ago, than the almost single devotion which he pays to the subject of possible export-trade extension."[28]

But if U.S. leading manufacturers believed foreign markets could be secured through colonial acquisitions, they kept the information to themselves. The idea of gaining additional markets led the topic of conversation in intellectual circles for years. For decades, political and intellectual leaders such as Mahan and Henry Cabot Lodge supported the idea that the country needed an imperialistic program for industrial and commercial development. Many in the business community opposed this idea because they believed it grew out of the dangerous jingoistic rhetoric that swept the country during the late 1890s.[29]

In the U.S. business community, a small group favored expansion in foreign lands. A minuscule group of business leaders supported plans for constructing a Nicaraguan canal with the aid of the U.S. government and in this small group, many considered the annexation of the Hawaiian Islands a very good thing. But beyond these two projects, most U.S. businessmen wanted to reign in any movement toward foreign expansion.[30]

The majority of business journals did not support construction and annexation schemes. Two of the most influential U.S. business news journals, the *New York Journal of Commerce* and the *Commercial and Financial Chronicle*, fervently opposed the canal construction and the annexing of the Hawaiian Islands. The *New York Journal of Commerce* made a parody of the arguments put forth by the proponents of both schemes. The nation's leading business journal jested: "we must certainly build the canal to defend the islands, and it is quite clear that we must acquire the islands ... in order to defend the canal."[31]

The *New York Journal of Commerce*'s satire vacillated between the humorous and the serious. The editor stated that the canal was not only unnecessary, but unless it became secure at each end and constantly patrolled by naval forces, it would become an albatross around the nation's neck. The *Journal* went on to comment that such a protective shield comes with the "price of jingoism" and would "easily cost us $25,000,000 a year, besides the lump sum that will be required for the original investment, and there is absolutely no excuse whatever in our commercial or our political interests for a single step in this long procession of expenses and of complications with foreign powers."[32]

Concerning Hawaii and Cuba, instability ruled out self-government for both, and the Constitution of the United States did not contain a mechanism for governing colonies. The Hawaiian Islands' only military value lay in the United States establishing a Pacific naval force capable of creating a security shield around the island. The *Commercial and Financial Chronicle* showed colonies as expensive outposts that would severely weaken the overall security of the United States, while the St. Louis *Age of Steel* cautioned that the expansion of export trade likely would "lead to territorial greed, as in the case of older nations, the price of which in armaments and militarism offsets the gain made by the spindle and the forge."[33]

To many business experts, colonies represented a dangerous expense that would entail commercial failure. Did not the colonies of Great Britain provide us with the most valuable goods of our export market? Did we not have favorable trade with Guiana, a British colony? "Most of our ideas of the commercial value of conquests, the commercial uses of navies and the commercial advantages of political control," commented the *Journal of Commerce*, dated back to times when colonial policies' very existence involved monopolization of the colonial trade market for the benefit of the mother country.[34]

Leading business journals became highly contemptible of foreign countries' positive sentiments regarding U.S. colonial possibilities. The *Commercial and Financial Chronicle* felt that European enthusiasm for colonies involved false premises; for even if trade remains loyal to the flag, "the trade is not always with the home markets of the colonies. England and the United States are quite as apt to slip in with their wares under the very custom-house pennant of the French or German dependency."[35]

Outright opposition of U.S. business journals to European opinion represented a small majority of the sentiment prevalent in the business community. Silence comes the closest to describing the common trait on this subject. Positive and negative evidence together point to the conclusion that the U.S. business community generally consisted of either those with complete indifference to imperialism or unconditional opposition to imperialism.

Trust in the continued expansion of the export trade centered on confidence in the principles of *laissez-faire* in a global market that revolved around a system of free trade. Leading manufacturers in the United States had enough confidence in their products that they could compete, in price and quality, with other industrial nations of the world. U.S. businessmen believed that, given a level playing field, their products would rise to the top in demand. The U.S. government could facilitate the success of these businesses, not by acquiring colonial markets but by eliminating or modifying the trade barriers that restricted imports of new materials and exchange commodities.

In spite of the long history of paying strict attention to the tariff as businesses had, the amount of free-trade sentiment grew during the months of late 1897 and early 1898. Congressional fascination with the rising duties associated with the Dingley Act was disconcerting to industrialists who favored and had a great interest in the export trade. The *Journal of Commerce* noted how pathetic it was "to see the national legislature bending its whole force to readjusting the trammels of a system which can only obstruct, and closing its eyes to the manifest, through unconscious, struggling of industry for a freedom that will enable it to compete successfully in any market of the world."[36]

Numerous business journals became aware of the uselessness of expecting exports to increase while limiting imports, and believed that a change in U.S. free-trade policy would soon materialize. The *Iron Age* exclaimed, "we are gradually losing our fear of the bugaboo of cheap foreign labor and slowly realizing that we hold the key of the position, since there are no indications that European manufacturers will ever displace us in the van of progress."

The *American Machinist* noted that the recent gains in export trade indicated that the tariff as a sharp tool on the international market had become dull and ineffective, that commodities could be sold within the domain of foreign competitors and no longer needed a protective shield on the domestic front, and leading business entities would likely pressure congress "toward action which will equalize these matters." The Chattanooga *Tradesman* firmly believed that growth in the export trade would result in a "broad and radical" effect on U.S. international business policies, and the president of the Baltimore Chamber of Commerce prophesied that "the day is not so far distant when free trade, in some measure, at least, will become part of our political faith."[37]

In a free-trade oriented system, the value of colonies would be insignificant. But if nations that U.S. manufacturers looked to for their products suddenly adopted restrictive trade policies, then a change in the U.S. business attitude on international trade markets may have occurred. Two developments in the latter part of 1897 hinted that the global sphere might not continue its friendly behavior toward U.S. products as it has in the past. The first development came in an address given by Count Goluchowski, Austro-Hungarian foreign minister, to the Austro-Hungarian delegations, detailing how destructive the trade policies of transoceanic countries had on European products and warned that "Europeans must fight shoulder to shoulder against the common danger, and must arm themselves for the struggle with all the means at their disposal."[38]

The Austro-Hungarian foreign minister cloaked his proclamation in terms of protection for Europe's future. The twentieth century, the Count declared, represents "a period marked by a struggle for existence in the politico-commercial sphere." He further insisted that Europe must unite when he stated that "the European nations must close their ranks in order to successfully defend their existence."[39]

Many leading industrialists in the United States believed the Count's declarations targeted the United States and its business leaders. The foreign minister's comments generated great interest in the United States but little serious alarm. Many business news journals did not believe in the feasibility of European commercial cooperation aimed at excluding U.S. products, pointing out that eliminating trade between the United States and Europe would negatively affect the Europeans more than it would the Americans because the United States provided Europe with material necessities, whereas Europe only provided the United States with commodities that the U.S. could produce.[40]

The viability of securing markets other than those in Europe occupied the thoughts of many U.S. businessmen. The *New York Commercial* stated that if the Europeans decided to exclude U.S. products from their markets, the United States would seek markets that the European cherished. The Philadelphia *Ledger* echoed similar sentiments, and acknowledged that a concerted effort on the part of Europe to limit U.S. products would incapacitate our markets there. But, the *Ledger* added, U.S. trade in the Far East and in South America would not "be directly disturbed through any European alliance."

Although the view of the *Commercial* and the *Ledger* gained traction in the U.S. business world, many leading journals looked at the situation in a more realistic manner. The *New York Journal of Commerce* stated that, in their determination to corner markets, the industrial nations of Europe started a slow descent down two paths: colonial acquisition and the enactment of unfair tariff policies. Up to that time, each European nation worked alone, but now many of these countries leaned toward joining a tariff alliance aimed at altering the preexisting tariff policy. Because Austria-Hungary had a $10,000,000 per year trade surplus with the United States, the *Journal of Commerce* surmised that an outside source (likely Russia) initiated this plan for a European tariff coalition, since Count Goluchowski did not want to lose this trade surplus and Russia had its own ulterior motives for wanting the tariff alliance.[41]

When the *Journal of Commerce* voiced its concern about the underlying motives of the Count's speech, in all likelihood the paper's editors believed the speech revealed a threat to U.S. markets in the Far East. Within days of the Count's declaration, a German force expelled the Chinese garrison at Tsingtau, seized the forts, and occupied the port. Within a week of this excursion, the German government presented its formal demands to China, including the sole right to build railways, open coal mines in Shantung, and take control of the naval station on Kraochow Bay. China yielded to these demands and in early March 1898 a ratified treaty codified the demands.

European aggression did not stop with the German excursion. Within a week of Germany taking possession of Tsingtau, the naval forces of Russia arrived at Port Arthur, and by May 1898, China had relinquished Port Arthur, Dalny, and most of the interior territories located in the vicinity of the Liaotung peninsula. France and Great Britain demanded and received compensation for the German and Russian expropriation of the Chinese territory. These events seem to suggest that the *New York Journal of Commerce* correctly believed that a grand scheme by a European alliance to take over and control global market places was taking shape.

However, the actions of Germany and Russia went far beyond proving the *New York Journal of Commerce* right; they also showed that actions spoke louder than words. These actions by Europe's two leading nations awakened a sensitive spot in the U.S. business community's psyche because even though U.S. trade with China represented less than two percent of its total foreign trade in 1897, the export ratio to China had double these numbers in 1896, indicating that China became a vital global marketplace for U.S. surplus products. Even with this knowledge, some business news outlets did not take the consequences from the Chinese crisis seriously, whereas others only saw positive advantages for the United States if China's development came under European influence. The most extreme view of the Chinese crisis came from a sector of U.S. industrialists who believed that, in all probability, U.S. trade would likely find itself discriminated against or, at most, excluded from global markets by the participating members of the European alliance.[42]

Former government officials added their professional opinions to the Chinese crisis and its implications for U.S. foreign trade. Charles Denby, former Minister to China, cautioned that with the seizure of territory, U.S. trade protocols with China "falls to the ground, and spheres of influence hostile to American commerce spring into existence." The *New York Journal of Commerce* vehemently expressed the same sentiments. Although this journal voiced pacifist and anti-imperialist views in its columns, it noted that the foundation of global trade became endangered as a result of Europe's partition of China.[43]

9. Voices of Concern

The *New York Journal of Commerce* espoused a detailed plan for taking corrective action. It declared that opening the markets of China would resolve the problem of U.S. surplus production, but for this to become successful, U.S. manufacturers must have complete equality of rights in China with the European nations. The *Journal* also called for the creation of an isthmian canal, the acquisition of Hawaii, and an expansion of U.S. naval forces: three measures that the journal previously opposed.[44]

Countering the State Department's lack of interest in the China crisis, the *Journal of Commerce* launched a campaign to bring the Chinese situation to the attention of the President. Following the *Journal*'s recommendation, a committee on U.S. interests in China was created to facilitate coordinated actions by the nation's chambers of commerce. As a result of this persuasive advertising, on February 3, 1898, a committee from the Chamber of Commerce of the State of New York presented a report on "American Treaty Rights in China" along with a memorandum to President McKinley. The report recapitulated the treaty history of Sino–American commercial rights and argued that these rights were jeopardized by the aggressive actions of the European nations.

The report also detailed the inherent dangers that the China crisis posed to U.S. businesses. U.S. products, it noted, were literally banned from French Cochinchina: a warning of what to expect if other European powers solidified their position on Chinese soil. "The Administration at Washington," the report exclaimed, "seems to be supine about the present menace to those important interests of our citizens in China.... Under these circumstances it would seem that unless those concerned in our export trade take steps to agitate the matter and to have their interests safeguarded, nobody else will do it."

The memorandum to President McKinley highlighted how vital U.S. trade relations with China were and the formidable obstacles that threatened it, and urged that measures be taken "for the prompt and energetic defense of the existing treaty rights of our citizens in China, and for the preservation and protection of their important commercial interests in that empire."[45]

A little less than three weeks later, a number of chambers of commerce and boards of trade across the nation took identical action. Not satisfied with this action, on March 3 a group of businessmen, meeting at 59 Wall Street in New York, formed an organization specifically for

Resistance to the Spanish-American and Philippine Wars

the protection of the eastern trade. Within a week, with the generous help of the New York Chamber of Commerce, this group of merchants organized the American, China, and Japan Association to act as a protective shield for the interests of U.S. citizens and to secure information relating to international trade. The organization also acted as a springboard to disseminate information to those nations that held the same trade sentiments as the United States.[46]

The inner workings of the organization were not completed until June 16. By the time that the internal mechanism of the organization was perfected, the battle of Manila Bay had given the United States a panoramic view of the East and the organization followed suit by changing its title to the American-Asiatic Association and including "the Philippine Islands" and other "Asia and Oceania" nations in the U.S. trade interest. Once the association had some stability, it informed the State Department that the United States government was free to use its services and resources for consultation.[47]

In consideration of this extraordinary interest in preserving the Chinese market, one can understand why U.S. businesses, that previously displayed intense anti-war and anti-imperialist sentiments, showed great enthusiasm at the news of Admiral Dewey's naval victory at Manila Bay. Not only did the news dispel the fears of a costly and infinite war, stock prices rose to record heights. Additionally, from a business perspective, the victory at Manila Bay allowed trade in the East to come under the control of the United States.[48]

The U.S. press advertised the naval attack on the Spanish fleet well before the military action took place. Many newspapers surmised that the value of the islands would lead to an attack at Manila Bay and that a victory would change the U.S. view of the quandary in China. However, most newspapers did not come to this speculation until after the Spanish fleet's destruction and the United States had complete control over Manila Bay. Interestingly enough, after the Dewey naval victory, businessmen joined the jingoes in their acclaim of imperial conquests.[49]

This patriotic coalition is seen by the statements made by influential members of the jingoes and the press. One of Congress' most powerful Senators, Henry Cabot Lodge from Massachusetts, held "the other side of the Pacific, and the value to this country ... almost beyond recognition." Lodge represents the same fervent rhetoric that many conservative business journals expressed in their columns. It was not the material value of the Philippines that caught the attention of U.S. supporters, although the intrinsic value of the island did not go unnoticed. These U.S. supporters built their support on the belief that the Philippines' unique locations allowed it to become a gateway to the Eastern marketplaces.[50]

The aggressive actions of the European nations in China compelled the *New York Journal of Commerce* to reexamine its position on expansionism and support a position that included a U.S.-built isthmian canal, acquisition of Hawaii, and a drastic expansion of U.S. naval forces. Taking a 360-degree turn from its previous foreign policy position, the *Journal of Commerce* took the lead in espousing a foreign policy that would use the Philippines' strategic position to uphold U.S. rights in China. The paper lamented that such a move might be disturbing, but it became a necessity and a major "factor in the protection of our interests in that part of the world." The *Journal of Commerce* added that the United States "allowed Great Britain to fight our battle for an open market in China; with our flag floating within 500 miles of Hong Kong we shall be able to give that policy something more than merely moral support in the future."

The paper highlighted the point of U.S. moral duty with a ringing statement. To allow the islands to be returned to Spain or to let them come under England's or any other European nation's power "would be an act of inconceivable folly in the face of our imperative future necessities for a basis of naval and military force on the western shores of the Pacific."[51] Support and approval of these views came rapidly from other business news venues. On May 5, the *Wall Street Journal* commented that some leading business experts

> believe that the United States should retain enough interest in the Philippines to be sure of a coaling station and a naval base in Asiatic waters, under belief that the breaking up of China will make it necessary for this country to be in a position to protect, not only the existing trade with the far east, but the enormously greater trade likely to be developed in the next 25 years.

The *American Banker*, while exempting the United States from charges of entering the war for ulterior motives, stated unequivocally that the United States could not relinquish the territories it had been compelled to seize. The *Banker* added "that a war with Spain should have transpired at precisely this time, when Europe is tending to divide a considerable section of the inhabited earth, is a coincidence which has a providential air." The *Banker and Tradesman* also declared that the hand of God bestowed the Philippines on the United States at a time when a European alliance threatened U.S. trade in China, and asked if the United States had the right to disregard "a possession which would be of such great advantage to us in maintain and defending our interests in this part of the globe?" The *Banker and Tradesman* later argued that the answer to China's open door "was given, as European nations very well know, when Dewey entered Manila Bay and won his glorious victory."[52]

Similar views found their way into the editorial columns of other renowned business journals. The *Age of Steel*, the *Iron Age*, the *United States Investor*, and the *Financial Record* affirmed the sentiments expressed by the *Banker and Tradesman*. *Bradstreet* firmly believed that control of Manila would stimulate the growth of U.S. trade in Asia and envisioned a day when the city "might in time even rival Hong Kong as a distributive trade center." The *New York Commercial*, relying on data supplied by Washington's Bureau of Statistics, noted that countries in close proximity to the Philippines contained well over 800,000,000 people, and purchased over $1 billion in commodities annually, mostly products grown or manufactured in the United States.[53]

Other members of the U.S. business community commented extensively on this subject. The New York Chamber of Commerce, reporting on "American Interests in China," asserted that, in the face of the prospect that European influence on Chinese territory might become permanent, the only recourse the United States could take to protect her interests was to become an active participant in the "politically dangerous ground of the Far East"; a participation that could be "hastened through our possible occupation of the Philippines Islands."[54]

The various regions of the country insisted that the Philippine Islands stay under U.S. control for the sake of facilitating commercial trade to Asiatic markets. In the South, merchants believed that retaining the Island would ensure a marketplace for cotton goods. The *Mining and Scientific Press* contended that Pacific coast cities could be transformed into first-class competitors in the trade industry. As so eloquently put by the *Mining and Scientific Press*, "the guns that destroyed the Spanish fleet in Manila Bay thundered a warning to the nations of our approaching commercial supremacy in the Orient."

Other regional business journals jumped on board to express their

9. Voices of Concern

opinions about the Philippines. The *Commercial Bulletin* of southern California considered the acquisition of the Philippines a way to accelerate the growth of trans-Pacific trade and proclaimed that "Pacific coast people so generally favor territorial expansion." The *Daily Commercial News and Shipping List* believed that Americans living on the Pacific coast would use political influence to ensure the United States retain the Philippines. The Chamber of Commerce of Seattle, the Chamber of Commerce Merchant Association, and Manufacturer and Producer Association of San Francisco appealed to the President for retention of the Islands, "and all other lands which are now, or may hereafter be acquired in the present war with Spain," for humanitarian reasons and continuation of Asia trade to the United States.[55]

The voices of U.S. leading financiers rang loud in announcing their opinions about the nation's policy in Asia. James J. Hill, previously an aggressive opponent of the war with Spain, informed a newspaper reporter that if he had anything to do with it, he would make sure that the United States kept the Philippines. The financial giant further stated, "if you go back in the commercial history of the world you will find that the people who controlled the trade of the Orient have been the people who held the purse strings of nations."[56]

The business community also generated a fair amount of opposition and indifference when it came to the subject of retaining the Philippine Islands. The *New York Journal of Commerce* condemned the idea that apprehensive people rejected the idea of imperialism and that "the businessmen of the country are maintaining a deathlike silence" on the issue of keeping the Philippines. The *Commercial and Financial Chronicle* pointed out that the United States needs to be careful when considering acquiring any overseas territory, because acquiring foreign territory had been Spain's Achilles' heel in her foreign policy. The Baltimore *Journal of Commerce*, which vehemently opposed annexation, held that no one yet knew whether "our position as wet nurse to Cuba, proprietors of Porto Rico, and pantata to the Philippines is likely to bring us profit or loss."[57]

The overall value of the Philippine Islands became a major concern for those who opposed expansionism. The *Iron Age*, which previously supported expansionism, held nagging doubts about the real value of the Philippines to the U.S. business community. President Everett Frazer of the American Asiatic Association, who personally wanted to annex the Philippines, delayed taking any action on a resolution that supported the notion of annexation. The *San Francisco Call*, acting as a proxy for the California-Hawaiian sugar interests of the Spreckels family, opposed adding the Philippines by arguing that tropical colonization inherently involves health risks that could negatively affect the population of the United States and that California's sugar-beet growers faced stiff competition from the cane-sugar farmers in the Philippines.[58]

Accurately determining the strength of those businesses that voiced their support for or against the retention of the Philippine Islands is difficult. Judging from expressions that emanated from the business community, it seems safe to conclude that the U.S. business world of late 1897 and early 1898 opposed war with Spain and either opposed territorial expansion or did not comprehend the problems inherent to acquiring a global colonial market. It seems equally safe to conclude that after Dewey's victory in Manila Bay, U.S. business became more imperialistic in its global outlook. It also seems certain that the business community's opinion changed concerning the acquisition of the Philippine Islands when the European threat to U.S. global markets materialized.

Having concluded that acquisition of the Philippines could do more good than harm, the U.S. business community believed that additional expansion was in order. The Philippine experiments strengthened the business community's demand to annex Hawaii. The *Journal of Commerce* announced that "the battle of Manila Bay makes it imperative that we should establish permanent arrangements which will make the [Hawaiian] islands a halfway house on the road to the Philippines." When President McKinley, in early July, signed a congressional resolution for annexation, the U.S. business world praised the measure as a step toward economic expansion.

Influential voices in the business community also believed that the resolution represented a step that the United States needed to take to assume her rightful place in world affairs. *Bradstreet* believed that the resolution "gave a new direction to the impulse toward expansion, which is seldom missing among the characteristics of great nations." Some business journals let it be known that there were other Pacific islands just as attractive as the Philippines. The Philadelphia *Press* proclaimed that the United States should "bridge the Pacific" with the Philippines so that the chains of expansionism could become a complete circle.[59]

9. Voices of Concern

These same voices announced the value and security that expansionism brought to the United States. In the Caribbean, business interests argued that the United States needed Puerto Rico for its military strategic position and commercial value, and suggested that upholding the guidelines in the Teller Amendment, which promised that the United States would not annex Cuba, might prove impossible to fulfill. The *Journal of Commerce*, expressing graves doubts concerning the Cubans' ability to govern themselves, stated that "the Teller amendment ... must be interpreted in a sense somewhat different from that which its author intended it to bear." In short, the United States must exert her influence over Cuba to ensure that an orderly government is established and maintained.[60]

U.S. desirous conduct included other foreign territories besides the Spanish islands. During the early part of March 1898, the *New York Commercial* supported the idea that the United States purchase the territory of St. Thomas, in the Danish West Indies, as part of an ongoing strategy to bolster the nation's naval forces. Two months later, signs indicated that the British West Indies would likely accept the possibility of U.S. rule, and the *Journal of Commerce* urged the nation not to miss this golden opportunity. In endorsing this idea, the influential business journal proclaimed: "Our people are now in an expansive mood and there is a deep and strong American sentiment that would rejoice to see the British flag, as well as the Spanish flag, out of the West Indies."[61]

Many U.S. businesses now viewed colonial possessions as a solution to the problem of disposing of U.S. surplus products. The *New York Commercial* remarked that European nations' outwardly antipathy toward U.S. products led them to acquire colonial markets. The *Commercial* further commented that the acquisition of the Spanish islands would stimulate the demand for U.S. products and become an outlet for U.S. surplus goods. The distinguished business journal endorsed the idea that to facilitate this system, the United States should require these islands to shape their customs in such a manner that these customs would resemble the United States' own traditional business principles.[62]

This plan, espoused by the *New York Commercial*, did not garner wide support from other powerful business news journals. The *Journal of Commerce*, the *Commercial*, the *Financial Chronicle*, and other business-oriented journals and organizations dismissed this process, and believed the United States must adhere to the same business principles she applied to the "open door" policy in China. The *Railway World* went a step further and announced that "one way of opening a market is to conquer it." The *World* added that "already our enterprising merchants are beginning to organize to take possession of the markets which our army and navy have opened to them."[63]

Some business journals believed U.S. merchants quickly took advantage of this newfound occasion. The Chicago *Inter-Ocean* raved that merchants and manufacturers were "very generally waking up to the opportunities which the war has brought at a moment when the immense increase of our manufacturing capacity has rendered foreign outlets absolutely necessary to us."

U.S. business eventually yielded to the necessity of a war with Spain, facilitated in part by the deteriorating conditions during the Cuban crisis. The business community had not anticipated the colonial responsibilities that could result from war. However, Dewey's electrifying victory during May of 1898 offered the business community a far-eastern base in China that promised additional opportunities for trade. As the year came to a close, leading business spokespeople praised the "incalculable expansion of the influence of the United States among other nations" or announced that the year had "witnessed a complete change in the temper and aspirations of the American people.... Our commercial horizon has been broadened."[64] The *Banker and Tradesman* went a step further by noting, "Our ideas of the work which is before us have been greatly magnified, and we have begun to be slightly conscious of the field of development into which this nation is evidently destined to enter."[65]

During the heated days of the late nineteenth century, no sector of U.S. society had transformed as much as the U.S. business community.

10

A War Without Benefits

The anti-war press believed that a successful war against Spain would not only cost the United States financially, it also offered no material benefits. After winning the war against Spain, lamented the anti-war advocates, Cuba would fall under the control of the United States and shortly thereafter America would regret Spain's departure. The anti-war press believed that the racial make-up of Cuba would increase America's regret, demonstrating their strong social Darwinism.

Most pro-war advocates studiously avoided any reference to the racial make-up of the Cuban island; when they did talk about the racial component, it was in conciliatory tones. The *Atlanta Constitution* wrote that native Cubans had comparatively little "Negro or Indian" blood in their veins and that the leaders within the rebel government contained "very competent men belonging to some of the best families of Cuba."[1] The senior rebel representative in the United States announced that no members of the governing assembly belonged to the "colored race." Literature that supported the Cuban insurgency either ignored the issue of race or stressed the fact that blacks occupied the subordinate positions within the rebel army.

The anti-war newspapers were more than willing to share information on the Cuban island's racial make-up to persuade the American public to oppose going to war with Spain. The anti-war press reminded their readers that the Cuban population consisted of "one-half Negroes" transported directly from Africa with the remaining half of the population descending from "the Spaniards."[2] The editors of the *San Francisco Chronicle* flatly stated that the Cuban insurgency consisted of "Negroes and half-breeds," while the *Chicago Times–Herald* noted that the Cuban insurgency contained a crude mixture of "Spanish, Indian, and Negro." Clearly, the anti-war press played on the America public's racial fears to keep the nation at peace with Spain.

Resistance to the Spanish-American and Philippine Wars

The anti-war press further used racial dynamics to support their argument that Cuba should remain under the rule of Spain. The *New York Herald* proclaimed that the term "*Cuba Libre*" means another "Black Republic" in the vicinity of the western hemisphere. The *Herald* also noted that the American people did not want such a republic so near and already had one in the form of "Hayti."[3] An independent Cuba, echoed the *Boston Herald*, would gradually transform into a second Haiti that would place a "terrible burden" on the U.S. people if the United States annexed the island. In short, the anti-war press believe that annexing the Cuban island would bring the standards of the United States down and force the nation to deal with a racial problem she did not want to address.

The American public did not want to annex territory that housed inferior people, they did not want to annex any Spanish colony or the Philippines. As the public engaged in a heated debate over the costs and benefits of waging war with Spain, the status of the Philippines came up only as a strategic liability for Spain rather than a blessing for the United States. The *New York Times* wrote that at the beginning of hostilities, the Philippine Islands would likely become "an easy and tempting" target for a U.S. military strike or an opportunity for Japan to add territory to her empire.[4] Showing skepticism toward these sentiments, the anti-war *New York Herald* noted that the Philippines would give the United States a voice in the East and the nation would be wise to add the islands to her strategic plans.

In a surprising show of solidarity with the anti-war press, the pro-war *New York Journal* echoed these sentiments. The *Journal* wrote that the United States should "reimburse ourselves" for the cost of waging war with Spain by compelling Spain to surrender the Caroline and Philippine islands and using this territory as property to sell to other nations.[5] The editor of the *New York Journal* further noted that this would meet the other nation's need for new territory. Until the outbreak of hostilities between the United States and Spain no one in the press, Congress, or in the White House even hinted at the value or liability of annexing the Philippine islands.

The most influential U.S. newspapers of the late nineteenth century opposed the war because of the lack of spoils associated with a military victory and for other practical reasons. As the war with Spain entered its second week, *Harper's Weekly* wrote that no war in history, other than

10. A War Without Benefits

America's war with Spain, has ever promised nothing but loss to the nation who started it.[6] The editor of this article went further in condemning the Spanish-American War by pointing out a key anti-war position: the cost in terms of money and American lives greatly outweighed any benefits the United States could gain by engaging in such a war. In essence, many newspapers felt the United States had nothing to gain and everything to lose in the war with Spain.

Many of the contemporary U.S. newspapers of the late nineteenth century supported the assertion about the costs of the war outweighing any benefits the United States could gain. The *New York Journal of Commerce* editorialized that the anti-war advocates consists of industrialists, railroad investors, and business merchants who kept the economy running with their "plethoric" bank accounts. A war with no visible gain attached to it would stress these financial titans and place the United States on the road to financial catastrophe.[7] The *Wall Street Journal*, a newspaper that did not take a strong position on America's war with Spain, wrote that conservative men in the United States would welcome any steps that would "relieve the Cuban dilemma" while at the same time maintain the peace. In assessing America's costs in fighting a war with Spain, the specter of economic destruction clearly ran through the editorials of the anti-war press.

More indirectly, these same sentiments were confirmed in the pro-war press. At the height of the American public's emotional response to the sinking of the Maine, the *New York Journal* spoke out against the call for war by the "money-grubbing" financial sector at the expense of American lives and to the dishonor of the American flag. The *New York Journal* noted that the financial giants' lust for money not only blinded them to the suffering that Americans would incur during a war with Spain, but also to the irreversible harm of wartime costs. The *Chicago Journal of Commerce* visually portrayed these sentiments when it printed a political cartoon showing President McKinley holding a scale with one end holding a human corpse and the other holding a heavy sack full of money.[8]

11

A Shift in Public Opinion

The destruction of the U.S.S. *Maine* hardened American citizens' feelings toward Spain and increased the ranks of the pro-war advocates. Many of the staunchest anti-war newspapers of late-nineteenth-century America dramatically changed their positions after the destruction of the *Maine*. Some of the most prominent reasons that these anti-war newspapers changed their viewpoint involve fear that continuing uncertainty about the events surrounding the sinking of the *Maine* would depress the business sector, suspicion that Spain might have actually caused the *Maine*'s explosion, and pressure from public opinion. However, the one overriding reason that the anti-war newspapers changed positions was domestic politics.

The *Chicago Times–Herald*, one of the most influential anti-war news outlets, reversed its position for political reasons leading many other newspapers across the nation to follow suit. This independent Chicago newspaper wrote that the United States must intervene in the Cuban crisis peacefully if possible or "forcibly if we must," but some type of intervention was required.[1] The editor of the *Times–Herald* also stated that President McKinley's peace initiatives would lead the Bryan elements of the Democratic Party to certain victory in the November congressional elections. In a choice between Cuban liberty and the prospects of a Bryan Presidential election, the *Chicago Times–Herald* seem to support a war with Spain.

The *New York Times* also concluded that the United States had no choice but to go to war with Spain. The *Times* wrote that the United States should concentrate not on what Spain had done, but what she had not done.[2] The editorial explained Spain's complete failure to put down the Cuban rebellion coupled with the "savage repression" she applied in attempting to do so. This had caused the American people to sympathize with the Cuban insurgents. The *New York Times* further noted that this

11. A Shift in Public Opinion

dissatisfaction on the part of the American people might not gain the approval of the U.S. government, but it did auger grave political consequences when it came time for the American citizens to cast their votes.

The *New York Times* joined other anti-war newspapers in tying the fate of political elections to the issue of going to war with Spain. The *New York Herald*, a leader in the ranks of the war opposition, noted that the *Maine*'s destruction inflamed public sentiment against Spain and facilitated congressional revolt against McKinley's peace policies. The *Herald*, who had categorically opposed the notion of a independent Cuba, wrote that any peace measures had to include independence for Cuba. If the Spanish government refused such a proposition, war became the only option.

While the *New York Herald* gave in to the strong tide of war fever, it did so reluctantly. The editor of the *Herald* stated that war is not something the United States should seek and any victory over Spain may seem empty, but war between the United States and Spain becomes the only real option given the circumstances of Spain's belligerency. The *Herald* linked Spain's situation to that of the American South during the Civil War. If the North could not solve its problems with the South without going to war, how could the nation solve its problems with Spain any other way?

The ranks of the anti-war newspapers shrank again when the *Commercial Advertiser* joined forces with the pro-war newspapers. The *Advertiser* accepted the concept of war not because of some moral duty, but because the "stimulus" of public sentiment and pressure from congressional members gave the anti-war newspapers no alternative.[3] The editor of the *Advertiser* noted that continued resistance to public opinion concerning going to war with Spain would result in an electoral victory for the Bryan forces in the congressional elections. In other words, political expediency overrode the *Commercial Advertiser*'s reservations for to war with Spain.

Among the anti-war advocates changing their positions about going to war with Spain, the *Chicago Chronicle* represents a special case. The fact that the newspaper heavily favored the Democratic Party should not go unnoticed. During the months prior to the start of hostilities between the United States and Spain, the editor of the *Chicago Chronicle* harshly criticized the McKinley Administration for its failure to aid the Cuban insurgency. The *Chronicle* noted that lack of aid to the Cuban rebels by the McKinley Administration caused respectable people in the United States to question the dignity of McKinley's foreign policy.[4]

Regardless of this public call to assist the Cuban rebels, the *Chicago Chronicle* opposed war with Spain. The main reason lies in the fact that the *Chronicle* considered the Spanish forces a formidable military opponent. The newspaper had little faith in the U.S. battleships, feared the Spanish torpedo boats, believed the Spanish soldiers would fight with tremendous courage, and feared some European nation would come to Spain's aid. The *Chicago Chronicle* painted a public picture of President McKinley as wishy-washy: pulled in one direction by the pro-war elements of the Republican Party and pulled in another direction by the big business giants who opposed war with Spain.

Even at the height of public hysteria over the explosion of the *Maine*, the *Chicago Chronicle* remained steadfast in its anti-war stance. While other prominent newspapers of the era condemned the "cowardly act of Spain," the *Chronicle* heaped praise upon the Spanish for assisting the *Maine*'s surviving crew. The editor of the *Chronicle* went as far as to write that perhaps the Cuban rebels destroyed the *Maine*.[5] Within this spirit, the *Chronicle* urged the American public not to let "the tide of warfare" override their sense of caution over an incident that had no clear villain.

However, as if the *Chicago Chronicle* had seen the light, its editors changed their position on going to war with Spain. In March of 1898, the editor of the *Chronicle* noted that "bloodletting clears the mind and the United States cannot submit to dishonorable acts at the hands of cowards." Shortly thereafter, the *Chronicle* decided that Spain caused the explosion of the *Maine* and the United States must go to war with Spain. The editors of the *Chicago Chronicle* did not disclose the reason the newspaper felt Spain had a hand in the *Maine*'s explosion, but by late March of 1898 the *Chronicle* acknowledged that the United States should wage war with Spain or its political leaders risk annihilation at the polls.

Like many of the anti-war newspapers across late-nineteenth-century America, the business newspapers also softened their opposition to war with Spain. While the shift of the business community toward pro-war sentiments developed slowly, it nevertheless materialized. However, this materialization of support for war with Spain had a lukewarm quality to it. The leading business newspapers of the era, *Bradstreet's* and the *Commercial Advertiser*, either expressed no opinion on the

11. A Shift in Public Opinion

Cuban crisis as it related to U.S. foreign policy or very little opinion on the coming war with Spain.

The destruction of the *Maine* had a direct effect on President McKinley's foreign policy. Between March and April of 1898, the United States gave the Spanish government a series of ultimatums. The most pressing demand called for Spain to conclude an armistice with the Cuban insurgents and enter into negotiations with them via the office of the President of the United States. If the terms of a peace settlement were not realized, the President of the United States would act as the final arbiter in the peace negotiations. Shortly thereafter, William McKinley notified Congress that his peaceful settlement of the Cuban crisis had failed, leaving the specter of war in the hands of Congress.[6]

Up to March of 1898, McKinley had resisted all calls for war, even risking a political revolt within his own party to avoid war with Spain. This risk of revolt within the Republican Party opened the door to an easy Democratic electoral victory in the Congressional elections. Since the Democrats in Congress believed firmly in going to war with Spain (with many Republicans supporting these pro-war Democrats) the real possibility of Congress defying McKinley's peace initiatives and voting for military intervention existed. But McKinley managed to maintain control over both his party and Congress by masterfully announcing war with Spain was inevitable.[7]

The United States earned an easy victory over Spain in the Spanish-American War, ultimately challenging the prewar fears of the anti-war advocates. This easy victory over Spain did not prove the fallacies of the anti-war advocate's arguments. In their assessment of the U.S. military strength, the U.S. Navy did not belong in the category of a powerful naval force and its performance in the two major naval battles with Spain did not leave that impression. Correspondingly, the U.S. Army's readiness for a major military campaign remained questionable. The real mistake of the anti-war advocates lay in the fact that they grossly overestimated the strength of Spain's naval forces as the U.S. fleet proved at Manila Bay.

The strength of the Spanish Army should also be considered. The U.S. Army fought only two battles of any significance: the battle at El Caney and the battle of San Juan Hill. The Spaniards, outnumbered almost twelve to one, fought bravely and their overall losses (654) paled in comparison to the U.S. Army's losses (1385).[8] Even the jingoistic

Resistance to the Spanish-American and Philippine Wars

Rough Rider Theodore Roosevelt wrote in a letter to his friend Senator Henry Cabot Lodge that the U.S. Army "are within measurable distance" of a great military disaster.

Spain entered the war with the United States convinced she would lose, but she knew that to give up Cuba without a fight would likely start a civil war at home. The diplomatic corps in Madrid knew this fear very well. McKinley received a diplomatic communication informing him that the Spaniards would take their chances with a war rather than incur a revolt against their dynasty. Spain firmly felt that being defeated in a war with the United States meant only a loss of Cuba, while a civil war in Spain had more dire consequences.

Spain's loss to the United States represented nothing more than a defensive mechanism against a domestic revolution. If Spain had relentlessly pursued a military victory as it had during the Mexican–American War, America's "splendid little war" would had devolved into a military quagmire.

12

Dissent, Alleged War Crimes and the Philippines War

Membership in the Anti-Imperialist League significantly dropped after the ratification of the Treaty of Paris and William McKinley's reelection to the presidency. Within two years of McKinley's reelection, the League's offices across the nation closed their doors. Boston once again became the epicenter of the anti-imperialist movement after the Chicago office shut it doors. Many labor groups who had opposed expansionism looked for new ways to keep cheap foreign labor from competing with American labor once the foreign policy of expansionism was a cold reality.[1] The majority of the black press who had displayed anti-imperialist sentiments supported McKinley's reelection to the presidency and after the election paid very little attention to the issue of expansionism. The American Left resumed its attack upon the evils inherent in the capitalist system. When the death of McKinley elevated Theodore Roosevelt to the presidency, the issue of American control of the Philippines had more or less been settled. However, in the spring and summer of 1902, reports began to circulate concerning the war crimes that the American military committed against the Filipino insurgents and the topic of imperialism began making headlines once again.

While the Treaty of Paris had officially transferred the Philippines to American control, the enforcement of this provision would be made in blood. The insurgents, under the leadership of Emilio Aguinaldo, waged an effective campaign to achieve the sovereignty they had declared in June 1898. With the promise of independence as an incentive, the Filipino rebels had allied with the American military forces when it came to fighting and defeating the Spanish forces in the islands. Shortly before the war had started, the United States had coaxed Aguinaldo out of exile for the express purpose of helping to energize the local population against Spain.[2] There is speculation that Aguinaldo believed that the United States would support independence for the Philippines if the rebels aided American in her fight against Spain. United States Consul General E. Spencer lured the insurgent leader back to the islands by saying, "Ally yourself with America and you will surely defeat the Spanish."[3] When Aguinaldo asked about America's plan for the Philippines once the war was over, he was informed, "You need not worry about America."[4] The Filipino leaders encouraged their supporters at home to aid the Americans because they are "our redeemers."[5]

Aguinaldo sailed to Manila aboard the U.S.S. *McCulloch*. Once he reached Manila, he was invited aboard the *Olympia* where Admiral Dewey welcome him with, "Go ashore and start your army."[6] Many years later, Aguinaldo recalled Dewey urging him to make a Philippine flag and raise it once the Spanish had been defeated.[7] What the rebel leader did not realize was the fact that at the moment that Dewey was encouraging Philippine independence, the Admiral had also received a communication from the Secretary of the Navy instructing him to avoid making any political commitments to the Filipinos.[8]

Although the U.S. military achieved a quick and decisive victory over the Spanish fleet, the American military forces did not capitalize on their victory. The Americans had to wait for support forces before making an amphibious assault. In the interim, the Filipino rebels had bedeviled the Spanish forces. To Dewey's great surprise, Aguinaldo had an effective fighting force of several thousand men.[9] While the exact number is not known, the number was sufficient to convince the Spanish that the rebel's numerical superiority would require them to seek reinforcements, but the American naval forces negated this option. Unwilling to surrender to their former colonial subjects, the remaining Spanish forces on the island of Luzon surrendered to the American forces once Dewey's fleet was reinforced with troops from the United States.[10]

When the Spanish-American War had ended, the Filipinos had established a primitive but functional government. Most Filipinos felt that their freedom was largely won through the shedding of Filipino blood. Although Dewey had overwhelmed the Spanish naval forces, American forces had not landed in the Philippines until the ground fighting was virtually over. As the terms of the Treaty of Paris crystalized, the newly established Filipino government insisted on independence for the Philippines. However, it became abundantly clear that occupation

12. Dissent, Alleged War Crimes and the Philippines War

was the United States' true plan once the reinforcement troops landed. As a reactionary move to these plans, the Malolos Congress decided to act and declared war on the United States on June 2, 1899.[11]

The first shots of the Philippine–American War were fired on February 4, 1899.[12] During this episode, one Filipino soldier was killed. An outbreak of fighting throughout the city of Manila compelled General Arthur MacArthur to bring in reinforcement forces to suppress the uprising.[13] American determination to retain control became very clear when the Filipinos attempted to negotiate peace terms. The peace entreaties offered by the Filipinos was dismissed by the U.S. ground commander, General Elwell Otis.[14]

President McKinley essentially blamed the Filipinos for the events that led to war. He stated, "The insurgents had attacked Manila," and this act had led to hostilities. Aguinaldo was branded a desperado and additional American forces were ordered to the islands to end what the Americans considered an uprising against a lawful colonial government.[15]

The fighting continued before a truce was reached on July 4th, 1902.[16] In terms of casualties rate, the war exceeded the Spanish-American War. The Filipinos suffered nearly 16,000 killed in combat, while the United States lost 4,000 killed in action.[17] The war caused untold misery on the civilian population in terms of collateral damage. It is estimated that roughly a quarter million Filipino civilians died during the conflict.[18] Disease played a major role by disrupting the food supply and forcing many Filipinos into concentration camps. Many villages were burned to the ground, reflecting a strategy that would be echoed by the American forces many years later during the Vietnam War. Similar to Vietnam, reports of atrocities committed against both the rebels and the civilian population began to circulate.

Many of these reports slowly made their way back to the States. Some of the most diehard anti-imperialists' periodicals did report such war crimes. The *New York Evening Post* published an article, in the spring of 1899, alleging that American troops of the 20th Kansas Regiment under the command of Major Wilder Metcalf had killed innocent Filipinos at the Battle of Caloocan.[19] In the summer of 1899, the Anti-Imperialist League published excerpts from the letters of an anonymous American soldier that detailed war crimes committed by American forces.[20] While the excerpts were shocking, they were nonetheless anonymous, limiting their political effectiveness. Although limited in their effectiveness, these excerpts still caught the attention of the War Department, who decided to investigate their veracity.[21] Because *The New York Post* and the Anti-Imperialist League failed to get signed official statements from the anonymous source concerning these atrocities, the War Department dismissed the claims of American war crimes as overzealousness on the part of the anti-imperialists.

For a time, the anti-imperialist press refused to publish any other claims of American war crime in the Philippines. However, new reports of atrocities eventually regained the interest of the anti-imperialist press. The *Albany Press-Knickerbocker* published an article that alleged that Colonel Frederick Funston had executed rebels without due process.[22] The *New York World* chimed in on the side of the *Press-Knickerbocker* article, giving the claim another avenue of circulation.[23] The *Omaha World* published stories of what became known as the "water cure." The water cure involved forcing an individual to drink water until they could not drink any longer and then kicking and jumping on the individual's stomach. The story originated from an account given by a Private Miller, who was a member of the 32nd Volunteer Infantry. The story Miller detailed was reprinted in such well-known anti-imperialist papers as *The Friend's Intelligencer* and *City and State*.[24] Despite the notoriety that these papers gave to Miller's account, many of the mainstream press refused to believe that American forces were capable of committing such horrendous acts. H. L. Wells epitomized the general attitude of many when he said it was a source "of great satisfaction to know that the earlier reports of misconduct of our soldiers are disproved."[25]

The anti-imperialist press continued to publish stories about alleged war crimes. The *Outlook* published an article by George Kennan detailing exactly how the water cure worked.[26] Kennan wrote that this form of torture was only used by American Filipino scouts on other Filipino nationals and not by American forces. He also noted that American forces did not condemn the practice either.[27]

The reasons that little attention was paid to such allegations in the American press are numerous. One factor involves the fact that General Elwell Otis censored the activities of the press, severely limiting what the correspondents could actually report back to the editors and restricting reporters' travel itineraries.[28] Later, even when the restrictions on the reporters were lifted, most newspapers had few correspondents in

12. Dissent, Alleged War Crimes and the Philippines War

the Philippines. There was a tendency of the press to believe that the American military could not commit such brutalities. The very thought that American soldiers could commit such crimes went against the principles that the nation was founded upon.[29]

The anti-imperialists were excited about using these reports as a political instrument against expansionism, but it was not clear who was to blame for these crimes. No real evidence suggested that the American government knew or sanctioned these acts. As noted by Richard Welch, "The chief inhibition ... lay in an uncertainty about the proper target of attack."[30] The fact that eyewitnesses either refused or were reluctant to sign affidavits supporting their version of the events made the reports of these accounts little more than hearsay and scuttlebutt.

Herbert Walsh, editor of *City and State*, was intent on keeping the problems of the Philippines in the public eye. He was particularly shocked by the use of the water cure tactic against the Filipinos,[31] and believed that, if the level of brutality was exposed to the American public, the United States would eventually be forced to leave the Philippines.[32] Welsh used agents to locate former American military personnel who had been stationed in the islands and who had been eyewitness to these criminal acts. These agents searched the American landscape and eventually found soldiers living in the states of Kansas, Maryland, and Massachusetts who would talk about their service in the Philippines.[33] He tried to get these witnesses to testify before the Senate's Committee on the Philippines.[34] In addition to this, Walsh's editorials continued to attack America's presence in the Philippines. He distributed pamphlets across the nation highlighting the American military's abuses on the island and suggesting that these were not isolated incidents but instead a part of America's grand strategy to defeat the insurgency.[35] While Walsh's efforts had minimum success, he did manage to keep the issue before the public around the same time that the Senate became interested in these alleged crimes.

Finally, Senator George F. Hoar, an influential member of the Anti-Imperialist League, proposed legislation calling for the creation of a special committee to look into the military activities of the American forces.[36] The Senate voted against the legislation and instead assigned the issue over to the Committee on the Philippines. The Committee on the Philippines evolved out of the Peace Commission that was established after the war with Spain had ended. That commission's purpose was to advise President McKinley on the benefits of annexing the Philippines. The commission, by a split vote, advised that the island not be annexed. But once the McKinley Administration had decided to add the Philippines to its empire, the Senate created the Committee on the Philippines and gave it the power to oversee U.S. efforts to civilize the country.[37]

The Committee commenced hearings on American activities in the Philippines on January 31, 1902, and ended its inquiry on June 28 of the same year.[38] The chief members of the committee included the chairman, Republican Henry Cabot Lodge, Republicans William Boyd Allison of Iowa, Albert Jeremiah Beveridge of Indiana, Julius Caesar Burrows of Michigan, Charles Henry Dietrich of Nebraska, and Louis Emory McComas of Maryland. The Democrats on the committee consisted of Edward Ward Carmack of Tennessee, Charles Allen Culberson of Texas, Fred Thomas Dubois of Idaho, Thomas MacDonald Patterson of Colorado, and Joseph Lafayette Rawlings of Utah.[39]

A number of the committee members strongly supported the administration's position. Lodge, a leading proponent of imperialism, was a personal friend of President Roosevelt. The majority of the witnesses called to testify supported America's policy in the Philippines. Only a third of the hearings even considered the issue of war crimes.[40] Among the most prominent witness to testify at the hearings were included General Elwell Otis, Admiral Dewey, and close friend of President Roosevelt and civilian governor of the Philippines William Howard Taft.[41] Dewey denied making comments to Aguinaldo suggesting America's support for Filipino independence. Patterson aggressively questioned Dewey in spite of Lodge's attempt to block such query. Patterson read into the hearings' record Dewey's earlier dispatches concerning the Filipinos' abilities to govern themselves. Dewey's dispatches stated in part, "In my opinion these people are far superior in intelligence and more capable of self-government than the natives of Cuba, and I am familiar with both races."[42] Dewey's testimony at the hearings was inconsistent at best. Concerning the issue of possible war crimes, Dewey said very little.

The committee gained insight into the horror of the war from the testimony of General Robert P. Hughes:

>SENATOR RAWLINGS: What did I understand you to say would be the consequence of that?

12. Dissent, Alleged War Crimes and the Philippines War

GENERAL HUGHES: They usually burned the village.
SENATOR RAWLINGS: All of the houses in the village?
GENERAL HUGHES: Yes; every one of them.[43]

Regarding who was specifically and negatively affected by these tactics, Hughes remarked:

> The destruction was as a punishment. The punishment in that case would fall, not upon the men, who could go elsewhere, but mainly upon the women and little children. The women and children are part of the family, and where you wish to inflict a punishment you can punish the man probably worse in that way than any other.[44]

As General Hughes' testimony continued, it became abundantly clear that the warfare in the Philippines had come to the point where atrocities were considered standard operating procedure.

The Committee continued its interrogative questioning:

SENATOR RAWLINGS: ... is that within the ordinary rules of civilized warfare? Of course, you could exterminate the family, which would be still worse punishment.
GENERAL HUGHES: These people are not civilized.
SENATOR RAWLINGS: But is that within the ordinary rules of civilized warfare?
GENERAL HUGHES: No, I think it is not.
SENATOR HALE: You made a very interesting statement some time ago that from year-to-year ... the conduct of the war was sterner, stiffer, as you called it. You are describing what took place the second summer, not the first?
GENERAL HUGHES: Yes. In the first campaign the rules of civilized warfare were rigidly enforced.[45]

But by the second year things had drastically changed.

GENERAL HUGHES: The next year we found that we had to arrest a great many people who were not in uniform, the evidence being that they were in the habit of assisting the enemy in different ways.[46]

What the General's testimony revealed is the classic manner in which a traditional trained military force responds and attempts to defeat the nontraditional tactics used by a guerrilla army. Hughes, along with the pro-imperialist members of the committee, believed that the actions of the Filipino rebels justified the use of extreme measures by the American forces. The general was asked directly about the use of the "water cure" that was reported in the editorials of the anti-imperialists' presses. Hughes denied having knowledge about such a tactic and downplayed its severity.[47] But the testimony of Charles S. Riley refuted Hughes' testimony.

Riley, a former member of the 1st Connecticut regiment, had served in the Philippines in from 1898 to 1899. After being questioned about the mistreatment of Filipino prisoners of war, Riley was asked directly about the tactic that became known as the water cure. Senator Lodge specifically asked him about the fate of the leading official of the town of Igaras:

> RILEY: He was taken and placed under the tank, and the faucet was opened and a stream of water was forced down ... his throat; his throat was held so that he could not prevent swallowing the water.
> SENATOR LODGE: Was anything done besides forcing his mouth open and allowing the water to run down?
> RILEY: When he was filled with water it was forced out of him by pressing a foot on his stomach.[48]

As Riley's testimony progressed, it was clear that abusive practices by the American forces were a common occurrence. In some cases, the junior officers directed these practices and at other times they was done by Filipinos working with the American forces. Riley's statements were supported by the testimony of Daniel J. Evans, who had served on the island of Luzon from 1899 to 1901.[49] Evans gave a detailed account of an incident in which a small number of American troops and their Filipino allies questioned an insurgent prisoner in the north of Luzon:

> EVANS: ... one of the scouts ... grabbed one of the men by the head and ... took a tomato can and poured water down his throat until he could hold no more. And when the native could hold no more water, then they forced a gag into his mouth; they stood him up and tied his hands behind him. Then one man, an American soldier, struck this native in the pit of the stomach as hard as he could, just as rapidly as he could.[50]

Evans went on to state that at least thirty men witnessed this action.[51]

As the hearings proceeded, it became quite clear to the pro-imperialist members of committee that numerous war crimes had been committed by either the American forces or by Filipino allies under the supervision of the U.S. military.[52] William Howard Taft, governor general, testified that he had no knowledge of these incidents but concluded that it was a not impossible that they could have occurred.[53] The tone

12. Dissent, Alleged War Crimes and the Philippines War

of the proceedings became heated at times as senators became embroiled in arguments over the lines of questioning asked of the witnesses.[54] Later, much of the information revealed at the proceedings was augmented by a report developed by Major Cornelius Gardner, civil governor of Tayabas.[55]

As information flowed from the hearings, American newspapers were delighted. Democrats on the committee leaked information on the proceedings to the newspapers.[56] The "Bell revelations" led to some twenty editorials being published in newspapers across the nation.[57] The *Springfield Daily Republican* and the *New York Evening Post* called the actions in the Philippines criminal.[58] Some newspapers that previously supported American efforts in the Philippines now withdrew their support.[59] Some newspapers went as far as to compare General Bell to the notorious Spanish General "Butcher" Weyler.[60] The revelation that concentration camps were used in the Philippines no doubt reminded many of the infamous Spanish General.

Despite this, the American military did have its share of supporters among the press. The *Pittsburgh Times* stated that General Bell did not intentionally starve those individuals in the camps.[61] Not surprisingly, the *Army and Navy Journal* severely criticized the anti-imperialist papers.[62] The pro-imperialists qualified their support by claiming the events in the Philippines were isolated incidents and should not detract from the overall goal of ensuring peace and democracy on the islands. One journalist from the *New York Herald* suggested that the Filipinos were better off in a concentration camp. This same correspondent also claimed that the concentration camps were more sanitary than the huts the Filipinos normally lived in.[63]

A number of courts-marshal were initialed that shed more light on American military actions in the Philippines. Due to these revelations, the public became critical of U.S. policy in the islands.[64] The controversy became even more intense when the Associated Press noted that one of the court-marshaled military officers, Major Walker, had been previously acquitted of charges because he had been following orders of his superiors.[65] General Jacob Smith was accused of issuing the orders that led to the confinement of Filipino civilians in concentration camps. Both the *New York Journal* and the *New York World* denounced Smith for his actions while other critics compared him to King Herod.[66] The *North American*, *Baltimore News*, *Boston Advertiser*, *Chicago News*, and *San*

Francisco Chronicle wrote editorials reflecting the same sentiments.[67] The *Buffalo Express* suggested that the General's actions epitomized the failure of America's imperialist policy in the Philippines.[68] Because of this negative publicity, President Roosevelt dismissed Smith from the military.[69]

Some newspapers were less severe in their condemnation. The *New York Times* painted the American forces' criminal acts as isolated incidents of overzealous junior officers and enlisted men.[70] The *Chicago Inter-Ocean, Philadelphia Press, Pittsburgh Gazette,* and *Kansas City Star* echoed these sentiments.[71] Some newspapers were supportive of the military. The editor of the *St. Louis Globe-Democrat* wrote:

> Well, suppose that the native barbarities have, in some cases, moved our soldiers to transgress the line of gentleness desirable for ordinary warfare? We are confident that, in view of the provocation received and peculiar nature of the task to be performed, the transgressions have been extremely slight.[72]

However, this sentiment was not representative of the general view of the American press concerning the allegations of war crimes.[73]

At the height of these revelations, the American public became incensed at stories of war crimes committed by the American military. The American public focused their anger upon the men who were responsible for these acts, not America's imperialist foreign policy in the Philippines. Many Americans felt that the Filipinos brought these crimes on themselves. The revelations of these incidents were seen as evidence of how fighting an uncivilized people can corrupt a normally moral fighting force such as the American military.[74] Regardless of who was the blame for the atrocities, the anti-imperialists used this negative information to force the nation out of the Philippines.

The movement that had been slowly fading away after the national elections of 1900 was now brought back to life. Two leading anti-imperialist representatives, Charles Adams and Carl Schurz, met in New York on April 28, 1902, and created a provisional committee for the sole purpose of investigating the alleged war crimes committed by the American military forces in the Philippines.[75] Julian Codman and Moorfield Storey developed pamphlets intended to inflame public indignation over the allegations of abuse and force American leaders to change U.S. foreign policy in the Philippines. They wanted America to leave the island as soon as possible. Codman and Storey followed the strategy of their compatriots from a few years earlier. They pressured Congress to create

12. Dissent, Alleged War Crimes and the Philippines War

a joint investigative committee tasked with ascertaining the full measure of the alleged brutalities in the Philippines.[76] Numerous tracts were printed in the spring of 1902. The most famous was entitled *Secretary Root's Record: "Marked Severities" in Philippines Warfare: An Analysis of the Law and Facts Bearing on the Action and Utterance of President Roosevelt and Secretary Root*. This pamphlet attacked the Roosevelt Administration's imperialist foreign policy, suggesting that the blame for the criminal acts be placed upon the shoulders of the President and the Secretary of State.

Since America's victory over Spain in 1898, the advocates of expansionism had matters going their way. The Senate had approved the Treaty of Paris, and the election of 1900 was a resounding victory for McKinley. But now, it seems as if public sentiment would turn against imperialism. Henry Lee Higginson wrote to Lodge concerning his doubts about the wisdom of American foreign policy in the Philippines, "A very considerable number of staunch republicans who have never looked at any other ticket, would like to get out of these islands."[77] Efforts to compel Congress to act were unsuccessful. The pamphlets motivated some members of Congress, but not nearly enough to pressure the Roosevelt Administration to pull out of the Philippines. Instead, the administration took its own action.[78]

Sensing the negative political effects of the publicity, the Roosevelt Administration along with Senator Lodge and other influential supporters started a campaign to rehabilitate American colonial policy in the minds of the American public. Lodge gave a speech stating that those individuals who were responsible for criminal acts in the Philippine campaign would be brought to justice. He further stated that those who opposed American foreign policy in the Philippines were aiding and abetting the enemy.[79] The Senator referred to the anti-imperialists as modern day Copperheads who were willing to believe the worse about America, accepting as the truth allegations of atrocities committed by American soldiers while ignoring the reports of brutalities committed by the Filipino insurgents.[80] Lodge argued that the vast majority of the Filipinos looked favorably on the Americans and that those opposing U.S. conduct of the war should keep in mind the great sacrifices that Americans were making to civilize a "semi-civilized people, with all the tendencies and characteristics of Asiatics."[81]

Members of President Roosevelt's cabinet voiced their support of the administration's foreign policy to the press. The President himself defended America's actions in the Philippines, claiming that U.S. forces were doing noble work by bringing liberty to the Filipinos.[82] Roosevelt called critics of the administration's policy ungrateful and stated that they attacked "brave men ... their faces marred by sweat and blood— who were engaged in this great redemptive task."[83]

The imperialists built their arguments upon two premises: They claimed that the incidents of brutalities were exaggerated in number and frequency and that these acts were provoked by the lawlessness of the insurgents. Some in the press found the President's arguments valid. An editorial in the *Providence Sunday Journal* noted that it was necessary to "fight fire with fire."[84] Several notable military figures support the American forces. Two of these figures were Major General O. O. Howard and General Frederick Funston, the latter having been accused of war crimes by the anti-imperialist press and vilified by Mark Twain.[85] The editor of *Harper's Weekly* asserted that American soldiers had been suffering untold indignities and that the insurgents' tactics compelled them to counter with harsh measures.[86]

By the end of the summer of 1902, the reports about American war crimes in the Philippines had dropped significantly. The public lost interest in these reports for a number of reasons. Lodge had done a very good job of keeping Congress in check during while the scandals were in the public's consciousness. The Senator had succeeded in limiting testimony concerning American abuses in the Philippines when witnesses made their statements before the Committee on the Philippines. In addition to this, much of the testimony given by witnesses made it appear that the abuses were isolated incidents unsanctioned by the military chain of command. Essentially, the Senate's Committee on the Philippines had successfully quarantined the reports and kept them from damaging the Roosevelt Administration. Roosevelt displayed great political instincts when he dealt with the Philippine abuse problem. The President and his cabinet condemned some for the abuses and promised to bring them to justice; they minimized the frequency of military misconduct and simultaneously blamed the insurgents for any abuse that may have taken place. Finally, they equated anti-imperialism with unpatriotic sentiment.

Some anti-imperialists continued to work in vain. Henry Welsh attempted to gather additional eyewitness accounts from veterans of the

12. Dissent, Alleged War Crimes and the Philippines War

war. The *Springfield Daily Republican* kept trying to keep the abuse issue alive, but the public slowly lost interest.[87] The window of opportunity for anti-imperialists to make an impact upon the country concerning the abuses had slowly closed. Political skill displayed by President Roosevelt, his allies in Congress, and the President's supporters in the press all played pivotal roles in defusing the issue. The American public generally accepted Roosevelt's version of the events. Numerous letters written to the press indicated that somehow the Filipinos were responsible for the abuses and that America was engaged in an honor crusade. Many Americans were willing to believe that the Filipinos could not behave according to the standards of the rules of war; thus, the American military had to take the extraordinary steps to "fight fire with fire."[88] A few members of the anti-imperialist camp even saw the reports of American atrocities as evidence that nonwhites had succeeded in undermining the moral values of the white man.[89] Possibly the best reason that allegation of abuses by American forces quickly disappeared as a political issue was the war's short duration.

Widespread reports of war crimes did not gain press circulation until the war was closing. Americans were reluctant to believe that their sons could commit such heinous acts. The public did not voice a strong indignation about the reports. If the abuses and the war had lasted longer, there might have been enough time to mount a vibrant anti-war movement against the Roosevelt Administration. But the Philippine–American War was short and the leadership of the anti-imperialist movement was well past their prime, which affected their ability to mount a successful campaign that would change American foreign policy.

Conclusion

Comparing the arguments of the anti-imperialist advocates in Congress with those in the press highlights two major differences. The anti-imperialist advocates in Congress never really explained the real reasons they opposed the war with Spain; their analysis usually involved political platitudes about moral duty. Very few members of Congress considered the cost of a war with Spain and those who did offered only general statements. However, the essence of the anti-imperialist presses' arguments consisted of balancing the material cost of war with Spain with any benefit the war may bring to the United States.

The anti-imperialist press argued aggressively and with specific points about the military strength of Spain and how much damage she would inflict upon the United States. The European press and military experts had similar views concerning a war between the United States and Spain. These views involved a faulty assessment of Spain's naval strength and of Spain's determination to resist. A more accurate examination of Spain's military capabilities and the threats posed by diseases native to the Cuban island represented a more realistic picture of the problems the United States faced when confronting Spain in war.

The anti-imperialist advocate's argument concerning the financial toll on the United States if it went to war with Spain had concrete points. A protracted war, noted a majority of the anti-imperialist press, would take a high toll on both American lives and property. Such a war, these advocates asserted, would affect not only the country's ability to recover from the economic downturn of the 1890s, but also the nation's ability to stabilize its finances. The essence of the anti-imperialist advocates' argument involved seeing a war between the United States and Spain as a socioeconomic crisis that would invariably play into the hands of Bryan and his political cohort.

The anti-imperialist press fervently believed that a victory over

Conclusion

Spain would not give the United States any material benefits. They stressed that the United States had personal interest in neither Cuban independence nor annexing the island to warrant a war with Spain. The public debate over war with Spain occurred at a time when America's own race relations remained unsettled. Many whites in America did not want another "Haiti" in the western hemisphere, nor did they welcome the prospect of acquiring territory where blacks represented the majority group.

It is very difficult to determine the relative weight of two of the anti-imperialist advocates' considerations (the high cost of war and the lack of benefits) to assess whether some anti-imperialist advocates used the racial issues of the Cuban crisis to exaggerate Spain's military strength and strengthen their case. However, the comments in the contemporary press suggest that while both issues had a basis in reality, the cost of a U.S. war with Spain predominated in the thoughts of the anti-imperialist newspapers. While the cost of waging war became the center of their arguments, the anti-imperialist press still believed in a U.S. victory over Spain. Spain may hurt the United States materially, but the anti-war press firmly doubted Spain's ability to wage a successful war.

Just as the anti-imperialist press had wrongly assessed the cost of going to war with Spain, they had also underestimated the fruits of victory for the United States. The anti-imperialist press and their supporters believed that victory over Spain would bring either Cuban independence or a U.S. annexation of the island. They did not foresee the Platt Amendment that transformed, at gunpoint, the Cuban island into a protectorate. In many ways this gave the anti-war advocates and many Americans something they could live with: attaining Cuba without the Cubans. In analyzing the anti-imperialist press and its supporters, it becomes clear that they became victims of the harsh realities of their times more than the fallacies of their own arguments.

But as a movement, why did the anti-imperialists fail? The anti-imperialists were not the instrument of change they hoped to be for a number of reasons. They did not organize their forces until the late stages of the game. They were fragmented, not unified. The political strategy they employed relied upon education and a belief that the public would heed the warnings against expansionism made by the leaders in academia, men of letters, and the Mugwumps. They completely miscalculated the public's mood.

Conclusion

Bad timing seems to have played a role in the anti-imperialists' failure to achieve their objectives. They did not actively campaign against expansionism until the United States had been victorious in a hugely popular war. It became easy for the expansionist to characterize the anti-imperialists as out of touch with the times and unpatriotic. McKinley was able to defend the acquisitions of the Philippines on moral, strategic, and economic grounds. The anti-imperialists asserted that the Filipinos were capable of governing themselves, and even if they could not, what sovereign right did the United States have to dictate how a foreign people should govern themselves? The expansionists countered this argument by reasoning that the United States had the right because she eliminated a colonial system imposed by Spain and thereby had a moral imperative to liberate the Filipinos. To leave them without adequate oversight would invite chaos and internal conflict. Essentially, what the expansionists suggested was that the Filipinos needed guidelines on how to be a civilized nation.

The efforts to stop McKinley's reelection were fruitless. McKinley had guided the nation to victory during a war that most Americans supported, and oversaw a nation in an economic recovery from the depression that had ravaged the economy a few years earlier. During the 1900 presidential election, the anti-imperialists had given their support to William Jennings Bryan, but Bryan turned out to be more divisive than effective. Failure in the 1900 presidential election seems to be the final blow to the anti-imperialists' hopes. The public's interest in expansionism waned, and the Anti-Imperialist League's membership dropped dramatically. The war in the Philippines renewed public interest in expansionism, but not for long.

The atrocities committed by the American military brought expansionism to light once again. Public anger over such abuses could have provided the anti-imperialists with the weapon they needed to mount a serious challenge to American expansionist foreign policies. But the public's uproar was short-lived and the issue once again faded from the public's consciousness. In the final analysis, the anti-imperialist movement was a complete failure. In the struggle to define the nation's identity and it future role in world affairs, the expansionists were much more successful.

Suggested Readings

Over the past 110 years, the development of late nineteenth century American foreign policy has prompted a great deal of introspection among historians. This self-examination has centered on the many events that influenced the United States' foreign policy as it related to the development of the Spanish-American and Philippine–American Wars. Many scholars have clarified the overall context of the times by examining the Spanish-American and Philippine–American Wars from military, cultural, political, and global perspectives. This is a partial list of works related to American imperialism, anti-imperialism, and the Spanish-American and Philippine–American Wars that may be useful for further study.

The explosion of the *Maine* has always been central in the historiography of the Spanish-American War. Contemporary historical accounts of the *Maine*'s destruction emphasize the battleship's prominence in the war's development. In the geopolitical science study *Spanish-American Diplomatic Relations Preceding the War of 1898*, progressive historian Horace Edgar Flack writes that the destruction of the *Maine* compelled the United States to intervene in the Cuban crisis. In the work *The United States in War with Spain*, Trumbull White notes that the sequence of events regarding the *Maine* explosion pulled the United States toward war with Spain.[1]

During the early part of the twentieth century, a vast and diverse literature pointed to the destruction of the *Maine* as the principal cause of the Spanish-American War. Both policymakers and political leaders proclaimed the role of the *Maine*'s explosion in the war's development. Theodore Roosevelt, in his post-presidency *Autobiography*, and Russell A. Alger in his book *The Spanish-American War*, wrote that the destruction of the *Maine* facilitated America's war with Spain.[2] Thus, some contemporary accounts placed the *Maine*'s destruction as the chief cause of the Spanish-American War.

Suggested Readings

The historical debate over the role of the military development of the war between the United States and Spain has animated the historiography of the Spanish-American War over the last one hundred years. In the compendium *Crucible of Empire: The Spanish-American War and Its Aftermath*, James Bradford presents the Spanish-American War as a transformative event that revolutionized American military affairs and foreign relations.[3] The work's main focus involves naval operations, the role of the Navy in its support of the Army's and the U.S. Marines' operations, and the impact of Asiatic service upon the careers of U.S. Naval Officers. The nine essays presented in this work indicate that the United States conducted a highly successful war.

Various authors in the *Crucible of Empire* examine the command relationships of the Army and Naval officers. Graham A. Cosmas gives an insightful analysis of the overall conduct of joint military operations. Due to a geographically distant war, military cooperation between the Army and the Navy in the Spanish-American War became a necessity. Primitive communications and a lack of landing crafts compelled many Naval and Army officers to improvise to find solutions to war-related problems.[4]

Five of the essays in the compendium analyze different aspects of military cooperation and joint operations. For example, authors Diane E. Cooper and David Trask survey American intelligence collection, both concluding that Army and Navy officers received enough good intelligence to plan and implement successful campaigns.[5] In essence, the *Crucible of Empire* shows how the Spanish-American War systematically changed the way the nation conducted war.

In the politico-military history *Empire by Default: The Spanish-American War and the Dawn of the American Century*, Ivan Musicant notes that both Grover Cleveland and William McKinley did their best to avoid any global issues that might hinder America's recovery from the Depression of 1893.[6] Musicant notes that despite a U.S. desire for quasi-isolation, Spain's inability to find a feasible political or military solution to the Cuban insurrection forced the United States onto the world stage. The author highlights the point that even without yellow journalistic efforts on the part of Hearst and his cohort, the sinking of the *Maine* made war inevitable. This view compares favorably to the historical perspective given by the Progressive school of thought.

In *Empire by Default*, Musicant shows that American military oper-

Suggested Readings

ational and logistical performance went beyond expectations despite contemporary Army and Naval forces' limited experience fighting such a distant war. The author notes that the biggest Achilles' heel involved the administration of the war: Raising a large army to fight a distant war entailed bureaucratic nightmares. Musicant also writes that American business and industry had a much more benign influence on foreign affairs than history recorded.

In the military-cultural study *War and Genocide in Cuba, 1895–1898,* John Lawrence Tone dispels the historical notion that the Cuban rebellion came from a mass uprising against Spanish rule by a united Cuban people relying on emotions to defeat Spain.[7] Tone notes that, in reality, the Cuban Liberation Army consisted of a small rebellion force that rarely exceeded 5,000 troops in strength at the height of the Cuban crisis. This exceedingly low number compelled the Cuban Liberation Army to resort to guerrilla tactics that protected them from engaging in major clashes with Spanish regulars. Tone writes that about 60,000 Cubans served Spain as volunteers and attachment units and distrusted the Cuban Liberation Army due to its large contingent of black troops.

According to Tone, the Cuban rebels had a natural ally that helped them against the superior forces of Spain: tropical diseases. Between February 1895 and August 1898, over forty thousand Spanish soldiers succumbed to tropical diseases. The author further notes that, by 1898, every Spanish soldier had spent some time under medical care due to disease. As a result, the nearly 190,000 Spanish troops deployed to Cuba during the mid to late 1890s became inactive for military service in some way.

While tropical diseases and the Cuban insurgency hindered Spain's military success, the effect of disease on the military forces also caused internal political challenges for the Spanish government and altered the way it prosecuted the war. The politico-military history *Empire by Default* by Ivan Musicant seems to support Tone's assessment of Spain's internal political problems. Both Tone and Musicant contend that Spain's inability to find a feasible military solution to the Cuban insurrection led directly to Spain's defeat in the Spanish-American War. The works of Tone and Musicant also show how acts of nature and political turmoil impeded Spain's quest for military success.

The politico-military study *The Spanish-American War: An American Epic, 1898* by G. J. A. O'Toole highlights McKinley's deep desire to

Suggested Readings

maintain peace with Spain and the domestic pressures that both Spain and the United States faced from internal warmongers. O'Toole sights German intervention in the Cuban crisis as an important factor in the United States' entrance into the Cuban crisis when Spain failed to agree with America's peace proposals. In the politico-cultural work *Manifest Destiny and the Mission in American History*, Frederick Merk makes a similar assertion: An expansionist ideology coupled with the destruction of the *Maine* led to the Spanish-American War.[8]

In the military-social history *The Spanish-American War: Conflict in the Caribbean and the Pacific, 1895–1902*, Joseph Smith examines the causes and consequences of the Spanish-American War within a strategic ideological context. According to Smith, popular American attitudes toward war added a social dimension to the Spanish-American War and gave a greater weight to its strategic consequences.[9] *The Spanish-American War* has similarities in presentation and views to the Barry Hughes socio-military work *The Domestic Content of American Foreign Policy*. Hughes argues that the American public influenced and, in many ways, directed foreign policy.

During the centennial of the Spanish-American War, the concepts of social and cultural history emerged. In *1898: The Birth of the American Century*, David Traxel covers the events that shaped the year 1898: the dominance of industry, the influence of war fever upon the American populace, and the celebration after the war with Spain ended in victory.[10] However, Traxel's analysis is weakened because he fails to sufficiently examine the pro-war and anti-war atmospheres of late-nineteenth-century American society and merely reports on the facts he collected from the period. Traxel also fails to elaborate on the free silver issues that would destroy the industrial economy, echoing instead the claim of earlier researchers that business leaders of the era viewed the Cuban crisis as potentially destructive to the gains made in the economy since the panic of 1893.

Many culturally themed works center on the elevation of America's world status through the rescue of chivalric male virtues. In the work *Fighting for American Manhood: How Gender Politics Provoked the Spanish-American and the Philippine–American Wars*, Kristin Hoganson examines the parallel themes between European imperialism and American imperialism within the context of manliness.[11] Hoganson writes that anxieties associated with the concept of American manhood led the United States down the road to war in search of marital identity. The author notes that this search not only involved manly defenders of the nation's honor, but also involved increasing America's standing on the global stage.

As a compelling event, the *Maine* explosion introduced the American public into the decision-making process, radically changing an issue of foreign policy into a question of domestic politics. As the events that surrounded the Cuban crisis came to a head, the American public resigned itself to the war and actively demanded the nation's leaders to prepare for the coming hostilities. This proposition asserts that once the American public became influential in the course of events, the move toward war became irreversible. Linking public opinion to the explosion of the *Maine* indicates how powerfully aroused the American mass could become.

Many works on the Spanish-American War centered on domestic characteristics to explain foreign-policy decisions. Walter LaFeber's insightful study, *The American Search for Opportunity, 1865–1913*, thoroughly outlines the interrelationship among U.S. political ideology, U.S. industrial growth, the cultural and financial upheaval of the 1890s, and the development of the political collaboration between the Republican Party and the U.S. business community. The political alliance of the Republicans and business leaders propelled McKinley into the White House. The backdrop of McKinley's election involved a strong foreign policy, an active search for foreign markets, and an extensive naval force serving as a major instrument of imperial power.[12]

The infrastructure of the political alliance between the Republicans and the business community rested on three primary components. The intellectuals, leaders in the business and financial industries, and the upper echelon of the executive branch occupied permanent spots in this hierarchy. For these elites, education and experience became the backdrop of decision making. As noted in *Creation of the American Empire*, these top players became instrumental in integrating various groups under their leadership.[13]

However, the role of these top-tier leaders went far beyond the title of group unifier. These *cosmopolitans*' major role revolved around empire building, and they used *functionals*—emissaries such as a strong naval force, leading capitalists, consumer-goods manufacturers, and agrarians—to achieve their goals. The cosmopolitans and functionals collab-

Suggested Readings

orated to develop a national consensus for international marketplace expansion, empire, and, ultimately, war.[14]

Many scholars have strived to identify specific regional components of the United States related to its behavior in late-nineteenth-century international affairs that may define the cultural, economic, and political allegiance that helped shape the nation's decision to go to war with Spain. *The American Search for Opportunity*, by Walter LaFeber, created a regional context for U.S. intervention in the Cuban crisis. LaFeber's central theme builds on whether the United States sought order in the western hemisphere or sought global influence and economic opportunity. LaFeber asserts that order did not occupy a high place on the nation's list of priorities. Rather, he contends that the United States endorsed a certain level of disorder if the end results led to economic expansion.

As the 1890s ended, the United States dominated the western hemisphere, a region defined by intense U.S. authority over its less powerful neighbors. The United States saw the western hemisphere as a central base for U.S. prosperity and security that needed constant vigilance and control. South America became a "natural market" for U.S. goods and for developing U.S. core values of democracy that would help fledging nations develop along the U.S. model, and create loyal allies for the United States. In short, the lesser nations of the western hemisphere would become a vital U.S. asset.

The main goal of late-nineteenth-century U.S. foreign policy centered on the need to stop European influence in the western hemisphere. The United States promoted Pan-American movements of the 1890s, attempting to encourage Latin America nations to support U.S. efforts to blunt all "competitive European metropole power" in the western hemisphere. The Venezuelan crisis showed that the United States had one message for the nations of the continent: stay out or else. The Spanish-American War definitively stated that European influence in the western hemisphere would not be tolerated.

Another characteristic of late-nineteenth-century U.S. regional policy that shaped our view of the Spanish-American War involves the U.S. refusal to confer with Latin American nations about their own circumstances. This revelation indicated that the United States acted impiously toward the sovereign rights of the smaller nations. For instance, in the Venezuelan controversy, the United States ignored the Venezuelans during the negotiations with Britain that resulted in a settlement of the

Suggested Readings

boundary dispute. In *An Unwanted War*, John Offner informs us that "once the war [against Spain] began, McKinley cut the Cubans out of wartime decisions and peacemaking negotiations."[15]

In the seminal work *Cuba and the United States*, Louis Perez showed how much the United States valued Cuba as a vital link in U.S. regional plans.[16] Geographical closeness played a major part. In 1898, President McKinley stated that the United States inherently took interest in Cuba since the island nation was "right at our door." Perez noted that the United States viewed Cuba as a major strategic security point and as a commercial market for its goods: "North Americans considered Cuba essential to the politicomilitary security of the United States and Cubans looked upon the United States as vital to the socioeconomic well-being of the island."

Perez elaborated further on U.S. security and U.S. actions to protect her safety. Perez suggested that the primary goal for the United States in Cuba involved keeping Cuba's sovereignty from being transferred to any European nation or to any Cuban extremist groups. Perez asserted that controlling Cuba's sovereignty was a top U.S. priority and when Spain failed to sell the island and her reforms failed, the United States interceded to stop another revolution from developing that would endanger U.S. interests.

U.S. actions seem to support Perez's argument. Occupation of the island, coupled with the Platt amendment, points to U.S. efforts to sustain Cuba's sovereignty. Some scholars highlighted U.S. humanitarianism and the moral responsibility of stopping wholesale carnage as the defining focus of the U.S. preoccupation with Cuba. However, Perez's central thesis, that the United States diligently confronted the European and social revolutionists' threats to Cuba's sovereignty, seems credible.

The Perez thesis concerning the activities of potential Cuban social revolutionists is a stolid argument, especially if coupled with U.S. historical ideas about revolutions. The stormy clouds associated with the U.S. domestic scene of the 1890s compelled many American leaders to fear a major social upheaval within the nation's borders. But long before the radical strikes and other turmoil of the 1890s, Americans viewed revolutions with skepticism. Many Americans were alarmed by the tumultuous French Revolution of 1793, whereas Latin American revolutions of the early nineteenth century disillusioned them because they believed the Latins were incapable of self-rule and would not honor the liberties for which they had fought. Although the revolutions of 1848 raised hopes, they were dashed by expropriation of private property by the 1871 Paris Commune.

In *Ideology and U.S. Foreign Policy*, Michael Hunt noted that Americans viewed Cuba as a breeding ground for "perilous revolution."[17] In other words, U.S. leaders became apprehensive about Cubans and Filipinos because they felt these groups could do great harm, strategically and economically, to U.S. goals and interests. Hunt contended that for late-nineteenth-century America to accept a revolution at face value, the revolution that took place must be orderly, protect property rights, and work slowly toward a constitutional-style government. Even with these criteria, social revolutions became something of a curse to the United States; as revolutions spouted up throughout the world, the United States grew even more anti-revolutionary, especially with regard to nations in the western hemisphere.

Connecting the destruction of the *Maine* with public opinion and linking both with the coming of war creates a causal sequence that has shaped the interpretation of the Spanish-American War and has become a central problem in the historiography of the development of the war. The connection drawn between the coming of the Spanish-American War on one hand and the *Maine* destruction–public-opinion matrix on the other shows the division of the different interpretations of the development of the Spanish-American War. Explanations in the vast Spanish-American-War literature implicitly rely on the theoretical functions of public opinion in a political democracy: The general electorate, which bestows political legitimacy and holds elected officials responsible, represents the force that dictates events and influences the course of foreign policy.

In this context, the *Maine* explosion–public-opinion–anti-war matrix advances the notion of the Spanish-American War as a functional tool in the democratic process, mandated by political considerations and authorized by constitutional statues. Shown as the will of the people, war serves as an allegory for the triumph of popular democracy. The explosion of the *Maine* generated public pressure for war that obliged elected officials to bow to these demands for war. In essence, an unwilling legislative branch and a reluctant executive branch went to war to meet the demands of the American public.

The interpretation that public opinion compelled public officials to take action in the Cuban crisis has become pervasive in the Spanish-American-War historiography. Early in that historiography, this proposition developed into the dominant thematic staple of the literature. In his seminal work, *The War with Spain*, Henry Cabot Lodge wrote that public sentiment drove Congress forward to meet the demands of public opinion: Congress could only fulfill the desires of the citizenry through war.[18] Henry Watterson, in *A History of the Spanish-American War*, drew a similar conclusion by noting that all avenues to peace became nullified by the "rude hand of a popular demand for reprisal."[19]

The correlation between the explosion of the U.S.S. *Maine* and the arousal of public sentiment also explains President McKinley's political decisions. He felt mounting pressure from public sentiment and from a pugnacious Congress to avenge the *Maine*'s destruction. Although in some historical accounts the White House represented a bastion of reason during a time of war-fever irrationality, in the end, the President became obliged to capitulate to the sentiments of the American people and to the demands of their congressional representatives. As political historian Randolph Greenfield Adams noted in *A History of the Foreign Policy of the United States*, McKinley leaned more toward a peaceful settlement of the Cuban crisis, but both Congress and the populace at large became bent on war and forced the his hand.[20]

Many variations of this thematic staple, some favorable to McKinley and others not, run through the Spanish-American War historiography. Historically, McKinley's role in the events leading up to the Spanish-American War is still debated by scholars. This historical debate originates from a general assumption that the explosion of the *Maine* created a climate of hostility in the minds of the American public that ultimately reduced McKinley's policy options to a difficult few. In essence, McKinley personally became committed to peace, but public sentiments toward the destruction of the *Maine* forced the President to act on events beyond his control.

Various Spanish-American-War writers depict McKinley as aware of the political ramifications associated with ignoring public opinion and resisting pressure from Congress to take action in the Cuban crisis. As noted by Thomas A. Bailey in *Diplomatic History of the American People*, the President wanted desperately to avoid hostilities with Spain, but the need to heed the voice of the people prevailed. Richard E. Welch, Jr., asserts in "William McKinley: Reluctant Warrior, Cautious Imperialist" that the destruction of the *Maine* not only intensified war hysteria in both the American press and the public's minds, but also persuaded President McKinley that events overtook all possibilities of bringing the Cuban crisis to a peaceful end, compelling McKinley to acknowledge that the United States must bow to public pressure and intervene in the Cuban crisis with military force. Thus, while McKinley personally wanted peace, he could not resist the public demand for war without drastic political consequences.[21]

Acknowledging the political fallout from failure to comply with the public's wishes concerning intervention in the Cuban crisis, McKinley did resist public pressure as long as he could. As noted by William E. Leuchtenburg in "The Needless War with Spain," most historians easily condemn McKinley for not holding out against going to war with Spain, but, in the final analysis, the President displayed an enormous amount of courage in "bucking the tide" of war fever. The diplomatic historian Richard W. Leopold agreed with this assertion in *The Growth of American Foreign Policy*, writing that McKinley exhibited an extraordinary amount of restraint when it came to yielding to the popular clamor for war. Taking this into account, the conventional historical argument that McKinley could have defied both the public's sentiments and the Congressional war hawks in late-nineteenth-century America does not seem plausible because Congress, at the request of the citizenry, had the power to vote a declaration of war over McKinley's objections.[22]

The destruction of the U.S.S. *Maine* represents a central element in forging a popular consensus for the United States going to war with Spain. The vast differences that existed between the public, press, and governmental representatives in American society did not impede these groups from uniting in the face of a national crisis. Setting aside their differences allowed for the creation of a nonpartisan consensus that required war as a politically acceptable instrument of foreign policy. John Weems' insightful military study, *Fate of the Maine*, contends that the sinking of the *Maine*, without a doubt, "unified Americans for war."[23]

The literature concerning the development of the Spanish-American War does not support a strict interpretation of how Spain and the United States went to war over the Cuban crisis, but it does show the dynamics that helped push the two nations toward war. In the cultural-political work *Twelve Against Empire: The Anti-Imperialists, 1898–1900*, social historian Robert Beisner shows how the social, cultural, and political disaffection of late-nineteenth-century American anti-imperialism affected the nation's desire to remain isolated from international problems and the need for the United States to fulfill its *manifest destiny*.[24] According to Beisner, the anti-imperialists operated and became a motivating force in the political-social consensus of the era. However, the author notes that this consensus, more than any other societal force, drove expansionism. Richard Welch's *Response to Imperialism* is another study that should be consulted. This book covers the impact of the Filipino insurrection on American society and politics and gives a detailed analysis of the public opinion response to the war.

The book *Liberty and American Anti-Imperialism: 1898–1909* by Michael Patrick Cullinane is worth considering. In this study, Cullinane brings light to the anti-imperialist movement and explains the historical consensus that surrounded its activities at the start of the twentieth century. The author asserts that the movement has been examined in a restrictive manner, and a focus on the anti-imperialist's abstract political principles in current scholarship has not given an in-depth understanding of the anti-imperialist's activities. Cullinane suggests that the movement was more successful than historical consensus has suggested.

Race Over Empire: Racism and U.S. Imperialism, 1865–1900 by Eric T. L. Love examines the racial component of American imperialism. In this work, Love asserts that traditional scholarship erroneously suggests that late-nineteenth-century American imperialism was motivated by the desire to assume the "white man's burden." The author contends that racism played a role in the expansion process, but not to the extent that scholars have maintained. This work gives a better understanding of imperialism as it relates to race during the era of late-nineteenth-century America.

While the majority of the scholars in this study examined a number of prominent issues surrounding public opinion and the development of the Spanish-American and Philippine–American Wars, reassessing the term imperialism as it relates to both public opinion and the development of the Spanish-American and the Philippine–American Wars would help historians better understand the concept of American exceptionalism. In historical accounts relating to public opinion and the development of the Spanish-American and Philippine–American Wars, the notion of anti-imperialism has little relevance for the complete understanding of America's development as a world power.

Chapter Notes

Chapter 1

1. Richard E. Welch, Jr., *The Presidencies of Grover Cleveland* (Lawrence: University Press of Kansas, 1988), 167–68.
2. *San Francisco Examiner*, November 27, 1888.
3. James D. Richardson, ed., *A Compilation of the Messages and Papers of the Presidents, 1789-1897* (Washington, D.C.: Government Printing Office, 1897–1907), 5390.
4. *The Nation*, January 31, 1889, 81, 84–85; Carl Schurz to Thomas F. Bayard, January 30, 1889, Carl Schurz Papers, Division of Manuscripts, Library of Congress, Washington, D.C.
5. Instructions of Blaine to the Conference Delegates, April 11, 1889, in Department of State, *Papers Relating to the Foreign Relations of the United States, 1895-1898* (Washington, D.C.: Government Printing Office, 1896–1901), 195–204.
6. Charles S. Campbell, *The Transformation of American Foreign Relations, 1865-1900* (New York: Harper and Row, 1976), 77; George C. Herring, *From Colony to Superpower: U.S. Foreign Relations Since 1776* (New York: Oxford University Press, 2008), 296.
7. Theodore Woolsey, "An Inquiry Concerning Our Foreign Relations," *Yale Review* 1, August (1892): 173.
8. *Ibid.*, 174.
9. Herring, *From Colony to Superpower*, 296.
10. *Ibid.*, 297.
11. *Ibid.*
12. *New York Tribune*, February 22, 1893. Senator Vest later suggested an amendment to the Treaty of Paris in 1898, stating that annexing the Philippines was unconstitutional; Blount was a rabid anti-imperialist and later vice-president of the Anti-imperialist League; *New York Times*, February 18, 1895.
13. *New York Evening Post*, February 3, 1893; *The Nation*, February 9, 1893.
14. Grover Cleveland to Carl Schurz, March 19, 1893, Carl Schurz Papers; Thomas J. Osborne, *"Empire Can Wait": American Opposition to Hawaiian Annexation, 1893-1898* (Kent, OH: Kent State University Press, 1981), 63; Welch, *Presidencies of Grover Cleveland*, 171.
15. Carl Schurz, "Manifest Destiny," *Harpers' New Monthly Magazine*, October (1893): 738.
16. *Ibid.*
17. *Ibid.*
18. *Ibid.*
19. *Ibid.*, 738–39.
20. *Ibid.*
21. *Ibid.*, 740. Schurz proved to be correct on this point. The war to free Cuba did lead to taking Puerto Rico as a matter of course.
22. *Ibid.*
23. *Ibid.*
24. *Ibid.* While Schurz does use the term "Germanic blood," his argument is built upon the belief that no race can achieve democracy in the tropics due to the inhospitable climate of the area.
25. *Ibid.*, 740.
26. Alfred Thayer Mahan, *The Influence of Sea Power upon History* (Boston: Little, Brown, 1890), 84.
27. Schurz, "Manifest Destiny," 740.
28. *Ibid.*, 743–44.
29. *Ibid.*, 745.
30. Herring, *From Colony to Superpower*, 260.
31. John Blount, "Report to President Grover Cleveland," Department of State, *Papers Relating to the Foreign Relations*, 567–605.
32. James Schouler, "A Review of the Hawaiian Controversy," *The Forum* 16, February (1894): 670–89. Schouler was a leading anti–imperialist in 1898.

Notes—Chapter 1

33. *Ibid.*, 672–84, 688.
34. *The Nation*, June 17, 1897, 489.
35. *Ibid.*
36. *Ibid.*
37. *Ibid.*
38. Alfred Thayer Mahan, *The Interest of America in Sea Power, Present and Past* (New York: Houghton, Mifflin, 1890).
39. James Bryce, "A Policy of Annexation for America," *The Forum* 22, June (1897): 388.
40. *Ibid.*, 394–95.
41. *Congressional Record*, 55th Cong., 2nd Sess., 6572–74, 7321–24. Sulzer was a leading proponent of expansionism and favored an aggressive imperialist policy.
42. *Ibid.* Shafroth was an ardent supporter of anti-imperialism and later became vice-president of the Anti-imperialist League.
43. *Ibid.*, 7321–24.
44. William L. Scruggs, *British Aggressions in Venezuela, or the Monroe Doctrine on Trial*, 1895, Reprint (Ann Arbor: University of Michigan Library, 2004), 20.
45. Welch, *Presidencies of Grover Cleveland*, 182.
46. Department of State, *Papers Relating to the Foreign Relations*, 564–66, 575.
47. *Ibid.*, 542–45.
48. *Ibid.*
49. Theodore Roosevelt letter to Henry Cabot Lodge, December 20, 1895, Elting E. Morison, *The Letters of Theodore Roosevelt, 1868–1898*, vol. 1 (Cambridge: Harvard University Press, 1951–1954), 500.
50. George S. Boutwell, *The Venezuelan Question and the Monroe Doctrine* (Washington, D.C.: Gibson, 1896), 7. The article was first published in the *Boston Herald*, February 2, 1896.
51. *Ibid.*, 12. President Cleveland held similar views.
52. *Ibid.*, 17, 20.
53. *Ibid.*, 22.
54. Richardson, *Messages and Papers*, vol. 13, 6258.
55. In the cases of Santo Domingo and Samoa, the American people, for the most part, assumed that the United States was acting as a protectorate with the consent of the indigenous population and the issue of self-determination was not a major concern.
56. *The Nation*, June 17, 1897, 448.
57. Andrew Carnegie, "Distant Possessions: The Parting of Ways," *North American Review* 167, no. 501 (1898): 242–43.

58. The intellectual history of self-determination is barely known. James Crawford, "The Right of Self-Determination in International Law: Its Development and Future," in *Peoples' Rights*, ed. Philip Alston (Oxford: Oxford University Press, 2001), 7–67.
59. To definitively say that the term "imperialism" was not used by Americans in the debates over foreign policies in the 1890s is impossible. Examining a number of primary sources from the era, including the *Congressional Record*, *The Nation*, and the *New York Evening Post* leads to the conclusion that the term was not used; Richard Koebner and Helmut D. Schmidt, *Imperialism: The Story and Significance of a Political Word, 1840–1960* (Cambridge: Cambridge University Press, 1964), 36; *Congressional Record*, 41st Cong., 3rd Sess., 225–26.
60. A. H. Thompson, "British Imperialism and the Autonomous Right of Races," *Kansas City Review of Science and Industry* 3 (1879): 229. The term imperialism was also used to portray the upper class in the United States during the latter part of the nineteenth century. Sarah E. V. Emery, *Imperialism in America: Its Rise and Progress* (Lansing, MI, 1892), 507.
61. Koebner and Schmidt, *Imperialism*, 196–220, 221–49.
62. William Graham Sumner, "The Fallacy of Territorial Expansion," *The Forum* 21, June (1896): 414, 416.
63. *Ibid.*
64. *Ibid.*, 417.
65. *Ibid.*, 418.
66. Campbell, *Transformation of American*, 84–106; Herring, *From Colony to Superpower*, 309; Musicant, *Empire by Default*.
67. Goldwin Smith to Bourke Cockran, November 10, 1899, quoted in R. Craig Brown, "Goldwin Smith and Anti-Imperialism," *Canadian Historical Review* 43, June (1962): 95.
68. Ernest R. May, *American Imperialism: A Speculative Essay* (New York: Atheneum Books, 1968), 216–17; Dorothea R. Muller, "Josiah Strong and American Nationalism: A Reevaluation," *Journal of American History* 53, no. 3 (1966): 487–503. For information concerning Fiske, see the *New York Times*, June 12, 16, 1898; Erving Winslow letter to Moorfield Storey, July 6, 1898, Moorfield Storey Papers, Division of Manuscripts, Library of Congress, Washington, D.C.; John

Chapter 2

1. Robert L. Beisner, *Twelve Against Empire: The Anti-Imperialists, 1898–1900* (New York: McGraw Hill, 1968), 6.
2. Ibid.
3. Ibid.
4. Ibid., 18.
5. Ibid., 19.
6. Ibid., 22.
7. Ibid.
8. Carl Schurz, *Speeches, Correspondence, and Political Papers of Carl Schurz*, vol. II (Philadelphia: J.B. Lippincott, 1865).
9. *Harper's Weekly*, March 19, 1898.
10. Beisner, *Twelve Against Empire*, 27.
11. "Thoughts on American Imperialism," *Century Magazine*, September (1898).
12. Schurz, *Speeches, Correspondence, and Political Papers*, vol. II, 213.
13. Beisner, *Twelve Against Empire*, 31.
14. Ibid., 108.
15. Ibid.
16. Charles Frances Adams, *Charles Frances Adams, 1835–1915: An Autobiography* (Boston: Houghton Mifflin, 1916), 15–16.
17. Beisner, *Twelve Against Empire*, 112.
18. Charles Frances Adams, "Imperialism and the Tracks of Our Fathers," *A Paper Read by Charles Francis Adams Before the Lexington, Massachusetts Historical Society*, December 20, 1898 (Boston: Dana Estes, 1899), 9.
19. Ibid.
20. *Springfield Daily Republican*, May 18, 1899.
21. Ibid., May 18 and 19, 1899.
22. "The Anti-Imperialist League," *Philippine Social Science Review* 3, August (1930): 38.
23. Beisner, *Twelve Against Empire*, 55.
24. Ibid.
25. Morison, *The Letters of Theodore Roosevelt*, vol. I (Cambridge: Harvard University Press, 1951–1954), 75.
26. Beisner, *Twelve Against Empire*, 62.
27. Ibid., 70.
28. *The Nation*, July 20, 1895, 36.
29. E. L. Godkin, "Diplomacy and the Newspaper," *North American Review* 160, May (1895): 571–72, 576–79.
30. *The Nation*, April 1899.
31. Ibid.
32. Ibid.
33. Kermit Vanderbilt, *Charles Eliot Norton: Apostle of Culture in a Democracy* (Cambridge: Belknap Press, 1959), 109.
34. William Roscoe Thayer, "The Sage of Shady Hill," *The Unpartizan Review* 15, January–March (1921): 84.
35. Beisner, *Twelve Against Empire*, 81.
36. Ibid.
37. C. E. Norton to William James, September 1, 1902; Norton to W. A. Croffut, September 5, 1902, William A. Croffut Papers, Library of Congress, Washington, D.C.
38. Beisner, *Twelve Against Empire*, 89.
39. *Boston Evening Transcript*, May 3, 1899.
40. *New York Times Sunday Herald*, August 1, 1900.
41. Beisner, *Twelve Against Empire*, 90.
42. Grover Cleveland Papers, Library of Congress, Washington, D.C., President Cleveland's memo dated February 15, 195.
43. Edward Atkinson, "Jingoes and Silverites," *North American Review* 161, November (1895): 559–60.
44. Beisner, *Twelve Against Empire*, 94.
45. Ibid.
46. Ibid., 95.
47. *The Anti-Imperialist* 1, May 27, 1899, 23. "Addenda to 'The Hell of War and Its Penalties.'"
48. Edward Atkinson to William McKinley, November 14, 1898, Andrew Carnegie Papers, Library of Congress, Washington, D.C.
49. Beisner, *Twelve Against Empire*, 98.
50. Ibid.
51. Ibid., 99.
52. *The Anti-Imperialist* 1, May 27, 1899.
53. Beisner, *Twelve Against Empire*, 99.
54. Ibid., 100.
55. Ibid.
56. Ibid., 101.
57. Ibid., 102.
58. Edward Atkinson, "Eastern Commerce: What it is Worth?" *North American Review* February (1900): 295–304.
59. Beisner, *Twelve Against Empire*, 141.
60. George F. Hoar, "Popular Discontent with Representative Government," *Annual Report of the American Historical Association for the Year 1895* (Washington, D.C: Government Printing Office, 1896), 24.

Notes—Chapter 2

61. Theodore H. White, *The Making of the President* (New York: Pocket Books, 1962), 429.
62. Beisner, *Twelve Against Empire*, 146.
63. *Ibid.*
64. George F. Hoar, *Autobiography of Seventy Years*, 2 vols. (New York: Charles Scribner & Sons, 1903), vol. II, 306.
65. *The Hoar Papers*, Speech by Hoar in Worchester, MA, November 1, 1898.
66. *Ibid.*, Letter to Beverly K. Moore, Secretary of the Boston Merchants' Association, December 29, 1898.
67. *The Nation*, November 10, 1898, 342.
68. William Jennings Bryan et al., *Republic or Empire? The Philippine Question* (Chicago: Independence, 1899). See the McEnery and Bacon Resolutions.
69. *Ibid.* George F. Hoar Speech to the U.S. Senate, 161.
70. Hoar, *Autobiography of Seventy Years*, vol. II, 304.
71. Beisner, *Twelve Against Empire*, 193–94.
72. George S. Boutwell, *The Crisis of the Republic* (Boston: Dana Estes, 1900), 7–25.
73. George S. Boutwell, "Hawaiian Annexation," *Honorable George S. Boutwell's Address before the Boot and Show Club of Boston, December 22, 1897* (Boston: J.E. Farwell, 1898), 5–12.
74. Richard E. Welch, Jr., *Response to Imperialism, the United States and the Philippine American War* (Chapel Hill: University of North Carolina Press, 1979), 46.
75. Beisner, *Twelve Against Empire*, 197–98.
76. *Ibid.*, 198.
77. *Congressional Record*, 54th Cong., 1st Sess., February 28, 1896, 2244–47.
78. Margaret Leech, *In the Days of McKinley* (New York: Harper & Brothers, 1959), 102, 151.
79. William Allen White, *Mask in a Pageant* (New York: Macmillan, 1929), 326.
80. Thomas B. Reed, "The Safe Pathway of Experience," *North American Review* 163, October (1896): 389.
81. *Congressional Record*, 55th Cong., 2nd Sess., June 15, 1898, 6018–19.
82. William A. Robinson, *Thomas B. Reed, Parliament* (New York: Dodd, Mead, 1930), 369–70.
83. *Ibid.*
84. John T. Morgan, "What Shall We Do with the Conquered Islands?" *North American Review* 166, June (1898): 641–650.
85. *Ibid.*
86. Bryan et al., *Republic or Empire?* 10.
87. *Democratic Campaign Book* (Democratic Party, 1898).
88. *Ibid.*
89. *Literary Digest*, October 1898, 481.
90. *Ibid.*
91. *Literary Digest*, July 1898, 32.
92. *New York Times*, October 4, 1898.
93. *Literary Digest*, July 2, 1898.
94. *Ibid.*, July 9, 1898, 32.
95. *New York Times*, October 5, 1898.
96. *Ibid.*, October 21, 1898.
97. Speech by Bryan at Savannah, Georgia, December 13, 1898, reprinted in Robert I. Fulton and Thomas C. Trueblood, eds., *Patriotic Eloquence Relating to the Spanish-American War and Its Issues* (New York: Scribner, 1900), 42–44.
98. Speech by Bryan at Cincinnati, OH, January 6, 1899, *Ibid.*, 39–42.
99. Bryan Speech at Ann Arbor, Michigan, February 18, 1898, *Ibid..*, 45.
100. William Jennings Bryan, *Memoirs of William Jennings Bryan, by Himself and His Wife* (New York: John C. Winston, 1925), 120–21.
101. R. F. Pettigrew, *Imperial Washington* (Chicago: C. H. Kerr, 1922), 270; Hoar, *Autobiography of Seventy Years*, vol. II, 321–23.
102. *The Chicago Liberty Meeting*, Central Anti-Imperialist League, 1899.
103. Letter to Erving Winslow and Edwin Burnett Smith, October 11, 1899, from George S. Boutwell in Boutwell, *The Crisis of the Republic*, 211.
104. W. Bourke Cochran, *Address Delivered at Faneuil Hall*, Boston, February 23, 1900, published under the auspices of the New England Anti-Imperialist League.
105. Allan Nevins, *Grover Cleveland: A Study in Courage* (New York: Dodd, Mead, 1933), 747.
106. Frederic Bancroft, ed., *Speeches, Correspondence, and Political Papers of Carl Schurz*, VI (Charleston, SC: BiblioBazaar, 2009), 191–92, 199–203, 264–65, 275–76.
107. Letter from James Creelman to Bryan, May 24, 1900, quoted in M. R. Werner, *Bryan* (New York: Harcourt, Brace, 1929), 125–27.
108. *Ibid.*
109. *Official Proceedings of the Democratic National Convention*, Chicago, 1900, 36.
110. *Ibid.*, 115.
111. *Ibid.*, 121–22.
112. *Ibid.*, 132–33.

Notes—Chapter 2

113. *National Democratic Campaign Book, Presidential Election* (Democratic Party, 1900).
114. *Official Proceedings of the Democratic National Convention*, 1990, 115.
115. *Literary Digest* 21, September 1, 1900, 243.
116. Bryan, *Memoirs*, 125.
117. *Report of the Second Annual Meeting of the New England Anti-Imperialist League*, Boston, 1900, 7.
118. *Literary Digest* 21, August 25, 1900, 216.
119. *National Democratic Campaign Book*, Chapter 13.
120. Thomas A. Bailey, "Was the Presidential Election of 1900 a Mandate on Imperialism?" *Mississippi Valley Historical Review* 24 (1937): 43–52.
121. *Report of the Second Annual Meeting of the New England Anti-Imperialist League*, 8, 22–23.
122. *Report of the Second Annual Meeting of the New England Anti-Imperialist League*, 5.
123. *Democratic Campaign Text-Book, Congressional Elections*, 1902.
124. Bryan et al., *Republic or Empire?* 263.
125. *Ibid.*, 271.
126. *Ibid.*, 130.
127. David Starr Jordan, *Imperial Democracy: With a New Introduction*, Gerald E. Markowitz, ed. (New York: Garland, 1972).
128. Jacob Gould Schurman, *Philippine Affairs: A Retrospect and an Outlook* (New York, 1902), 14, 107–9.
129. Welch, *Response to Imperialism*, 118.
130. Beisner, *Twelve Against Empire*, 44.
131. Ralph Barton Perry, *The Thought and Character of William James, As Revealed in Unpublished Correspondence and Notes, Together with His Published Writings* (Boston: Little, Brown, 1935), vol. II, 208. See his letter to J. Mark Baldwin, dated April 22, 1898.
132. *Ibid.*, 309–10.
133. *Boston Evening Transcript*, April 1899.
134. *North American Review* 17, February (1901): 161–76.
135. *Ibid.*, May 1902. This piece was also quoted in Philip S. Foner and Richard C. Winchester, eds., *The Anti-Imperialist Reader: A Documentary History of Anti-Imperialism in the United States*, vol. I (New York: Holmes & Meier, 1984).
136. *Puck* 49, March 13, 1901.
137. *New York Times*, February 15, 1899, reprinted in Ernest Crosby, *Sword and Plowshares* (New York: Funk and Wagnalls, 1902), 33–34.
138. *Atlantic Monthly* 85, May 1990.
139. *Atlantic Monthly* 87, February 1900, 288.
140. Morrison I. Swift, *Imperialism and Liberty* (Los Angeles: Ronbroke Press, 1899), 4.
141. *Ibid.*, 4–8, 92–103.
142. Foner and Winchester, eds., *The Anti-Imperialist Reader*, vol. I, 111.
143. F. Scrishaw, *The Weekly People*, December 29, 1895.
144. *The People*, March 6, 1898.
145. *The People*, April 24, 1898, Algernon Lee.
146. *The People*, June 19, 1898.
147. *Ibid.*
148. *Literary Digest*, 21, November 3, 1900, 518.
149. "Why Colored Troops Were not Sent Earlier," *The Richmond Planet*, July 30, 1898.
150. *The Advance*, August 31, 1899.
151. *Richmond Planet*, April 2, 1898, quoted in George P. Marks, *The Black Press Views American Imperialism, 1898–1900* (New York: Arno Press, 1971), 3–4.
152. *Washington Bee*, August 27, 1898; *Ibid.*, 88.
153. *Christian Recorder*, February 9, 1899, quoted in Foner and Winchester, *The Anti-Imperialist Reader*, 153.
154. *Salt Lake City Broad Axe*, April 25, 1899.
155. *Ibid.*
156. *The Colored American*, April 8, 1899.
157. *Ibid.*, May 27, 1899.
158. *Ibid.*, December 2, 1899.
159. *Ibid.*, March 24, 1900, "Negro Anti-Imperialists National Organization May Meet in Kansas City."
160. Foner and Winchester, *The Anti-imperialist Reader*, 168–70.
161. *Ibid.*, 172.
162. *The Recorder* (Indianapolis), September 1, 1900, quoted in Marks, *The Black Press*, 182.
163. *Ibid.*
164. *Literary Digest* 19, September 30, 1899, 188.
165. Welch, Jr., *Response to Imperialism*, 92.
166. *Literary Digest* 19, September, 30, 1899, 409–10.
167. Welch, Jr., *Response to Imperialism*, 92.

168. *Springfield Daily Republican*, May 1, 1899.
169. Bryan et al., *Righteous Empire?* 689.
170. *Ibid.*, 690.
171. *Springfield Daily Republican*, May 1, 1899.
172. Welch, Jr., *Response to Imperialism*, see note 13 on 175.
173. *Ibid.*, 95.
174. Bryan et al., *Republic or Empire?* 432.
175. *Ibid.*, 433.
176. *Ibid.*, 434.
177. *Ibid.*, 696.
178. *Ibid.*, 702.
179. *Ibid.*, 703.
180. *Ibid.*, 704.

Chapter 3

1. Albert Ellery Bergh, ed., *Letters and Addresses of Grover Cleveland* (New York: Unit, 1909), 374.
2. Philip S. Foner, *Spanish-Cuban-American War and the Birth of American Imperialism* (New York: Monthly Review Press, 1973), 17–18, 178–81.
3. Walter Q. Gresham, Secretary of State, to Hannis Taylor, Minister to Spain. March 14, 1895; Taylor to Gresham, April 11, 1895; Carlos O'Donnelly Abreu, Duque de Tetuán, Minister of Foreign Affairs, to Taylor, April 18, 1895, Department of State, *Papers Relating to the Foreign Relations*, 1895, 1177, 1179, 1180, 1183.
4. Richardson, *Messages and Papers*, 6023–24.
5. The figures are taken from two articles in *Revue du Droit International Public* 5 (1898): 358, 499.
6. Edwin F. Atkins, *Sixty-Years in Cuba: Reminiscences* (Cambridge: Harvard University, 1926), 146–50.
7. Elbert J. Benton, *International Law and Diplomacy of the Spanish-American War*, 1908, Reprint (Charleston, SC: Nabu Press, 2013), 45–49.
8. A list of prisoners can be found in Department of State, *Papers Relating to the Foreign Relations*, 746–50.
9. Fitzhugh Lee to William W. Rockhill, December 31, 1896, Department of State, *Papers Relating to the Foreign Relations*, 843–44; *Congressional Record*, 53rd Cong., 3rd Sess., 3039; *Washington Post*, February 25, 26, 27, 28, 1897.
10. *Congressional Record*, 54th Cong., 1st Sess., 11.
11. United States War Department, *Report on the Census of Cuba, 1899* (Washington, D.C.: Government Printing Office, 1900), 528–29.
12. Edwin Atkins and Company to Edwin F. Uhl, December 9, 1895, Department of State, *Papers Relating to the Foreign Relations*, 1895, 1217–18; Edwin Atkins son of Elisha Atkins of Boston who purchased the planation Soledad during the Ten Years' War, was a resident of Cuba for most of his life. Edwin had powerful connections in Washington, with Richard Olney and John D. Long being among his most influential friends; Edwin Atkins to Uhl, December 9, 1895, Department of State, *Papers Relating to the Foreign Relations*, 1895, 1217.
13. Department of State, *Papers Relating to the Foreign Relations*, 1896, 710–11.
14. *Congressional Record*, 54th Cong., 1st Sess., 1065–68.
15. *Ibid.*, 1927–78, 2054–67, 2105–18.
16. *Ibid.*, 1967–70, 1978, 2163–69, 2246–48.
17. Before the rights and duties of nations were codified by the United Nations in the interest of global security, many international law scholars of late-nineteenth-century America agreed with the opposition's arguments. John B. Moore, "The Question of Cuban Belligerency," *The Forum* 21, May (1896): 288–300; Joseph H. Beale, Jr., "The Recognition of Cuban Belligerency," *Harvard Law Review* 9, January (1896): 406–9; Thomas Woolsey, "The Consequences of Cuban Belligerency," *Yale Law Journal* 5, March (1896): 182–86.
18. *Congressional Record*, 54th Cong., 1st Sess., 2244–48.
19. The *New York Journal* was a part of the William R. Hearst newspaper syndicate and was one of the largest manufacturers of yellow journalism. The book Sherman used to support these arguments was supposedly written by Erique Donders, a former Spanish officer who defected to the United States after witnessing Spain's crimes.
20. *Congressional Record*, 54th Cong., 1st Sess., 2067, 2256.
21. *Ibid.*, 2256.
22. *Ibid.*, 2587–94.
23. *Ibid.*, 2723–28.
24. *Ibid.*, 3037.
25. *Ibid.*, 3574–77.
26. *Ibid.*, 3547–55, 3574–77, 3592–97.
27. *Ibid.*, 3578–80, 3581–83.

Notes—Chapter 4

28. *Ibid.*, 3589, 3586–87.
29. *Ibid.*, 3627–28.
30. Dupuy de Lome to the Duque de Tetuán, April 10, 1896, *Spanish Diplomatic Correspondence and Documents, 1896-1900: Presented to the Cortes by the Minister of State*, 1905, Reprint (Charleston, SC: Forgotten Books, 2015), 3.
31. Orestes Ferrar, *The Last Spanish War: Revelations in Diplomacy*, trans. William E. Shea (New York: Paisley Press, 1937), 14–78.
32. Fitzhugh Lee, a nephew of Robert E. Lee, served as a cavalry officer during the Civil War. He was a major force in Virginia politics after the war and eventually became governor. Small in stature, Lee was too biased and temperamental to be successful for the mission on which Cleveland sent him. Fitzhugh Lee, "Cuba under Spanish Rule," *McClure's Magazine* 11 (1898): 99–100.
33. Cleveland to Olney, July 16, 1896, Allan Nevins, ed., *The Letters of Grover Cleveland, 1850-1908* (New York: Houghton Mifflin, 1933), 448–49.
34. Thomas H. McKee, *The National Conventions and Platforms of all Political Parties, 1789-1900*, 1900, Reprint (Ann Arbor: University of Michigan Library, 2009), 301–3.
35. *Ibid.*, 297.
36. Joseph P. Smith, *McKinley: The People's Choice: Full Text of Each Speech or Address Made by Him from June 18 to August 1, 1896*, 1896, Reprint (Charleston, SC: Nabu Press, 2010).

Chapter 4

1. Fitzhugh Lee to Day, January 12, 13 1898, Department of State, *Papers Relating to the Foreign Relations*, 1024, 1025; *Washington Post*, January 13, 1898.
2. Lee to Day, January 12, 1898, *Consular Letters, Havana to the State Department*, vol. 131, Personal and unnumbered; Lee to Day, January 13, 1898, Department of State, *Papers Relating to the Foreign Relations*, 1025; Lee to Day, January 15, 1898, *Consular Letters*, 131, no. 747.
3. *Ibid.*
4. *New York Tribune*, January 21, 1898; *Washington Evening Star*, January 13, 1898.
5. Dupuy de Lome to Gullon, January 14, 16, 19, 20 1898, Ministerio de Estado, *Spanish Diplomatic Correspondence*, 63–67. Theodore Roosevelt's correspondence reflected the seriousness of the Cuban riots. During the height of the riots, Roosevelt sent out letters about organizing an army unit and reminded Long that naval forces would need a month's warning before hostilities broke out. Roosevelt to C. Whitney Tillinghast. January 13, 1898; Roosevelt to Francis V. Greene. January 13, 1898; Roosevelt to Long, January 14, 1898, Morrison, *The Letters of Theodore Roosevelt*, vol. 1, 358–59.
6. *Congressional Record*, 55th Cong., 2nd Sess., 582; *New York Tribune*, January 12, 1898.
7. *Congressional Record*, 55th Cong., 2nd Sess.
8. *Ibid.*, 761, 764, 766.
9. *Ibid.*, 767–69.
10. *Ibid.*
11. At a White House dinner on January 27, McKinley was quite cordial toward Dupuy de Lome. In front of the German, English, and French ambassadors, McKinley remarked to the Spanish minister, "I see that we have good news: I am well satisfied with what has occurred in the House, and with the discipline of the Republicans. You, who comprehend this, will understand how strong our position is and how much it has changed and bettered in the past year; you have no occasion to be other than satisfied and confident." Dupuy de Lome to Gullon, January 28, 1898, Ministerio de Estado, *Spanish Diplomatic Correspondence*, 71.
12. Long's diary revealed that he favored sending a warship in early 1897, but realized that such a move involved "a great deal of risk." Lawrence S. Mayo, *America of Yesterday as Reflected in the Journal of John Davis Long* (Boston: Atlantic Monthly Press, 1933), 154–55; "The Week," *The Nation* 65 (1898): 59–60; *Washington Post*, January 25, 1898; *Ibid.*
13. Lee to Day, January 24, 1898, Department of State, *Papers Relating to the Foreign Relations*, 1026; Charles D. Sigsbee, *The "Maine," An Account of Her Destruction in Havana Harbor, Personal Narrative* (New York: Century, 1899), 24–30; Lee to Day, January 26, 1898, *Consular Letters*, 131.
14. Day to Lee, February 4, 1898, Department of State, *Papers Relating to the Foreign Relations*, 1027–28; Sigsbee to Long, February 1, 1898, Department of State Archives, *Miscellaneous Letters*, National Archives, Washington, D.C.
15. *Washington Post*, January 26, 1898; Lee to Day, January 25, 1898, Department of State, *Papers Relating to the Foreign Relations*,

Notes—Chatper 5

1026; Segismundo Bermejo to Pascual Cervera, February 6, 1898, Pascual Cervera, "The Spanish-American War," in *Notes on the Spanish-American War*, Office of Naval Intelligence (Washington, D.C.: Government Printing Office, 1900), 16-18.

16. George A. Converse to the Navy Department, February 6, 1898, Department of State Archives, *Miscellaneous Letters*, unnumbered.

17. *Ibid*. U.S. charity did very little to alleviate the food crisis. By February 4 only $6,743.46 of the donated relief aid made its way to Cuba. Senate document 230, 55th Cong., 2nd Sess., 23.

18. Negotiating with the insurgents started when Blanco first arrived in Cuba, but he had very little success with it. *New York Tribune*, November 23, December 14, 1897, February 3, 7, 1898.

19. Sherman to Woodford, February 8, 1898, *Instructions, Department of State to Consuls* 22, no. 125, 126, State Department Archives; Edwin Atkins to Day, January 27, 1898, William Rufus Day Papers, Division of Manuscripts, Library of Congress, Washington, D.C. Woodford did not present the claims to Spain until after February 18. Woodford to Sherman, February 25, 1898, Stewart L. Woodford, *Dispatches from the Minister to Spain to the State Department* 133, no. 157, State Department Archives, The Petition was covered by a letter from George R. Mosle to Day, February 9, 1898, *Miscellaneous Letters*, unnumbered.

20. The Dingley Tariff raised tariff rates to historic highs (to as high as 57 percent). The bill was so blatantly protectionist that Republican leaders sought to cover the bill's details behind the issue of the Cuban crisis. F. W. Taussing, "The Tariff Act of 1897," *Quarterly Journal of Economics* 12, no. 1 October (1897): 42-69.

21. *Congressional Record*, 55th Cong., 2nd Sess., 1605, 1534-35.

22. Robert Dallek, *1898: McKinley's Decision, The United States Declares War on Spain* (New York: Chelsea House, 1969), 110; Kenneth Whyte, *The Uncrowned King: The Sensational Rise of William Randolph Hearst* (New York: Random House Canada, 2008), 320-21, 368-70; Dupuy de Lome to Don José Canalejas, Department of State, *Papers Relating to the Foreign Relations*, 1007-8.

23. *Ibid*.

24. *Washington Evening Star*, February 10, 1898; Sherman to Woodford, February 23, 1898, *Instructions*, 22, no. 137.

25. Day to Woodford, February 9, 1898, Department of State, *Papers Relating to the Foreign Relations*, 1008; Woodford to Sherman, February 11, 1898, *Ibid.*, 1009; Woodford to Gullon, February 14, 1898, *Ibid.*, 1012-13.

26. *Ibid*.

27. Woodford to McKinley, February 15, 1898, *Dispatches of Stewart L. Woodford, Minister to Spain to the President of the United*, vol. 131A, no. 32, State Department Archives, Washington, D.C.

28. Woodford to McKinley, February 23, 1898, *Dispatches of Stewart L. Woodford*, vol. 131A, no. 34; Woodford to Sherman, February 17, 1898, *Dispatches from the Minister to Spain to the State Department*, 133, no. 145; Woodford to Sherman, February 17, 1898, Department of State, *Papers Relating to the Foreign Relations*, 1015-16.

29. Marcus M. Wilkerson, *Public Opinion and the Spanish-American War: A Study in War Propaganda* (New York: Russell and Russell, 1967), 93-95; *Washington Post*, February 10, 1898; *Washington Evening Star*, February 12, 1898; "The de Lome Incident," *Literary Digest*, 16, 212-13.

30. *Congressional Record*, 55th Cong., 2nd Sess., 1605, 1703; *Ibid.*, 1576, 1578-83, 1585; Champ Clark noted in 1920 that the de Lome letter incident facilitated the cause of the war between the U.S. and Spain and united the Democrats and Republicans in upholding the office of the U.S. President. Champ Clark, *My Quarter Century of American Politics* (New York: Harpers and Brothers, 1920), vol. 1, 400-401.

31. *Congressional Record*, 55th Cong., 2nd Sess., 1681-82.

32. *Ibid*.

Chapter 5

1. L. White Busbey and Joe Cannon, *Uncle Joe Cannon: The Story of a Pioneer American* (New York: Henry Holt, 1927), 186.

2. *Ibid.*, 186, 192.

3. *Ibid*.

4. Lee to Day, March 1, 1898, *Consular Letters*, vol. 132, State Department Archives; Sherman to Woodford. March 7, 1898, Department of State, *Papers Relating to the Foreign Relations*, 679-80; Senate document 230, 55th Cong., 2nd Sess.; Stephen E. Barton

Notes—Chapter 6

to Day, March 15, 1898, William Rufus Day Papers, Division of Manuscripts, Library of Congress, Washington, D.C.

5. Lee to Day, March 8, 1898, *Consular Letters*, 132; *Washington Post*, March 12, 1898; *New York Tribune*, March 11, 1898; Theodore Roosevelt to Henry White, March 9, 1898, Morison, *The Letters of Theodore Roosevelt*, vol. 1, 790–91.

6. *Washington Post*, March 11, 13 1898; Edward Nelson Dingley, *The Life of Nelson Dingley, Jr.*, 1902, Reprint (Charleston, SC: Ulan, 2013), 455–56; James H. Wilson to John J. McCook, March 13, 1898, James H. Wilson Papers, Division of Manuscript, Library of Congress, Washington, D.C.

7. *Ibid.*

8. Oscar S. Straus, *Under Four Administrations: From Cleveland to Taft* (Boston: Houghton Mifflin, 1922), 122–24; Straus to McKinley, March 12, 1898; Straus to McCook, March 12, 1898; Oscar S. Straus Papers, Division of Manuscripts, Library of Congress, Washington, D.C.; McCook to McKinley, March 22, 1898, William McKinley Papers, Division of Manuscripts, Library of Congress, Washington, D.C.

9. *Ibid.*

10. Straus, *Under Four Administrations*, 124.

11. *Washington Post*, March 16, 1898; John C. Spooner to John G. Gregory, March 14, 1898, John C. Spooner Papers, Division of Manuscripts, Library of Congress, Washington, D.C.

12. Morison, *The Letters of Theodore Roosevelt*, 795; Hyman Rickover, *How the Battleship Maine was Destroyed* (Annapolis, MD: Naval Institute Press, 1995), 67.

13. Polo de Bernabe to Gullon, March 16, 1898, United States, Ministerio de Estado, *Spanish Diplomatic Correspondence and Documents*, 91–92.

14. Woodford to Sherman, March 17, 1898, *Dispatches from the Minister to Spain to the State Department*, 132, no. 187; Woodford to McKinley, March 17, 1898, Department of State, *Papers Relating to the Foreign Relations*, 685–88. Woodford's military assistant held the opposite view, writing on March 16 to his wife: "all the information we get here points to a speedy end to our stay in Madrid. The Spaniards expect war will come and are making preparations to meet it." Frederick Palmer, *Bliss, Peacemaker: The Life and Letters of General Tasker Howard Bliss* (New York: Dodd, Mead, 1934), 50–51.

15. While Woodford believed that such a plan would work, Moret had little faith in the ambassador's clandestine plan. Woodford to McKinley, March 18, 1898, Department of State, *Papers Relating to the Foreign Relations*, 689–90.

16. Woodford to McKinley, March 19, 1898, *Dispatches of Stewart L. Woodford*, vol. 131A, no. 45, 33.

17. *Ibid.*, 46.

18. Woodford to McKinley, March 19, 1898, Department of State, *Papers Relating to the Foreign Relations*, 693; Woodford to Sherman, March 21, 1898, *Ibid.*, 693–94.

19. Genevieve Tabouis, *The Life of Jules Cambon* (London: Jonathan Cape, 1938), 92–93; Approximately nine-tenths of McKinley's incoming mail was destroyed upon his death, but every incoming letter was answered by the President. Copies of all outgoing mail are on file in the McKinley papers, and most of these letters showed that a majority of the letter writers favored peace. McKinley's private secretary, John A. Porter, informed John Hay in March of 1898 that "every day brings [McKinley] a great number of messages of congratulations and expressions of confidence in the administration from all parts of the country." William McKinley Papers; Nelson Dingley, who fervently supported McKinley's administration, also received many letters in the six weeks following the *Maine* explosion, asking him to support the President's policies. Dingley, *Nelson Dingley*, 455.

20. *Washington Post*, February 26, March 14, 1898; *Washington Evening Star*, March 11, 14, 1898; Polo de Bernabe to Gullon, March 19, 1898, Ministerio de Estado, *Spanish Diplomatic Correspondence*, 93.

21. *Washington Evening Star*, March 14, 1898.

22. *Congressional Record*, 55th Cong., 2nd Sess., March 17, 1898, 2918.

23. *Ibid.*
24. *Ibid.*
25. *Ibid.*

Chapter 6

1. *New York Chronicle*, October 2, 1897, 596, Editorial.

2. *Chicago Tribune*, March 21, 1898, 6, Editorial.

3. David Lyon, *The First Destroyers* (Annapolis, MD: Naval Institute Press, 1996), 14.
4. *London Times*, April 14, 1898, 6, Editorial.
5. *Scientific America*, April 2, 1898, 216, 218.
6. French Ensor Chadwick, *The Relations of the United States and Spain: The Spanish-American War* (New York: Nabu Press, 1911), 46.
7. Alfred T. Mahan, *Lessons of the War with Spain and other Articles* (Boston: Little, Brown, 1918), 31.
8. *Chicago Inter-Ocean*, April 11, 1898, 6, Editorial.
9. *Washington Post*, April 4, 1898, 6, Editorial.
10. *San Francisco Chronicle*, April 4, 1898, 4, Editorial.
11. *Chicago Times–Herald*, April 1, 1898, 6, Editorial.
12. *New York Times*, April 9, 1898, 6, Editorial.
13. *Boston Journal of Commerce*, April 23, 1898, 54, Editorial.
14. *The Omaha Bee*, March 13, 1898, 12, Editorial.

Chapter 7

1. Letter of the Army's Adjutant General, April 7, 1898, *Congressional Record*, 55th Cong., 2nd Sess., 3678.
2. *Chicago Chronicle*, March 2, 1898, 6, Editorial.
3. *New York Journal of Commerce and Commercial Bulletin*, April, 13 1898, 6, Editorial.
4. *Saturday Review*, April 16, 1898, 513, Editorial.
5. *Baltimore American*, February 1898.
6. *Emporia Gazette*, March 31, 1898, 2, Editorial.

Chapter 8

1. *Westminster Gazette*, March 31, 1898, 1, Editorial.
2. Fred Lane, *Fortnightly Review*, April 1, 1898, 648.
3. *Nieuws van den Dag*, quoted by *Literary Digest*, March 26, 1898, 383.
4. *New York Times*, March 22, 1898, 6, Editorial.

5. *Chicago Tribune*, March 28, 1898, 6, Editorial.
6. *New York Chronicle*, February 12, 1898, 308, Editorial.
7. *New York Herald*, February 27, 1898, 3, Editorial.
8. *New York Tribune*, April 1, 1898, 6, Editorial.
9. *New York Journal of Commerce and Commercial Bulletin*, May 21, 1897, 4, Editorial.
10. *Bankers' Magazine*, March 1898, 358, Editorial.

Chapter 9

1. James Ford Rhodes, *The McKinley and Roosevelt Administrations*, 1922, Reprint (Charleston, SC: BiblioBazaar, 2009), 55; Walter LaFeber, *The Cambridge History of American Foreign Relations*, vol. 2, *The American Search for Opportunity, 1865–1913*, ed. Warren I. Cohen (Cambridge: Cambridge University Press, 1993), 129–59.
2. *Wall Street Journal*, December 3, 31, 1897, January 25, April 21, 1898; *Railway World*, January, February 26, 1898, 105, 217; *Banker and Tradesman*, February 23, 1898, 79; *American Banker*, March 30, 1898, 528; *Journal of Commerce and Commercial Bulletin*, November, 27, 1897; *Commercial and Financial Chronicle*, October 2, 1897, 597; *Daily Commercial News and Shipping List*, March 25, 1898.
3. Chamber of Commerce of the State of New York, *Fortieth Annual Report*, 1897–98, 127; Boston Chamber of Commerce, *Thirteenth Annual Report*, 1898, 115–16; Baltimore Board of Trade, *Report of President and Directors for the Year Ending September 30, 1898*, 67; Philadelphia Board of Trade, *Sixty-Sixth Annual Report, 1897*, 50–51; Cleveland Chamber of Commerce, *Fiftieth Year*, 66; Indianapolis Board of Trade, *Annual Report for the Year Ending June 1, 1898*, 20. The antiwar sentiment expressed in these reports varied. Some was strongly opposed to war, while others commended President McKinley's conservative approach to establishing a peaceful resolution to the Cuban crisis.
4. *American Banker*.
5. *Commercial and Financial Chronicle*, vol. 66, 641; *Boston Journal of Commerce*, vol. 52, 40.

Notes—Chapter 9

6. Welch, *Presidencies of Grover Cleveland*, 188.
7. *New York Commercial*, January 3, 1898.
8. *Commercial and Financial Chronicle*, July 24, December 4, 1897, 134, 1046; *Wall Street Journal*, December 23, 1897.
9. *Banker and Tradesman*, April 20, 1898, 297.
10. *The Iron Age*, December 9, 1897, 19-20, 22; *Railway World*, August 21, 1897, 837; *Daily Commercial News and Shipping List*, March 7, 1898.
11. *Commercial and Financial Chronicle*, October 1897, vol. 65, 597-99; *Banker and Tradesman*, April 27, 1898, 328.
12. *Ibid.; New Jersey Trade Review*, March 1, 1898.
13. *Railway Age*, April 1, 15, 1898, 215, 253.
14. *Commercial and Financial Chronicle*, February 12, 1898, 308; *Bankers' Magazine*, March 1898, 358; *United States Investor*, April 9, 1898, 529.
15. *Railroad Gazette*, April 1, 1898, 236; *Iron and Steel*, April 9, 1898, 10; *The Iron Age*, March 17, 1898, 21. As to the views held by the manufacturers of arms and ammunitions, it is interesting to note that a representative of a New York munitions firm wrote the Secretary of the Interior in March 1898, asking him to fight for a peaceful settlement of the Cuban crisis. M. Hartley to C. N. Bliss, March 16, 17, 1898, Department of State Archives, *Miscellaneous Letters*, vol. 2.
16. *Wall Street Journal*, November 18 and December 31, 1897; *New York Journal of Commerce and Commercial Bulletin*, May 21 and June 5, 1897.
17. *Commercial and Financial Chronicle*, May 22, 1897, 974, February 12, 1898, 308; *American Banker*, May 26, 1897, 912-13, March 9, 1898, 394; *United States Investor*, March 12, 1898, 368; *Rand-McNally Bankers' Monthly*, April 1898, 294.
18. *The Financial Record: An Investor's Manual*, November 4, 17, 1897.
19. The proposal of the Kansas City Board of Trade was forwarded, for endorsement, to the Philadelphia Board of Trade, who categorically rejected it. Philadelphia Board of Trade, *Sixty-Sixth Annual Report, 1897*, 15; Cincinnati Chamber of Commerce and Merchant's Exchange, *Fiftieth Annual Report, 1899*, 49; *The Economist*, February 26, March 19, 1898, 233, 322.
20. *Rand-McNally Bankers' Monthly*, March 1898, 199-201; *Age of Steel*. March 5, 12, 1898; *St. Louis Republic*, March 3, 1898.
21. *The Tradesman*, March 1, 1898, 58; In the May issue of the *Tradesman*, the editors denied that any permanent good to business could result from a war with Spain. May 1, 1898; *Mining and Scientific Press*, April 9, 1898. In the April 23 issue of the *Mining and Scientific Press*, the editor noted that war between the two chief copper-producing nations would result in a boom in that metal, 438.
22. *Wall Street Journal*, February 17 and 24, 1898.
23. *Dun's Review*, March 5 and 12, 1898; *Bradstreet's*, March 12, 1898, 161. Similar views were held by the *Dry Goods Economist*, April 9, 1898.
24. Department of State Archives, *Miscellaneous Letters*, May 1897, vol. 2. The memorandum is covered by a letter from George R. Mosle to John Sherman, May 17, 1897.
25. The memorandum was signed by seventy individuals or firms from New York and surrounding cities; forty from Philadelphia; and sixty-four from Mobile. The businessmen presented it to President McKinley on the morning of February 9, 1898, with George R. Mosle, William Moore Carson, and George Turnure leading the delegation.
26. Juragua Iron Co., Ltd. Josiah Monroe to Day, April 14, 1898, Department of State Archives, *Miscellaneous Letters*, vol. 2; Spanish-American Iron Co. (Per C. F. Rand, President) to Day, April 8, 1898, *Ibid.*, April 1898, vol. 1; Armstrong Cork Co., to Secretary Sherman. March 8, 1898, *Ibid.*, March 1898; John Duer to Department of State, March 28, 1898, *Ibid.*; R. H. Clarke to honorable J. Wheeler, March 26, 1898, *Ibid.*, March 1898, vol. 3; C. R. Fowlers to Secretary Alger, April 23, 1898, *Ibid.*, April 1898, vol. 3.
27. *Commercial and Financial Chronicle*, April 16, 1898, 732; *Journal of Commerce and Commercial Bulletin*, April 23, 1898; *Boston Journal of Commerce*, April 18, 1898; *United States Investor*, April 9, 1898, 529.
28. *Bradstreet's*, January 29, 1898, 66; *American Banker*, May 12, 1897, 817; *United States Investor*, March 19, 1898, 400-401; *Dry Goods Economist*, January 1, 1898; *American Wood and Cotton Reporter*, March 24, 1898, 380; *The Tradesman*, June 15, 1898, 52. The National Board of Trade at its annual meeting in Washington in December 1897 recommended various measures for the further ex-

Notes—Chapter 9

tension of export trade. National Board of Trade, *28th Annual Meeting, 1897*, December 1897, 337-38.

29. Theodore S. Woolsey, *America's Foreign Policy: Essays and Addresses* (Toronto: University of Toronto Libraries, 1898), 1-21.

30. The National Board of Trade consistently supported the construction of the canal. National Board of Trade, *28th Annual Meeting*, 335; The National Association of Manufacturers, at its January 1897 meeting, took "strong ground in favor of the Nicaragua canal." *Journal of Commerce and Commercial Bulletin*, January 25, 1897.

31. *Commercial and Financial Chronicle*, January 20, June 26, 1897, 211-13, 1205-7; *Journal of Commerce and Commercial Bulletin*, June 17, August 14, September 8, 1897.

32. *Journal of Commerce and Commercial Bulletin*, September 8, 1897.

33. *Ibid.*, June 17 and October 21, 1897. In a similar fashion, the *United States Investor* considered Hawaiian annexation as a "menace" and the *Banker and Tradesman* believed the people of Cuba were "incapable and unfit for self-government. ... This country does not want Cuba." *United States Investor*, January 8, 1898, 48; *Banker and Tradesman*, March 16, 1898, 161; *Commercial and Financial Chronicle*, March 5, 1898, 446-48; *Age of Steel*, January 1, 1898, 57.

34. Baltimore Chamber of Commerce, *Forty-Third Annual Report*, January 31, 1898, 11; *Journal of Commerce and Commercial Bulletin*, January 24, 1896.

35. *Commercial and Financial Chronicle*, December 1897, 1147-48.

36. *Journal of Commerce and Commercial Bulletin*, May 27, 1897. Similar comments were expressed by the *American Banker*, May 12, 1897, 817; *Railway World*, June 5, 1897, 572.

37. *American Banker*, December 1, 1897, 2328-29; *Dry Goods Economist*, January 15, 1898; *The Iron Age*, December 23, 1897; *American Machinist*, quoted in *Daily Commercial News and Shipping List*, September 17, 1898; *The Tradesman*, June 15, 1898, 52; Baltimore Chamber of Commerce, *Forty-Third Annual Report*, 11.

38. *Literary Digest*, December 11, 1897, 964.

39. *Ibid.*

40. *New York Commercial*, January 27, 1898; *Commercial and Financial Chronicle*, December 18, 1897, 1147-48.

41. *New York Journal of Commerce and Commercial Bulletin*, November 30, 1897.

42. *Journal of Commerce and Commercial Bulletin*, May 15, 1896, February 22, December 23, 1897, January 8, 1898; *San Francisco Bulletin*, January 4, 1898; *Financial Record*, December 29, 1897; *American Banker*, January 5, 1898, 9; *New York Commercial*, January 5 and 22, 1898; *Baltimore Sun Kansas City Journal* in *Literary Digest*, January 8, 1898, 31-38; *Commercial and Financial Chronicle*, January 15, 1898, 106-7.

43. *American Banker*, December 29, 1897, 2489; *Age of Steel*, January 8, 29, 1898; *United States Investor*, January 8, 1898, 48; *Birmingham Age-Herald*, March 25, 1898; *The Nation*, February 17, 1898, 122-23.

44. *Journal of Commerce and Commercial Bulletin*, December 28, 1897, January 7, 1898.

45. These documents were printed in a pamphlet entitled "Commercial Rights of the United States in China," a copy of which is in the Department of State Archives, *Miscellaneous Letters*, June 1898, accompanying a letter of E. Frazer to Secretary Day, June 17, 1898. Another document in the same source is a communication from about seventy mercantile and manufacturing firms and individuals in New York, Philadelphia, and Pittsburgh, urging the New York Chamber of Commerce to bring the situation in China to the attention of the State Department. The original of the memorandum to President McKinley is in *Miscellaneous Letters*, February 1898, vol. 1.

46. Philadelphia Board of Trade to the President, February 25, 1898; San Francisco Chamber of Commerce to the President, March 8, 1898; Baltimore Chamber of Commerce to Secretary Sherman, March 17, 1898; Boston Chamber of Commerce to the President, March 30, 1898; Seattle Chamber of Commerce to the President, April 1898. All in Department of State Archives, *Miscellaneous Letters*, February–April 1898.

47. Frazer to Day, June 17, 1898, Department of State Archives, *Miscellaneous Letters*, vol. 2, June 1898.

48. *Dun's Review*, May 7, 1898, stated that railway stocks had advanced on the average of $2.79 per share since receiving the news of Dewey's victory.

49. *New York Sun*, November 8, 1897, March 13, 1898; *United States Investor* believed that such victory even if the islands were not retained "might pave the way for

Notes—Chapter 9

future interventions on the part of the United States in the affairs of the East." *United States Investor*, April 30, 1898, 624; *Financial Record* thought that the Philippines "would be good trading material for getting our share of what is going in Asia." *Financial Record*, May 5, 1898.

50. *New York Commercial*, May 7, 1898. The *Commercial* stated that the Philippines were "treasure islands"—"the richest islands in the world." Their development by U.S. capital, it noted, in the June 7 edition, would stimulate the trade of the Pacific coast and promote the establishment of new industries in the west; *Daily Commercial News and Shipping List*, May 13, 1898.

51. *New York Journal of Commerce and Commercial Bulletin*, May 3, 4, 11, and 31, 1898. The *Journal of Commerce* consistently held this view. On August 24, 1898, it stated: "We can establish ourselves as one of the Oriental powers by acquiring a really important stake in the Philippines, or we may resign ourselves to seeing the open door shut gradually in our faces."

52. *American Banker*, May 11, 1898, 785; *Banker and Tradesman*, June 1, August 24, 1898, 456, 776.

53. *Age of Steel*, May 21, 1898; *The Iron Age*, June 23, 1898; *United States Investor*, July 2 and 16, 1898, 953, 1017; *Financial Record*, June 15, 1898; *Bradstreet's*, June 4, 1898, 356; *New York Commercial*, June 1, 1898. The *Commercial* stated that "with the Philippines as a three-quarter way house, forming a superb trading station, the bulk of this trade should come to this country."

54. *Journal of Commerce and Commercial Bulletin*, June 17, 1898.

55. *The Tradesman*, June 15, September 1, 1898; *Dixie*, June 1898, 27; *New Orleans Picayune*, quoted in the *New York Journal of Commerce and Commercial Bulletin*, May 18, 1898; *Mining and Scientific Press*, May 21, June 18, 1898, 534 and 643; *Commercial Bulletin of Southern California*, June 17, December 23, 1898; *Daily Commercial News and Shipping List*, August 10, 1898; *Seattle Post-Intelligencer*, August 8, 1898; Chamber of Commerce of San Francisco, *Forty-Ninth Annual Report, 1899*, 23-24. The quotation is from resolutions adopted July 29, 1898 by the San Francisco Chamber of Commerce in conjunction with the other Associations and entities above.

56. *Seattle Post-Intelligencer*, June 1, 1898; Albro Martin, *James J. Hill and the Opening of the Northwest* (New York: Oxford University Press, 1976), 471.

57. *New York Journal of Commerce and Commercial Bulletin*, August 11, 1898; *Commercial and Financial Chronicle*, May 7, 14 1898, 876-78, 922-24; *Baltimore Journal of Commerce*, July 16, September 10, 1898.

58. *The Iron Age*, September 29, November 24, 1898; Everett Frazer to President McKinley, November 11, 1898, Department of State Archives, *Miscellaneous Letters*, 1898. Other businessmen informed McKinley about their reservations of annexing the Philippines. T. G. Bush, president of the Mobile and Birmingham Railroad Co., believed that the United States only needed a coal and naval station in the Philippines. Wharton Barker, of Philadelphia, thought trade could best be built by a reciprocity treaty with the Americas, not by expanding into Asia. August 25, 1898, Paris Peace Commission, *Miscellaneous Letters sent to the President and the Secretary of State*, 1898; *San Francisco Call*, September 10, 17, December 15, 1898.

59. *Bradstreet's*, July 16, 1898, 450; *Financial Record*, July 13, 1898; *Commercial and Financial Chronicle*, July 16, 1898, 96. The *Commercial and Financial Chronicle* believed "that whether wisely done or not, the annexation of Hawaii has settled the general principle."

60. *Journal of Commerce and Commercial Bulletin*, May 11, 1898, Letters from businessmen to the State Department urged the annexation of Puerto Rico as a "garden spot," capable of financially contributing to U.S. commerce. J. H. Hamlin & sons to President McKinley, May 11, 1898, Department of State Archives, *Miscellaneous Letters*, vol. 2, May 1898; T. G. Bush to President McKinley, July 30, 1898, *Ibid.*, vol. 3, July 1898.

61. *New York Commercial*, May 12, 1898; *Journal of Commerce and Commercial Bulletin*, August 25, 1898. Henry Cabot Lodge promoted the idea that the United States receive from Spain the entire Philippine island group, retain Luzon, and trade the remainder to Britain "in exchange for the Bahamas and Jamaica, and the Danish Islands, which I think we should be entitled to ask her to buy and turn over to us." Lodge to Secretary Day, August 11, 1898, Department of State Archives, *Miscellaneous Letters*, vol. 2, August 1898.

62. *New York Commercial*, May 9, June 8, August 9, 1898.
63. *Journal of Commerce and Commercial Bulletin*, May 31, July 13, 1898, January 6, February 1, 1899; *Commercial and Financial Chronicle*, May 14, August 13, 27, November 26, 1898, 922–24, 290, 401, 1082–3; *United States Investor*, November 26, 1898, 1704–5; *Rand-McNally Bankers' Monthly*, December 1898, 464. The American Asiatic Association, in a number of resolutions adopted January 5, 1899, called for a continuation of the "open door" policy in the Philippines. American Asiatic Association to Secretary John Hay, January 7, 1899, Department of State Archives, *Miscellaneous Letters*, vol. 1, January 1899.
64. *Dun's Review*, December 31, 1898.
65. *Banker and Tradesman*, December 28, 1898, 1186.

Chapter 10

1. *Atlanta Constitution*, April 15, 1898, 4, Editorial.
2. *Chicago Chronicle*, February 4, 1898, 6, Editorial.
3. *New York Herald*, January 21, 1898, 8, Editorial.
4. *New York Times*, March 16, 1898, 6, Editorial.
5. *New York Journal of Commerce and Commercial Bulletin*, April 11, 1898, 6, Editorial.
6. *Harper's Weekly*, April 30, 1898, 411.
7. *New York Journal of Commerce and Commercial Bulletin*, March 5, 1898, 6, Editorial.
8. *Chicago Journal of Commerce*, February 28, 1898, 1.

Chapter 11

1. *Chicago Times-Herald*, March 4, 1898, 6, Editorial.
2. *New York Times*, March 15, 1898, 6, Editorial.
3. *The Commercial Advertiser*, March 31, 1898, 6, Editorial.
4. *Chicago Chronicle*, February 15, 1898, 6, Editorial.
5. *Ibid.*, February 18, 1898, 6.
6. Letter of Secretary of State William Day to U.S. Minister Stewart Woodford, March 28, 1898, William Day's Papers, Library of Congress, Washington, D.C.
7. Paul Holbo, "Presidential Leadership in Foreign Affairs: William McKinley and the Turpie–Foraker Amendments," *American Historical Review* July (1967): 1321–26.
8. Graham A. Cosmas, "San Juan Hill and El Caney, 1–2 July," in *America's First Battles, 1776-1965*, ed. Charles Heller and William Stofft (Lawrence: University of Kansas, 1986), 109–48.

Chapter 12

1. Richard E. Welch, *Response to Imperialism*, 87; Paul T. McCartney, *Power and Progress, American National Identity, the War of 1898, and the Rise of American Imperialism* (Baton Rouge: Louisiana State University, 2006), 237–38.
2. Henry F. Graff, *American Imperialism and the Philippine Insurrection, Testimony of the Times: Selections from Congressional Hearings* (Boston: Little, Brown, 1969), x.
3. *Ibid.*, xi.
4. *Ibid.*
5. *Ibid.*, xii.
6. *Ibid.*
7. *Ibid.*
8. *Ibid.*
9. *Ibid.*, xii.
10. *Ibid.*, xii–xiii.
11. Welch, *Response to Imperialism*, 24; *Pedro Paterno's Proclamation of War, June 2, 1899* (Washington, D.C.: U.S. Government Printing Office, 1899), vol. 30.
12. A. B. Feuer, *America at War, the Philippines, 1898-1913* (Westport, CT: Praeger, 2002), 35. There is some dispute as to when the war between America and Filipino guerillas began. The claim made by Feuer is based upon the testimony of Charles Mabey who apparently got his information from secondhand sources.
13. *Ibid.*
14. Welch, *Response to Imperialism*, 30.
15. *Ibid.*, 33; Brian McAllister Linn, *The Philippine War, 1899-1902* (Lawrence: University Press of Kansas, 2000), 11–12.
16. Feuer, *America at War*, xx.
17. Graff, American Imperialism, xiv.
18. *Ibid.*
19. *Ibid.*, 133.
20. *Ibid.*, 134.
21. *Ibid.*
22. *Public Opinion*, April 19, 1900, 486–87.

Notes—Suggested Readings

23. *Ibid.*
24. Welch, *Response to Imperialism*, 134.
25. *Ibid.*
26. *Ibid.*
27. George Kennan, "The Philippines: Present Conditions and Possible Courses," *The Outlook* 67, March 9 (1901): 576–84.
28. Linn, *The Philippine War*, 132–35.
29. Kristin L. Hoganson, *Fighting for American Manhood: How Gender Politics Provoked the Spanish-American and Philippine-American Wars* (New Haven: Yale University Press, 1998), 84.
30. Welch, *Response to Imperialism*, 134.
31. *Ibid.*, 135.
32. *Ibid.*
33. *Ibid.*, 136.
34. *Ibid.*, 134–35.
35. *Ibid.*
36. Graff, *American Imperialism*, vi–vii.
37. *Ibid.*, xiv.
38. *Ibid.*, xx; Welch, *Response to Imperialism*, 137.
39. *Ibid.*, xix–xx.
40. Welch, *Response to Imperialism*, 137.
41. Graff, *American Imperialism*, v.
42. *Ibid.*
43. *Ibid.*, 64.
44. *Ibid.*, 65.
45. *Ibid.*
46. *Ibid.*, 67.
47. *Ibid.*, 71.
48. *Ibid.*, 75.
49. *Ibid.*, 80.
50. *Ibid.*, 81.
51. *Ibid.*
52. *Ibid.*, 86–87, 88–89, 102–3.
53. *Ibid.*, 90–93.
54. Welch, *Response to Imperialism*, 137.
55. *Ibid.*
56. *Ibid.*
57. *Ibid.*
58. *Springfield Daily Republican*, January 28, 1902, 10; *New York Evening Post*, January 1902, 28.
59. *Literary Digest* 24, February 1902, 531; *New York World* April 19, 1902, 12, 16, and 18; *New York Evening Post*, April 18, 1902, 9.
60. Welch, *Response to Imperialism*, 138.
61. *New York World*, April 1902, 12, 16, 18; *New York Evening Post*, April 1902, 9, 18.
62. *Ibid.*
63. *New York Herald*, 8, February 1902, 1–2.
64. Welch, *Response to Imperialism*, 138.
65. *Ibid.*
66. Graff, *American Imperialism*, 139.
67. Welch, *Response to Imperialism*, 140–41.
68. *Ibid.*
69. Edmund Morris, *Theodore Rex* (New York: Random House, 2001), 129.
70. *New York Times*, April 1902, 17, 27, 29.
71. Welch, *Response to Imperialism*, 140–41.
72. *New York Times*, April 1902, 27.
73. Welch, *Response to Imperialism*, 140.
74. *Atlanta Constitution*, May 10, 1902.
75. Paul T. McCartney, *Power and Progress*, 245–47.
76. Welch, *Response to Imperialism*, 140.
77. H. L. Higginson to Lodge, 22 February 9, The Lodge Papers, Massachusetts Historical Society.
78. Morris, *Theodore Rex*, 104–5.
79. *Congressional Record*, 57th Cong., 1st Sess., May 4, 1902, 4030–40.
80. *Ibid.*
81. *Ibid.*
82. *Boston Journal of Commerce*, May 31, 1902.
83. *Ibid.*
84. *Providence Sunday Journal*, April 1902, May 1902.
85. *North American Review*, May 1902. Quoted in Foner and Winchester, eds., *The Anti-imperialist Reader*, vol. I, 1984.
86. *Harper's Weekly*, 46, June 7, 1902, 712.
87. *Springfield Daily Republican*, July 5, 1902.
88. Welch, *Response to Imperialism*, 147–49.
89. *Ibid.*

Suggested Readings

1. Horace Edgar Flack, *Spanish-American Diplomatic Relations Preceding the War of 1898* (Baltimore: John Hopkins University Press, 1906), 46; Trumbull White, *The United States in War with Spain* (Charleston, SC: Nabu Press, 2011).
2. Theodore Roosevelt, *Theodore Roosevelt, An Autobiography* (New York: MacMillan, 1913), 212; Russell A. Alger, *The Spanish-American War* (New York: Harper & Brothers, 1901), 4.
3. James C. Bradford, ed., *Crucible of Empire: The Spanish-American War and Its Aftermath* (Annapolis, MD: Naval Institute Press, 1993).
4. Graham A. Cosmas, "Joint Operations in the Spanish-American War," in *Cru-*

Notes—Suggested Readings

cible of Empire: The Spanish-American War and Its Aftermath, ed. James C. Bradford (Annapolis, MD: Naval Institute Press, 1993), 102.

5. Diane E. Cooper, "Diplomat and Naval Intelligence Officer: The Duties of Lt. George L. Dyer, U.S. Naval attaché to Spain," in *Crucible of Empire: The Spanish-American War and Its Aftermath*, ed. James C. Bradford (Annapolis, MD: Naval Institute Press, 1993), 1; David F. Trask, "American Intelligence During the Spanish-American War," in *Crucible of Empire: The Spanish-American War and Its Aftermath*, ed. James C. Bradford (Annapolis, MD: Naval Institute Press, 1993), 23.

6. Ivan Musicant, *Empire by Default: The Spanish-American War and the Dawn of the American Century* (New York: Henry Holt, 1998).

7. John Lawrence Tone, *War and Genocide in Cuba, 1895–1898* (Chapel Hill: University of North Carolina Press, 2006).

8. G. J. A. O'Toole, *The Spanish-American War: An American Epic, 1898* (New York: Norton, 1984); Frederick Merk, *Manifest Destiny and the Mission in American History* (Cambridge: Harvard University Press, 1970).

9. Joseph Smith, *The Spanish-American War: Conflict in the Caribbean and the Pacific, 1895–1902* (New York: Longman, 1994).

10. David Traxel, *1898: The Birth of the American Century* (New York: A. A. Knopf, 1998), 283–86.

11. Hoganson, *Fighting for American Manhood*.

12. LaFeber, *The American Search for Opportunity*; Walter LaFeber, *The New Empire: An Interpretation of American Expansionism, 1860–1998* (Ithaca: Cornell University Press, 1963).

13. Lloyd C. Gardner, Walter F. LaFeber, and Thomas J. McCormick, *Creation of the American Empire* (Chicago: Rand McNally, 1973), 193.

14. *Ibid.*, 204–11.

15. John Offner, *An Unwanted War: The Diplomacy of the United States and Spain over Cuba, 1895–1898* (Chapel Hill: University of North Carolina Press, 1992).

16. Louis A. Perez, Jr. *Cuba and the United States: Ties of Singular Intimacy* (Athens, GA: University of Georgia Press, 2003).

17. Michael H. Hunt, *Ideology and U.S. Foreign Policy* (New Haven: Yale University Press, 2009).

18. Henry Cabot Lodge, *The War with Spain* (New York: Harper & Brothers, 1899), 32.

19. Henry Watterson, *A History of the Spanish-American War* (Ithaca: Cornell University Library, 2009), 12.

20. Randolph Greenfield Adams, *A History of the Foreign Policy of the United States* (New York: MacMillan, 1924), 274.

21. Thomas A. Bailey, *Diplomatic History of the American People* (New York: MacMillan, 1948), 463; Richard E. Welch, Jr., "William McKinley: Reluctant Warrior, Cautious Imperialist," in *Traditions and Values: American Diplomacy, 1865–1945*, ed. Norman A. Graebner (Lanham, MD: University Press of America, 1985), 29–52.

22. William E. Leuchtenburg, "The Needless War with Spain," *American Heritage* 8, February (1957): 95; Richard Leopold, *The Growth of American Foreign Policy* (New York: Alfred A. Knopf, 1967).

23. John Weems, Fate of the "Maine" (Norwalk: Easton Press, 1990), 168.

24. Beisner, *Twelve Against Empire* (New York: McGraw Hill, 1968).

Bibliography

Adams, Charles Frances. *Charles Frances Adams, 1835–1915: An Autobiography.* Boston: Houghton Mifflin, 1916.

Adams, Charles Frances. "Imperialism and the Tracks of Our Fathers." *A Paper Read by Charles Francis Adams Before the Lexington, Massachusetts Historical Society. December 20, 1898.* Boston: Dana Estes, 1899.

Adams, Randolph Greenfield. *A History of the Foreign Policy of the United States.* New York: Macmillan, 1924.

The Advance. August 31, 1899.

Age of Steel. January 1898, March 1898, May 1898.

Alger, Russell A. *The Spanish-American War.* New York: Harper & Brothers, 1901.

American Banker. May 1897, December 1897, January 1898, March 1898, May 1898.

American Machinist. September 1898.

American Wood and Cotton Reporter. March 1898.

Andrew Carnegie Papers. Library of Congress, Washington, D.C.

The Anti-Imperialist. May 1899.

"The Anti-Imperialist League." *Philippine Social Science Review* 3, August (1930): 38.

Atkins, Edwin F. *Sixty-Years in Cuba: Reminiscences.* Cambridge: Harvard University, 1926.

Atkinson, Edward. "Eastern Commerce: What it is Worth?" *North American Review* February (1900): 295–304.

Atkinson, Edward. "Jingoes and Silverites." *North American Review* 161, November (1895): 559–60.

Atlanta Constitution. March–April 1898, May 1902.

Atlantic Monthly, February, 1900, May, 1990.

Bailey, Thomas A. *Diplomatic History of the American People.* New York: Macmillan, 1948.

Bailey, Thomas A. "Was the Presidential Election of 1900 a Mandate on Imperialism?" *Mississippi Valley Historical Review* 24 (1937): 43–52.

Baltimore American. February 1898.

Baltimore Board of Trade. *Report of President and Directors for the Year Ending September 30, 1898.*

Baltimore Chamber of Commerce. *Forty-Third Annual Report, 1898.*

Baltimore Journal of Commerce. July 1898, September 1898.

Baltimore Sun. January 1898.

Bancroft, Frederic, ed. *Speeches, Correspondence, and Political Papers of Carl Schurz, VI.* Charleston, SC: BiblioBazaar, 2009.

Banker and Tradesman. May 1897, February 1898, March 1898, April 1898, June 1898, August 1898, December 1898.

Bankers' Magazine. March 1898.

Beale, Joseph H. Jr. "The Recognition of Cuban Belligerency." *Harvard Law Review* 9, January (1896): 406–9.

Bederman, Gail. *Manliness and Civiliza-*

Bibliography

tion: *A Cultural History of Gender and Race in the United States*. Chicago: University of Chicago Press, 1995.

Beisner, Robert. *Twelve Against Empire: The Anti-imperialists, 1898–1900.* New York: McGraw-Hill, 1968.

Benton, Elbert. *International Law and Diplomacy of the Spanish-American War.* 1908. Reprint, Charleston, SC: Nabu Press, 2013.

Bergh, Albert Ellery, ed. *Letters and Addresses of Grover Cleveland.* New York: Unit, 1909.

Birmingham Age-Herald. March 1898.

Boston Chamber of Commerce. *Thirteenth Annual Report, 1898.*

Boston Evening Transcript. May 1899, April 1899.

Boston Herald. February 1896.

Boston Journal of Commerce. April 1898.

Boutwell, George S. *The Crisis of the Republic.* Boston: Dana Estes, 1900.

Boutwell, George S. "Hawaiian Annexation." *Honorable George S. Boutwell's Address before the Boot and Show Club of Boston, December 22, 1897.* Boston: J.E. Farwell, 1898, 5–12.

Boutwell, George S. *The Venezuelan Question and the Monroe Doctrine.* Washington, D.C.: Gibson, 1896.

Bradford, James C., ed. *Crucible of Empire: The Spanish-American War and Its Aftermath.* Annapolis, MD: Naval Institute Press, 1993.

Bradstreet's. January 1898, March 1898, June–July 1898.

Brown, R. Craig. "Goldwin Smith and Anti-imperialism." *Canadian Historical Review* 43, June (1962): 95.

Bryan, William Jennings. *Memoirs of William Jennings Bryan, by Himself and His Wife.* New York: John C. Winston, 1925.

Bryan, William Jennings, et al. *Republic or Empire? The Philippine Question.* Chicago: Independence, 1899.

Bryce, James. "A Policy of Annexation for America." *The Forum* 22, June (1897).

Burgess, John W. *Reminiscences of an American Scholar.* New York: Columbia University Press, 1934.

Busbey, L. White, and Joe Cannon. *Uncle Joe Cannon: The Story of a Pioneer American.* New York: Henry Holt, 1927.

Campbell, Charles S. *The Transformation of American Foreign Relations, 1865–1900.* New York: Harper and Row, 1976.

Carl Schurz Papers. Division of Manuscripts. Library of Congress. Washington, D.C.

Carnegie, Andrew. "Distant Possessions: The Parting of Ways." *North American Review* 167, no. 501 (1898).

Cervera, Pascual. "The Spanish-American War." In *Notes on the Spanish-American War.* Office of Naval Intelligence. Washington, D.C.: Government Printing Office, 1900.

Chadwick, French Ensor. *The Relations of the United States and Spain: Diplomacy.* New York: Charles Scribner Press, 1909.

Chadwick, French Ensor. *The Relations of the United States and Spain: The Spanish-American War.* New York: Nabu Press, 1911.

Chamber of Commerce of San Francisco. *Forty-Ninth Annual Report, 1899.*

Chamber of Commerce of the State of New York. *Fortieth Annual Report, 1897–98.*

Chicago Chronicle. February–March 1898.

Chicago Inter-Ocean. April 1898.

The Chicago Liberty Meeting. Central Anti-Imperialist League, 1899.

Chicago Journal of Commerce. February 1898.

Chicago Times-Herald. March–April 1898.

Chicago Tribune. March 1898.

Cincinnati Chamber of Commerce and Merchant's Exchange. *Fiftieth Annual Report, 1899.*

Clark, Champ. *My Quarter Century of American Politics.* New York: Harpers and Brothers, 1920.

Cleveland Chamber of Commerce. *Fiftieth Year.*

Cochran, W. Bourke. *Address Delivered at Faneuil Hall.* Boston, February 23, 1900. published under the auspices of the New England Anti-Imperialist League.

The Colored American. April 8, 1899, May 27, 1899, December 2, 1899, March 24, 1900.

Commercial and Financial Chronicle. January 1897, May 1897, June–July 1897, October 1897, December 1897, January–May 1898, July 1898, August 1898, November 1898.

The Commercial Advertiser. March 1898.

Commercial Bulletin of Southern California. June 1898, December 1898.

Congressional Record. 41st Cong., 3rd Sess., 53rd Cong., 3rd Sess., 54th Cong., 1st Sess., 55th Cong., 2nd Sess.

Consular Letters, Havana to the State Department, vols. 129–132. State Department Archives.

Cooper, Diane E. "Diplomat and Naval Intelligence Officer: The Duties of Lt. George L. Dyer, U.S. Naval attaché to Spain." In *Crucible of Empire: The Spanish-American War and Its Aftermath*, edited by James C. Bradford, 1–22. Annapolis, MD: Naval Institute Press, 1993.

Cosmas, Graham A. "Joint Operations in the Spanish-American War." In *Crucible of Empire: The Spanish-American War and Its Aftermath*, edited by James C. Bradford, 102–26. Annapolis, MD: Naval Institute Press, 1993.

Cosmas, Graham A. "San Juan Hill and El Caney, 1–2 July." In *America's First Battles, 1776–1965*, edited by Charles Heller and William Stofft, 109–48. Lawrence: University of Kansas, 1986.

Crawford, James. "The Right of Self-Determination in International Law: Its Development and Future." In *Peoples' Rights*, edited by Philip Alston, 7–67. Oxford: Oxford University Press, 2001.

Crosby, Ernest. *Sword and Plowshares.* New York: Funk and Wagnalls, 1902.

Daily Commercial News and Shipping List. March 1898, May 1898, August–September 1898.

Dallek, Robert. *1898: McKinley's Decision, The United States Declares War on Spain.* New York: Chelsea House, 1969.

Democratic Campaign Book. Democratic Party, 1898.

Democratic Campaign Text-Book, Congressional Elections. Democratic Party, 1902.

Department of State Archives. *Miscellaneous Letters.* National Archives. Washington, D.C.

Department of State. *Papers Relating to the Foreign Relations of the United States, 1895–1898*, 6 vols. Washington, D.C.: Government Printing Office, 1896–1901.

Dingley, Edward Nelson. *The Life of Nelson Dingley, Jr.* 1902. Reprint, Charleston, SC: Ulan, 2013.

Dispatches from the Minister to Spain to the State Department. Fitzhugh Lee and Stewart L. Woodford. vols. 132–133. State Department Archives.

Dispatches of Stewart L. Woodford, Minister to Spain to the President of the United States, vol. 131A. State Department Archives.

Dixie. June 1898.

Dry Goods Economist. January 1898, April 1898.

Dun's Review. March 1898, May 1898, December 1898.

The Economist. February–March 1898.

Emery, Sarah E. V. *Imperialism in America: Its Rise and Progress.* Lansing, MI, 1892.

Emporia Gazette. March 1898.

Ferrar, Orestes. *The Last Spanish War: Revelations in Diplomacy*, trans. William E. Shea. New York: Paisley Press, 1937.

Feuer, A. B. *America at War, the Philip-*

Bibliography

pines, 1898-1913. Westport, CT: Praeger, 2002.

The Financial Record: An Investor's Manual. November-December 1897, May 1898, June-July 1898.

Flack, Horace Edgar. *Spanish-American Diplomatic Relations Preceding the War of 1898.* Baltimore: John Hopkins Press, 1906.

Foner, Philip S., and Richard C. Winchester, eds. *The Anti-imperialist Reader: A Documentary History of Anti-imperialism in the United States,* vol. I. New York: Holmes & Meier, 1984.

Foner, Philip S. *Spanish-Cuban-American War and the Birth of American Imperialism,* vol. 1. New York: Monthly Review Press, 1973.

Fulton, Robert I., and Thomas C. Trueblood, eds. *Patriotic Eloquence Relating to the Spanish-American War and Its Issues.* New York: Scribner, 1900.

Gardner, Lloyd C., Walter F. LaFeber, and Thomas J. McCormick. *Creation of the American Empire.* Chicago: Rand McNally, 1973.

Godkin, E. L. "Diplomacy and the Newspaper." *North American Review* 160, May (1895): 570-79.

Graff, Henry F. *American Imperialism and the Philippine Insurrection, Testimony of the Times: Selections from Congressional Hearings.* Boston: Little, Brown, 1969.

Grover Cleveland Papers. Library of Congress, Washington, D.C.

Harper's Weekly. March 19, 1898, April 1898, June 1902.

Herring, George C. *From Colony to Superpower: U.S. Foreign Relations Since 1776.* New York: Oxford University Press, 2008.

Hoar, George F. *Autobiography of Seventy Years,* 2 vols. New York: Charles Scribner & Sons, 1903.

Hoar, George F. "Popular Discontent with Representative Government." *Annual Report of the American Historical Association for the Year 1895.* Washington, D.C.: Government Printing Office, 1896.

The Hoar Papers. Speech by Hoar in Worchester, MA. November 1, 1898.

Hoganson, Kristin. *Fighting for American Manhood: How Gender Politics Provoked the Spanish-American and Philippine-American Wars.* New Haven: Yale University Press, 1998.

Holbo, Paul. "Presidential Leadership in Foreign Affairs: William McKinley and the Turpie-Foraker Amendments." *American Historical Review* (1967): 1321-35.

Hunt, Michael H. *Ideology and U.S. Foreign Policy.* New Haven: Yale University Press, 2009.

Indianapolis Board of Trade. *Annual Report for the Year Ending June 1, 1898.*

Instructions. Department of State to Consuls, vols. 155-161. State Department Archives.

The Iron Age. December 1897, March 1898, June 1898, September 1898, November 1898.

Iron and Steel. April 1898, June 1898, September 1898, November 1898.

James H. Wilson Papers. Division of Manuscripts. Library of Congress. Washington, D.C.

Jefferson, Thomas. "Letter to Bowdin. 2 April 1807." In *The Writings of Thomas Jefferson,* edited by H. A. Washington. Cambridge: Cambridge University Press, 2011.

John C. Spooner Papers, 1855-1909. Manuscript Division. Library of Congress. Washington, D.C.

Jordan, David Starr. *Imperial Democracy: With a New Introduction,* Gerald E. Markowitz, ed. New York: Garland, 1972.

Journal of Commerce and Commercial Bulletin. January 1896, May 1896, January-February 1897, May-June 1897, August-December 1897, January 1898, April-August 1898, January-February 1899.

Bibliography

Kennan, George. "The Philippines: Present Conditions and Possible Courses." *The Outlook* 67, March 9 (1901): 576–84.

Kennedy, Paul. *The Rise and Fall of the Great Powers*. New York: Random House, 1987.

Koebner, Richard, and Helmut D. Schmidt. *Imperialism: The Story and Significance of a Political Word, 1840–1960*. Cambridge: Cambridge University Press, 1964.

LaFeber, Walter. *The Cambridge History of American Foreign Relations*. vol. 2, *The American Search for Opportunity, 1865–1913*, edited by Warren I. Cohen. New York: Cambridge University Press, 1993.

LaFeber, Walter. *The New Empire: An Interpretation of American Expansionism, 1860–1998*. Ithaca: Cornell University Press, 1963.

Lane, Fred. *Fortnightly Review*. April 1, 1898.

Lee, Fitzhugh. "Cuba under Spanish Rule." *McClure's Magazine* 11 (1898): 99–100.

Leech, Margaret. *In the Days of McKinley*. New York: Harper & Brothers, 1959.

Lemke, Douglas, and William Reed. "Regime Types and the Status Quo Evaluations: Power Transition Theory and the Democratic Peace." *International Interactions* 22, no. 2 (1996): 143–64.

Leopold, Richard. *The Growth of American Foreign Policy*. New York: Alfred A. Knopf, 1967.

Letter of Secretary of State William Day to U.S. Minister Stewart Woodford. March 28, 1898. William Day's Papers, Library of Congress. Washington, D.C.

Leuchtenburg, William E. "The Needless War with Spain." *American Heritage* 8, February (1957): 33–43.

Linn, Brian McAllister. *The Philippine War, 1899–1902*. Lawrence: University Press of Kansas, 2000.

Literary Digest. December 1897, January 1898, March 1898, July 1898, October 1898, September 1899, August 1900, September 1900, November 1900, February 1902.

Livezey, William E. *Mahan on Sea Power*. Norman, OK: University of Oklahoma Press, 1947.

Lodge, Henry Cabot. *The War with Spain*. New York: Harper & Brothers, 1899.

The Lodge Papers. Massachusetts Historical Society. Boston, MA.

London Times. April 1898.

Lyon, David. *The First Destroyers*. Annapolis, MD: Naval Institute Press, 1996.

Mahan, Alfred Thayer. *The Influence of Sea power upon History*. Boston: Little, Brown, 1890.

Mahan, Alfred Thayer. *The Interest of America in Sea Power, Present and Past*. New York: Houghton, Mifflin, 1890.

Mahan, Alfred Thayer. *Lessons of the War with Spain and other Articles*. Boston: Little, Brown, 1918.

Marks, George P. *The Black Press Views American Imperialism, 1898–1900*. New York: Arno Press, 1971.

Martin, Albro. *James J. Hill and the Opening of the Northwest*. New York: Oxford University Press, 1976.

May, Ernest R. *American Imperialism: A Speculative Essay*. New York: Atheneum Books, 1968.

May, Ernest R. *Imperial Democracy: The Emergence of America as a Great Power*. New York: Harcourt, Brace, and World, 1961.

Mayo, Lawrence S. *America of Yesterday as Reflected in the Journal of John Davis Long*. Boston: Atlantic Monthly Press, 1933.

McCartney, Paul T. *Power and Progress, American National Identity, the War of*

1898, and the Rise of American Imperialism. Baton Rouge: Louisiana State University, 2006.

McKee, Thomas H. *The National Conventions and Platforms of all Political Parties, 1789-1900*. 1900. Reprint, Ann Arbor: University of Michigan Library, 2009.

Merk, Frederick. *Manifest Destiny and the Mission in American History*. Cambridge: Harvard University Press, 1970.

Mining and Scientific Press. April-June 1898.

Ministerio de Estado. *Spanish Diplomatic Correspondence and Documents, 1896-1900: Presented to the Cortes by the Minister of State*. 1905. Reprint, Charleston, SC: Forgotten Books, 2015.

Moore, John B. "The Question of Cuban Belligerency." *The Forum* 21, May (1896): 288-300.

Moorfield Storey Papers. Division of Manuscripts. Library of Congress. Washington, D.C.

Morgan, John T. "What Shall We Do with the Conquered Islands?" *North American Review* 166, June (1898): 641-650.

Morison, Elting E. *The Letters of Theodore Roosevelt, 1868-1898*. Cambridge: Harvard University Press, 1951-1954.

Morris, Edmund. *Theodore Rex*. New York: Random House, 2001.

Muller, Dorothea R. "Josiah Strong and American Nationalism: A Reevaluation." *The Journal of American History* 53, no. 3 (1966): 487-503.

Musicant, Ivan. *Empire by Default: The Spanish-American War and the Dawn of the American Century*. New York: Henry Holt, 1998.

National Democratic Campaign Book, Presidential Election. Democratic Party, 1900.

The Nation. January 1889, February 1893, July 1895, June 1897, February 1898, November 1898, April 1899.

National Board of Trade. *28th Annual Meeting, 1897*. Washington, D.C.

Nevins, Allan. *Grover Cleveland: A Study in Courage*. New York: Dodd, Mead, 1933.

Nevins, Allan, ed. *The Letters of Grover Cleveland, 1850-1908*. New York: Houghton Mifflin, 1933.

New Jersey Trade Review. March 1898.

New Orleans Picayune. May 1898.

New York Chronicle. October 1897, February 1898.

New York Commercial. January 1898, May 1898, June 1898, August 1898

New York Evening Post. February 1893, January 1902, April 1902.

New York Herald. January-February 1898, February 1902.

New York Journal of Commerce and Commercial Bulletin. May 1897, June 1897, November 1897, March-May 1898, August 1898.

New York Sun. November 1897, March 1898.

New York Times. February 1895, March-April 1898, June 1898, October 1898, February 1899, April 1902.

New York Times Sunday Herald. August 1900.

New York Tribune. February 1893, January 1898, March-April 1898.

The New York World. April 1902.

North American Review, February 1901, May 1902.

The Omaha Bee. March 1898.

O'Toole, G. J. A. *The Spanish-American War: An American Epic, 1898*. New York: Norton, 1984.

Official Proceedings of the Democratic National Convention. Chicago, 1900.

Official Proceedings of the Democratic National Convention. Chicago, 1990.

Offner, John. *An Unwanted War: The Diplomacy of the United States and Spain over Cuba, 1895-1898*. Chapel Hill: University of North Carolina Press, 1992.

Olney, Richard. "On American Jurisdiction in the Western Hemisphere." In *Papers Relating to the Foreign Relations* of the United States, 1895. Washington, D.C.: Government Printing Office, 1901.

Osborne, Thomas J. *"Empire Can Wait": American Opposition to Hawaiian Annexation, 1893–1898*. Kent, OH: Kent State University Press, 1981.

Oscar S. Straus Papers. Division of Manuscripts. Library of Congress. Washington, D.C.

Palmer, Frederick. Bliss, *Peacemaker: The Life and Letters of General Tasker Howard Bliss*. New York: Dodd, Mead, 1934.

Paris Peace Commission, *Miscellaneous Letters sent to the President and the Secretary of State*. 1898.

Peceny, Mark. "A Constructivist Interpretation of the Liberal Peace: The Ambiguous Case of the Spanish-American War." *Journal of Peace Research* 34, no. 4 November (1997): 415–30.

Pedro Paterno's Proclamation of War, June 2, 1899. Washington, D.C.: U.S. Government Printing Office, 1899, vol. 30.

The People. March 1898, April 1898, June 1898.

Perez, Louis A., Jr. *Cuba and the United States: Ties of Singular Intimacy*. Athens, GA: University of Georgia Press, 2003.

Perez, Louis A., Jr. *The War of 1898: The United States and Cuba in History and Historiography*. Chapel Hill: University of North Carolina Press, 1998.

Perry, Ralph Barton. *The Thought and Character of William James, As Revealed in Unpublished Correspondence and Notes, Together with His Published Writings*. Boston: Little, Brown, 1935.

Pettigrew, R. F. *Imperial Washington*. Chicago: C. H. Kerr, 1922.

Philadelphia Board of Trade. *Sixty-Sixth Annual Report, 1897*.

Providence Sunday Journal. April 1902, May 1902.

Public Opinion. April 1900.

Puck, March 13, 1901.

Railroad Gazette. April 1898.

Railway Age. April 1898.

Railway World. June 1897, August 1897, January-February 1898.

Rand-McNally Bankers' Monthly. March–April 1898, December 1898.

Reed, Thomas B. "The Safe Pathway of Experience." *North American Review* 163, October (1896): 385–394.

Report of the Second Annual Meeting of the New England Anti-Imperialist League. Boston, 1900.

Report of the Third Annual Meeting of the New England Anti-Imperialist League. Boston, 1901.

Revue du Droit International Public 5 (1898).

Rhodes, James Ford. *The McKinley and Roosevelt Administrations*. 1922. Reprint, Charleston, SC: BiblioBazaar, 2009.

Richardson, James D., ed. *A Compilation of the Messages and Papers of the Presidents, 1789–1897*. Washington, D.C.: Government Printing Office, 1897–1907.

Rickover, Hyman G. *How the Battleship Maine was Destroyed*. Annapolis, MD: Naval Institute Press, 1995.

Robinson, William A. *Thomas B. Reed, Parliament*. New York: Dodd, Mead, 1930.

Roosevelt, Theodore. *Theodore Roosevelt, An Autobiography*. New York: Macmillan, 1913.

Rydell, Robert W. *All the World's a Fair: Visions of Empire at the American International Expositions, 1876–1916*. Chicago: University of Chicago Press, 1987.

Salt Lake City Broad Axe. April 25, 1899.

San Francisco Bulletin, January 1898.

San Francisco Call. September 1898, December 1898.

San Francisco Chronicle. April 1898.

San Francisco Examiner. November 1888.

Bibliography

Saturday Review. April 1898.

Schouler, James. "A Review of the Hawaiian Controversy." *The Forum* 16, February (1894): 670–89.

Schurman, Jacob Gould. *Philippine Affairs: A Retrospect and an Outlook.* New York, 1902.

Schurz, Carl. "Manifest Destiny." *Harpers' New Monthly Magazine,* October (1893).

Schurz, Carl. *Speeches, Correspondence, and Political Papers of Carl Schurz,* vol. II. Philadelphia: J.B. Lippincott, 1865.

Scientific America. April 1898.

Scrishaw, F. *The Weekly People.* December 29, 1895.

Scruggs, William L. *British Aggressions in Venezuela, or the Monroe Doctrine on Trial,* 1895, Reprint. Ann Arbor: University of Michigan Library, 2004.

Seattle Post-Intelligencer. June 1898, August 1898.

Senate documents. 55th Cong., 2nd Sess.

Sigsbee, Charles D. *The "Maine," An Account of Her Destruction in Havana Harbor, Personal Narrative.* New York: Century, 1899.

Smith, Joseph P. *McKinley: The People's Choice: Full Text of Each Speech or Address Made by Him from June 18 to August 1, 1896,* 1896. Reprint Charleston, SC: Nabu Press, 2010

Smith, Joseph P. *The Spanish-American War: Conflict in the Caribbean and the Pacific, 1895–1902.* New York: Longman, 1994.

Springfield Daily Republican. May 1899, May 1899, January 1902.

St. Louis Republic. March 1898.

Straus, Oscar S. *Under Four Administrations: From Cleveland to Taft.* Boston: Houghton Mifflin, 1922.

Sumner, William Graham. "The Fallacy of Territorial Expansion." *The Forum* 21, June (1896).

Swift, Morrison I. *Imperialism and Liberty.* Los Angeles: Ronbroke Press, 1899.

Tabouis, Genevieve. *The Life of Jules Cambon.* London: Jonathan Cape, 1938.

Taussing, F. W. "The Tariff Act of 1897." *Quarterly Journal of Economics* 12, no. 1 October (1897): 42–69.

Thayer, William Roscoe. "The Sage of Shady Hill." *The Unpartizan Review* 15, January–March (1921): 79–90.

Thompson, A. H. "British Imperialism and the Autonomous Right of Races." *Kansas City Review of Science and Industry* 3 (1879): 229.

"Thoughts on American Imperialism." *Century Magazine,* September, 1898.

Tone, John Lawrence. *War and Genocide in Cuba, 1895–1898.* Chapel Hill: University of North Carolina Press, 2006.

The Tradesman. March 1898, May 1898, June 1898, September 1898.

Trask, David F. "American Intelligence During the Spanish-American War." In *Crucible of Empire: The Spanish-American War and Its Aftermath,* edited by James C. Bradford, 23–46. Annapolis, MD: Naval Institute Press, 1993.

Traxel, David. 1898: *The Birth of the American Century.* New York: A. A. Knopf, 1998.

United States Investor. January 1898, March–April 1898, July 1898, November 1898.

United States War Department. *Report on the Census of Cuba, 1899.* Washington, D.C.: Government Printing Office, 1900.

Vanderbilt, Kermit. *Charles Eliot Norton: Apostle of Culture in a Democracy.* Cambridge: Belknap Press, 1959.

Wall Street Journal. November–December 1897, January–February 1898, April 1898.

Washington Bee. August 27, 1898.

Washington Evening Star. February–March 1898.

Washington Post. February 1897, January–April 1898.

Washington, H. A., ed. *The Writings of*

Thomas Jefferson. Cambridge: Cambridge University Press, 2011.

Watterson, Henry. *A History of the Spanish-American War*. Ithaca: Cornell University Library, 2009.

Weems, John. *Fate of the "Maine."* Norwalk: Easton Press, 1990.

Welch, Richard E., Jr. *The Presidencies of Grover Cleveland*. Lawrence: University Press of Kansas, 1988.

Welch, Richard E., Jr. *Response to Imperialism, The United States and the Philippine American War*. Chapel Hill: University of North Carolina Press, 1979.

Welch, Richard E., Jr. "William McKinley: Reluctant Warrior, Cautious Imperialist." In *Traditions and Values: American Diplomacy, 1865–1945*, edited by Norman A. Graebner, 29–52. Lanham, MD: University Press of America, 1985.

Werner, M. R. *Bryan*. New York: Harcourt, Brace, 1929.

Westminster Gazette. March 1898.

White, Theodore H. *The Making of the President*. New York: Pocket Books, 1962.

White, Trumbull. *The United States in War with Spain*. Charleston, SC: Nabu Press, 2011.

White, William Allen. *Mask in a Pageant*. New York: Macmillan, 1929.

"Why Colored Troops Were not Sent Earlier." *The Richmond Planet*. July 30, 1898.

Whyte, Kenneth. *The Uncrowned King: The Sensational Rise of William Randolph Hearst*. New York: Random House Canada, 2008.

Wilkerson, Marcus M. *Public Opinion and the Spanish-American War: A Study in War Propaganda*. New York: Russell and Russell, 1967.

William A. Croffut Papers, Library of Congress, Washington, D.C.

William McKinley Papers. Division of Manuscripts. Library of Congress. Washington, D.C.

William Rufus Day Papers. Division of Manuscripts. Library of Congress. Washington, D.C.

Woolsey, Theodore S. *America's Foreign Policy: Essays and Addresses*. Toronto: University of Toronto Libraries, 1898.

Woolsey, Theodore. "The Consequences of Cuban Belligerency." *Yale Law Journal* 5, March (1896): 182–86.

Woolsey, Theodore. "An Inquiry Concerning Our Foreign Relations." *Yale Review* 1, August (1892).

Index

academe: and anti-imperialism 52–55
Adams, Charles Francis 31–32, 72, 150
Adams, John Quincy 3
Adee, Alvey 84
Adler, Felix 52
Africa: and British territory 6
African Americans: and anti-imperialism 28–30, 56–59, 62
The Afro-American 59
Afro-American Press Association 59, 141
The Age 59
Age of Steel (St. Louis) 120, 128
agriculture: destroyed by military action 102
Aguinaldo, Emilio 54, 58–59, 61, 141–43
Albany Press—Knickerbocker, war crimes report 144
Alger Russell A. 159
Allen, William V. 70
Alliance (U.S. mail) 65, 67
Alliance mail ship incident 65, 67
Allison, William Boyd 146
Altgeld, John P. 19
A.M.E. Zion Review 59
The American (Chicago) 48
American Asiatic Association 126, 129–30
American Banker 114, 127
American Machinist 122
American Peace Society 36
Ames, Charles G. 60
Anglo-Saxons 56–57
annexation: characteristics of 57, 61; and Democratic Party platforms 43; and government stability 120; and Hawaii 15, 61, 120, 130; and the Philippines 129–30, 157; and Puerto Rico 15, 61; and Teller Amendment 51; views of—business journals 120, Grover Cleveland 13, John Quincy Adams 3, U.S. Congress 15–16, 43; *see also* expansionism/-ists; imperialism/-ists; jingoism; treaties
Annexation Club 7–8
anti-autonomy riots 77–78, 83

anti-expansionism/-ists: Adler 52; American Board of Missions 61; and the Black press 57–59; business community 129–30; and Canada 4; and Catholic Church 60; at end of 19th century 28; Godkin 34; and racism 30, 40, 51–52, 59, 61, 63; Schurz 11–12; Shafroth 16; and universities 52; and war crimes reports 145
anti-imperialism/-ists: and academic/literary world 52–55; Adams 31–32; Boston conference of 21–22; Carnegie 45, 47; on cost-benefits of war with Spain 155–56; and Democratic Party 42–52; diminishment of 12; at end of 19th century 28; failure of 156–57; labor unions 28–29; and leadership debility 41; and the left 55–56; limited influence of 45; and Mugwumps 29–38; and national security 62; opposition to 13; and the Philippines 129–30; and presidential election (1900) 33; and racism 28, 63; reasons for 62–63; of religious community 59–61; and Roosevelt administration 151–52; as unpatriotic 152; of various groups 28–29; and war crimes reports 144–45, 150; and war with Spain 156–57
The Anti-Imperialist 19
Anti-Imperialist League: and academe 28, 52–55; and Adams 32; and African Americans 58; and Atkinson 37; and Blount 171n12; and Boutwell 40; and Catholics 60; decline of 141; growth/development of 37, 46–47; and New Anti-Imperialist League 47; and Schurz 31; voting pattern of 33; and war crimes reports 143–45
anti-militarism 14, 41
Anti-Trust League: and African Americans 58
The Appeal 59
Army and Navy Journal: criticizes anti-imperialists 149
Asia 3–4, 11, 123, 128–29
Associated Press: on war crimes 149

197

Index

Astwood, H. C. 57
Atkins, Edwin 176n12
Atkinson, Edward 19, 35–38
Atlanta Constitution: as pro-war advocate 133
Atwood, Isaac M. 60

Bacon, Augustus O. 39
Bailey, Thomas A. 91
Baker, William 72
Baltimore American: on Cuban crisis 103
Baltimore News: on war crimes 149
Banker and Tradesman: on Philippine War 128, 132
Barker, Wharton 183n58
Barton, James L. 61
Barton, Stephen 89
Bayard, Thomas F. 22
The Bee: supports McKinley 59
Bell, J. Franklin 149
Bermejo, Sigismundo 81
Beveridge, Albert Jeremiah 146
Bierce, Ambrose 53
Bisbee, Robert E. 60–61
Bismarck, Otto von 5
Blaine, James G. 5–6
Blanco, Ramón 77, 82
Bliss, Howard 103
Blount, James 8–9, 13, 21, 171n12
Boer War of South Africa 19, 48
Boston: as anti-imperialist center 21–22, 141
USS *Boston* 8
Boston Advertiser: on war crimes 149
Boston Evening Transcript 35, 85
Boston Herald 61, 106
Boston Journal of Commerce 100
Boutelle, Charles A. 72
Boutwell, George S.: public service of 40; *The Venezuelan Question and the Monroe Doctrine* 19–20
Bradford, James: *Crucible of Empire* 160
Bradstreet 116, 119, 128, 130, 138–39
Britain *see* Great Britain
British Guiana: boundary dispute 17
British West Indies 131
The Broad Axe 57–58
Bryan, William Jennings 157; African American support of 58; and anti-imperialism 43, 46–47, 50, 155; as free silver proponent 45–49, 96; and Liberty Party 50; on Philippine independence 45; as presidential candidate 32–33; *see also* free silver movement
Bryce, James 14–15
Buffalo Express: on war crimes 150
Burgess, John W. 26

Burke, John Edward 58
Burrows, Julius Caesar 146
Bush, T.G. 183n58
business/industry *see* economy

Cambon, Jules 93
Campbell, Charles: *The Transformation of American Foreign Relations* 25
Canada: and U.S. expansionism 4
Canalejas, José 83
Cannon, Frank J. "Joe" 78–79, 83, 85, 88
capitalism 55–56, 141
Caribbean: and annexation 10–11; and expansionism 131; Schurz's proposal for 30; Seward's plan for 4
Carmack, Edward Ward 146
Carnegie, Andrew 19, 22, 45, 47
Catholic Church: and Anti-Imperialists League 60
Catholic Young Men's National Union 60
censorship of the press 59–61, 144–45
Central Cuban Relief Committee 89
Chamber of Commerce (Seattle) 129
Chamber of Commerce (New York): "American Interests in China" 128; "American Treaty Rights in China" 125–26
Chamber of Commerce Merchant's Association 129
Chicago Chronicle 101–2, 107, 137–38
Chicago Inter-Ocean 98, 102, 150
Chicago Journal of Commerce 135
Chicago News: on war crimes 149
Chicago Times-Herald 108, 133, 136
Chicago Tribune 96, 98, 101
China: as global marketplace 124–26, 132, 182n45
Christians 29, 59–62
churches: Philippine desecration of 60
Cincinnati Chamber of Commerce 115
City and State: war crimes reports 144–45
Clemens, Samuel Langhorne *see* Twain, Mark
Cleveland, Grover: and Cuban rebellion 20, 64, 66–67, 73–75; and overseas expansionism 8–9; on Samoa crisis 5; on Venezuelan boundary dispute 17
climate: as incompatible with democracy 11; and warfare 103
Cochran, Bourke 26
Cochran, William B. 4
Codman, Julian 150–51
Collier's Weekly 60
colonialism: African American opposition to 56–59; of Europe 123; and export trade 119–22, 131; problems of 130; Twain's views of 53–54; of USA 28

198

Index

The Colored American 58
commerce: and naval expansion 12
The Commercial see *New York Commercial*
Commercial Advertiser 137–39
Commercial and Financial Chronicle 115, 120–21, 131
Commercial Bulletin 129
Compeditor 67
Conde de Venadito (Spanish warship) 65
Converse, George A. 81
Cooper, Diane E. 160
Cornell University: and anti-imperialism 52
Cosmas, Graham A. 160
Crawford, James 22
Creelman, James 48
Crosby, Ernest: *Captain Jinks, Hero* 54
Cuba: destruction from military action 102; and expansionism 3, 56–58; famine in 81–82, 89, 94; Spanish occupation of 101; suzerainty plan failure 90; and Teller Amendment 51; trade agreement with Spain 82–83; as unfit for self-government 182n33; unstable government of 120; and Woodford negotiations 92
Cuba Libre 64
Cuban Americans 64, 66
Cuban crisis: anti-autonomy riots 77–78; anti-war sentiments 96–98, 105–8, 155, 180n3; business/industry affected by 116–17; European views of 74–75; and filibustering expeditions 64–65; media views of 101–2; and presidential campaign 87; Proctor report 93–94; and public opinion 87–88, 92–93, 105–9; and Spanish rule 20, 43, 136–37; and U.S. foreign policy 20–21, 24, 36, 64–65, 67–70, 73–74; as U.S. national issue 70–74; *see also* Spanish-American War
Cuban Junta 64, 69
Cuban Liberation Army 161
Culberson, Charles Allen 146
currency/money: and free silver 50, 76, 96, 108; and gold standard 108, 114–15

Daily Commercial News and Shipping List 129
Danish West Indies 131
Darrow, Clarence 19
Day, William Rufus 84, 89, 91
De Armond, David A. 79
Debs, Eugene 55
The Defender 57
De Leon, Daniel 55
de Lôme, Enrique Dupuy 73–74, 78, 83–85, 177n11, 1779n1

democracy: and Cuban belligerency 43; as incompatible with tropical climate 11
Democratic Campaign Book 43, 49
Democratic Party: and anti-imperialism 19, 28, 32, 42–52; on Cuban independence 70–71, 76; and Gold Democrats 47–49; Hearst's criticism of 44; platforms of 43–44, 48–50; and Populists 49; and William Jennings Bryan 32–33, 45, 48, 50, 96
Denby, Charles 124
Dewey, George 15–16, 142, 146
Dietrich, Charles Henry 146
Dole, Sanford 8
Donald, E. Winchester 60
Donders, Erique 176n19
Dubois, Fred Thomas 146
Dunne, Finly Peter 53
Dun's Review 116
Dupuy de Lôme, Enrique 73–74, 78, 83–85, 177n11, 1779n1

Economist (Chicago) 115
economy: and Cuban crisis 117–18; elitism, of Adams 31–32; expansion of 117–19; and labor unions 28–29, 141; stimulated by rumors of war 115–16; and warfare 113–17
Ellett, Tazewell 72
Emporia Gazette 103
England *see* Great Britain
Europe: and free trade 122–24; and Spanish-American War 105–9
Evans, Daniel J. 148
expansionism/-ists 7–10; and anti-imperialism/-ists 19, 23; and business community 119–20, 130; in the Caribbean 131; and China 132; development of 3–4; at end of 19th century 28; and imperialism/-ists 25–27; Nicaraguan canal 119–20; and Pacific bridge concept 130; on Philippine liberation 157; and trade 129, 132; *see also* anti-expansionism/-ists; imperialism/-ists
exports 124, 131–32

famine: in Cuba 81–82, 89, 94
Faunce, William H.P. 60
filibustering expeditions 64–66
Financial Chronicle 131
Financial Record 114–15, 128, 182n49
Fiske, John 26
Florida Times-Union 67
Foraker, Joseph 103
foreign policy *see* United States foreign policy
The Forum 13, 59
France: compensated for Chinese territory 124

199

Index

Frazer, Everett 129–30
free silver movement 43, 50, 76, 96, 108, 113–15
The Freeman 59
Freeman's Journal 60
The Friend's Intelligencer and Journal 60, 144
Funston, Frederick 54, 144, 152s

Gage, Lyman 114
Gardner, Cornelius 149
Germany 4–6, 123–24
Gildea, William 67
Gillette, Frederick H. 72
globalization 124, 130
The *Globe* 58
Godkin, Edwin Lawrence 33–34
Gold Democrats: as anti-imperialists 47–48
gold standard: and war speculation 107–8, 114–15
Goluchowski (count) 122–23
Gomez (Cuban insurgent) 68, 82
Gray, George 8
Great Britain: assessment of U.S. military 105; compensated for China territory 124; and Cuban crisis 74–75; imperialist policies of 22–23; on Monroe Doctrine 17–18; and Samoan crisis 4, 6; and Venezuelan boundary dispute 17–19
Gresham, Walter Q. 9, 65
Griggs, John W. 37
Grit, Bruce 58
Gullón y Iglesias, Pío 84

Hale, Eugene 69, 71
Harper's Weekly 103–4, 134–35, 152
Harrison, Benjamin 5, 8, 21
Harvard University: and anti-expansionism 52
Hawaiian Islands: and annexation movement 7–9, 11–12, 21–22, 30, 119–20; as gateway to Philippines 130; instability of 120; and Japanese pressure 15; and opium trade 7; Seward's view of 3; and U.S. reciprocity treaty 7; and U.S. security 14
Hearst, William Randolph 44, 48, 176n19
Herring, George 13, 25
Hersey, Scott F. 60
Higginson, Henry Lee 151
Hill, David Bennet 44, 49
Hill, James J. 129
Hitt, Robert R. 71, 79–80
Hoar, George F. 38–40, 69, 145
Hobson, John A.: *Imperialism: A Study* 23
Howard, O.O. 152

Hughes, Barry: *The Domestic Content of American Foreign Policy* 162
Hughes, Robert P. 146–47

imperialism/-ists: and annexation 22; and business community 121; and Cuban crisis 118–19; at end of 19th century 28; and globalization 130; Henry Cabot Lodge 146; and industrial/commercial development 119; and international trade 25; media views on 43–44; negative perceptions of 23, 151; and Philippines 141, 151–52; as political issue 44–45; and Santo Domingo 4–5; and Spanish-American War 53; and U.S. Constitution 24–25; usage of the term 172n59–60; and Venezuela 17; versus expansionism 25–27; and war crimes reports 149; *see also* anti-imperialism/-ists
industry *see* economy; mining industry; sugar industry
Inter-Ocean (Chicago) 132
Interstate Commerce Act (1887) 35
Iron Age 122

James, William 52–53
Jameson's raid 19, 23
Jane, Fred 106
Jefferson, Thomas: on annexing Cuba 3
jingoism 5, 10, 16, 53, 71–72, 101, 106, 108, 114–15, 119–20, 126
Journal of Commerce 121, 123, 130–31
Journal des Débat 106
Juragua Iron Company 68

Kansas City Board of Trade 115
Kansas City Star: on war crimes 150
Kennan, George 144
Kiefer, Andrew R 72
Kipling, Rudyard 23, 54
Kruger, Paul 19

labor unions 28–29, 141
Laborde, Alfredo 67
Ledger (Philadelphia) 123
Lee, Fitzhugh 75, 78–80, 89, 177n32
Lewis, James 95
Liberty Party 47, 50
Liliuokalani (queen) 7
literary world: and anti-imperialism 52–55
Lodge, Henry Cabot 19, 119, 126, 140, 146, 148, 151
London Engineer 105
London Times 102
Long, John D. 91, 177n12

Index

Lorimer, Rev. George C. 61
Louisville Courier Journal 43–44

Mabey, Charles 184n12
Mahan, Alfred Thayer 14, 26, 119; *The Influence of Sea Power upon History* 12
Mahany, Rowland B. 72
USS *Maine* 80, 86–87, 89–90, 138; and Spanish-American War 159
manifest destiny concept 1, 4, 9–10, 27
Manila Bay battle: and east-west trade 126
Manufacturers' and Producers' Association 129
Maria Cristina (queen regent) 93
Mason, William E. 83, 85
Matanzas, Cuba: famine 81–82
McComas, Louis Emory 146
McCook, John 90
USS *McCulloch* 142
McEnery, Samuel D. 39
McKinley, William: and annexation 13–15, 130; and Cannon meeting 88; and Cuban crisis 20–21, 78; and de Lôme letter 83; defeats Bryan 50–51; foreign policy of 137–38; and USS *Maine* incident 80–81, 90; praised by Hitt on House floor 79; presidential campaign of, as bitterest in history 87; reelection of 141, 157; and Spain 76, 86, 139; versus Charles Francis Adams 32; as wishy-washy 138
McKinley Tariff: and Hawaiian revolution 7
media: Afro-American Press Association 59, 141; as anti-imperialist 144, 155–56; anti-war presses 105, 107–8, 133; anti-war/pro-war views of 96–98, 136–40; censorship of 144–45; condemns Spanish-American war 135; on Cuban crisis 101–3; European press sentiments 105–9; and expansionism 127–28; and imperialism 121; on international trade 123–32; on Manila Bay victory 126; on the Philippines 126–27; and public opinion 93–94, 105–9; as racist 133–34; shift in attitude toward war 96, 98, 136–40; on Spanish-American War 105–9, 113–15, 155; on war crimes 148–50
Melton, Ona 67
Merk, Frederick: *Manifest Destiny and the Mission in American History* 162
Metcalf, Wilder 143
Metropolitan Truth Society 60
Miller, Pvt. 144
Mining and Scientific Press 115, 128
mining industry 115, 118
Monitor 60
Monroe Doctrine 17–20, 93

USS *Montgomery* 81
Moody, William Vaughn: "On a Soldier Fallen in the Philippines" 54
Moret y Prendergast, Segismundo 84, 92–93
Morgan, John T. 70, 42, 68–69, 85, 114
Mugwumps 29–38
Musicant, Ivan: *Empire by Default* 25, 160–61

The Nation 5, 8, 14, 21–22, 33, 54
National Association of Democratic Clubs 48
nationalism 5, 9; *see also* jingoism; manifest destiny
naval engagements: of Sino-Japanese War 99
naval expansion 12
naval strength 91–92, 96–100
Negro National Democratic League 58
The Negro World 58
New Anti-Imperialist League 47
New Monthly Magazine (Harper) 12
New York Chronicle 100, 107–8
New York Commercial 123, 128, 131–32
New York Evening Post 8, 143–44, 149
New York Herald 102–3, 107–8, 134, 137, 149
New York Journal 44, 48, 70–71, 83–85, 119, 134–35, 149
New York Journal of Commerce 102, 108, 114, 119–20, 123–25, 127, 135
New York stock market: and war speculation 116
New York Times 43, 100, 106, 134, 136–37, 150
New York World 144, 149
Nicaraguan canal 119–20, 182n30
Nieuws van den Dag (Netherlands) 106
North American 149
Norton, Charles Eliot 35–36, 52

The Observer 60
O'Hall, Frank 60
Olney, Richard 17, 73–74, 176n12
USS *Olympia* 142
Omaha Bee 100
Omaha World 144
Otis, Elwell 60, 143–44, 146
O'Toole, G.J.A.: *The Spanish-American War* 161–62
Outlook 144

Pacific Islands: as British territory 6
Parkhurst, Charles H. 60
Patterson, Thomas MacDonald 146
The People 55

201

Index

Pettigrew, Richard F. 8, 46–47
Philadelphia Press 130, 150
Philippine-American War 143–44, 157
Philippines: annexed by U.S. 31–32, 43–45, 56, 128, 142–43; and anti-imperialism 63; and anti-war sentiment 57–59; and colonialism 53, 56; declares war on U.S. 143; in Democratic Party platforms 43; and expansionism 16–17, 26, 39; as gateway to Eastern markets 127; intervention opposed 37; post-war government of 142; and resistance to war 77–86; as trade center/trade route 36–37, 128; and Treaty of Paris 141; as uncivilized 146–47, 150–51, 157; and war crimes 148–51, 153
Pittsburgh Gazette 150
Pittsburgh Times 149
Platt, Orville. H. 71
Polo de Bernabé y Borrás, José 91
Populist Party 40, 70
Potter, Henry C. 62–63
Proctor, Redfield 93, 95
Protestants: and expansionism 60
Providence Sunday Journal 152
public opinion: and Cuban crisis/debates 70–73, 87–88, 92–95; and pro-war fever 137
Puck 54
Puerto Rico annexation 42–43, 45, 131–32

Quigg, Lemuel F. 86

racism: and Anglo-Saxons 56–57; and anti-expansionism/-ists 30, 40, 51–52, 59, 61, 63; and anti-imperialism/-ists 28, 63; and anti-war media 133; against Asiatics 151; of Atkinson 36; and Cuban situation 72, 93–94, 133; of Godkin 34; and pro-war advocates 133; of Schurz 30; and social Darwinists 56; and war crimes 153; and war with Spain 156
Railway World 131–32
Rand-McNalIly Bankers' Monthly 114–15
Rawlings, Joseph Lafayette 146–47
The Recorder 59
Reed, Thomas Brackett 16, 41–43
Reid, Whitelaw 19, 90
Republican Party: and Afro Americans 59; and anti-imperialism 28, 38–42, 47–48; and Cuban crisis 70, 75–796; and expansionism 40, 75; and Hoar 38–39; and Mugwumpism 29
The Richmond Planet 57
Riley, Charles S. 148
riots: Cuban anti-autonomy 77–78, 83
Roosevelt, Theodore: and annexation 15; becomes president 141; and colonialism 151; as expansionist 19, 23; on naval forces 100, 177n5; and the Philippines 151–52; on role of USS *Maine* 159; on Spanish-American War 140; versus Godkin 33; and war crimes report 153
Root, Elihu 100, 151
Rubens, Horatio S. 84
Ruiz, Joaquin 82
Russia 123–24

St. Louis Globe-Democrat 150
St. Thomas: and expansionism 131
Samoan Islands 4–6
San Francisco Call 130
San Francisco Chronicle 99, 107, 133, 149–50
San Francisco Examiner 5
Sanguily, Julio 66–67
Santo Domingo: and imperialism 4–5
Saturday Review 102
Schouler, James 13, 21, 171n32
Schurz, Carl: and annexation 9–11, 21, 23, 30; as anti-expansionist 4–5, 12–13, 29–30, 171n21; as anti-imperialist 31; on Caribbean confederation 30; as Mugwump 29; as racist 30; "Thoughts on American Imperialism" 30; and war crimes investigation 150
Scruggs, William I.: *British Aggressions in Venezuela...* 17
Seattle Post-Intelligencer 99
self-determination concept 21–22, 172n59
Seward, William H. 3, 7–8
Shafroth, John F. 16, 172n42
Sherman, John 41, 70–71, 116–17
ships: battleships 98–99; cruisers 99–100; destroyed by hurricane 5; torpedo boats 99–100
Sigsbee, Charles 80–81
silver/silverites *see* free silver movement
Sino-Japanese War naval engagements 99
Smith, Charles Emory 37
Smith, Goldwin 26
Smith, Jacob 149–50
Smith, Joseph: *The Spanish-American War* 162
Socialist Labor Party 55–56
socialists: as anti-expansionists 55
South Africa, Boer War 19, 48
Spain: as belligerent 137; and Cuban insurrection 20, 70, 74, 140; and de Lôme's letter 85; impedes U.S. war effort 64–65; imprisons Cuban Americans 66; loss to the U.S. 140; and USS *Maine* 81 138; naval strength of 91–92, 97–98, 100, 139; occupation of Cuba 101; searches U.S. ships 69;

Index

surrenders at Luzon 142; trade treaty with Cuba 82–83; and and U.S.–Cuba arbitration 92; U.S. foreign policy 86, 96–97; and Woodford plan 92–93
Spalding, John L. 60
Spanish-American War: European press favors Spain 106; historiography of 159–69; and imperialism 53; and USS *Maine* explosion 86; opposed by business world 130; resistance to 77–86; *see also* Cuban crisis
Spencer, E. 142
Spreckels family 130
Springfield Daily Republican 149, 152
Stanford University: and anti-imperialism 52
Steere, J. Neal 52
Stevens, John L. 8, 13, 21
Stevenson, Adlai 51
Storey, Moorfield 150–51
Straus, Oscar S. 90
Strong, Josiah 26
sugar industry: and annexation 130; and autonomy 86; California versus Philippines 130; and Cuban crisis 118; military destruction of 102; and Republican platform 75; sugarcane harvest and Cuban insurgents 67–68; and U.S.–Hawaiian agreement 7
Sulzer, James 16
Sulzer, William 79, 85
Sumner, William Graham 23–24, 52
Swift, Morrison I. 55

Taft, William Howard 146, 148
tariffs: Atkinson opposed to 35; and European coalition 123; and Hoar 38; as ineffective 122; McKinley and Hawaiian revolution 7; and Mugwumpism 31; and Russia alliance 123
Teller Amendment 37, 51, 56, 131
territorial expansionism *see* expansionism
Tetuán, Duque de 74
Thompson, A. H. 22–23
Tillman, Benjamin R. 49
Tone, John Lawrence: *War and Genocide in Cuba, 1895–1898* 161
trade relations 37, 40, 82–83; American, China, and Japan Association 126; and colonialism 120–21; and Cuban crisis 117; and export-import ratio 119–20; and free trade 121–22; and Manila Bay battle 126; with non–European countries 123, 128; Spain-Cuba trade treaty 83; and U.S. surplus goods 131
Tradesman (Chattanooga) 115, 122

Transvaal, South Africa: Boers 19
Trask, David 160
treaties: not ratified 15; trade, Spain-Cuba 82–83; Treaty of Paris 39–40, 45–46, 141, 151; U.S./Germany/Great Britain on Samoa 6; U.S./Hawaiian Kingdom 7–9; U.S./Spain 61
tropical diseases and Spanish-American War 161
Turner, Henry G. 72
Twain, Mark: "A Defense of General Funston" 54, 152; "To the Person Sitting in Darkness" 53–54

Unitarian Church of New England 60
United Nations 176n17
United States: anti-war advocacy of 107–8; national security of 6–7, 62; occupation of Philippines 142–43; victory in Spanish-American War 139
United States Army: British assessment of 106; and Cuban crisis 101; losses of, to Spanish army 140–41
United States Congress: annexation treaty not ratified 15; appropriates funds for boundary commission 18; Cannon Emergency Bill 88–89; Committee on the Philippines 152; and Cuban crisis 64, 68–69, 73, 78–79, 83; debates—on Cuban crisis 8, 70–72, 79–80, on naval appropriations 99, and public opinion 70–73, and funding war effort 88–89; 87–88, 92–95; joint resolutions—on annexation 16–17, on Cuba 72–73; and McKinley's diplomacy 91; and Monroe Doctrine 17; Senate Committee on the Philippines 145–46— war crimes reports 145; and Spain-Cuba trade treaty 83; support for *Maine*'s voyage to Havana 80; Teller Amendment 37; and Treaty of Paris 39; war powers of 91
United States Constitution: and expansionism 10, 24–25, 61, 120
United States Department of War: dismisses war crimes report 144
United States economy: affected by warfare 109–10
United States foreign policy: adopts expansionism 141; and budget deficit 96; and Cuban crisis 69–70, 96, 139; at end of 19th century 28–29; free trade versus annexation 24; and imperialism 21, 24–26; and new manifest destiny 9; and overseas expansion 7–9; and public opinion 70–73, 87–88, 92–93; and self-determination concept 21; transformation of 6
United States government: budget deficit

203

Index

and foreign policy 96; economic depression (1890s) 96; filibustering expeditions of 64–65; and Germany 5; global advantage of 12; intervenes to save *Compeditor* crew 67; and militarism 14, 89; and Philippines 57, 61; public opinion and foreign policy 70–73, 87–88, 92–95; and Samoa 4, 6; and Spain-Cuba arbitration 92

United States Investor 8, 128

United States military: war crimes of 145–48; and war preparedness 89, 101–2

United States Navy: and annexation treaty 9; battleships' shortcomings 98–99; blockade of Cuba 102; British assessment of 106; and commercial expansion 12–14; Court of Inquiry report on USS *Maine* 95; and Cuban crisis 64, 81; and foreign manpower 98, 106; inadequacies of 97–98; media opinions of 99–100; and Samoa crisis 4; victory in Philippines 142; warfare crafts 97

United States State Department: and Cuban crisis 68, 82; and McKinley's views toward Spain 86; uninterested in China crisis 125

United States Supreme Court: and filibustering expeditions 65–66; legalizes imperial policy 40

University of Chicago 52

University of Michigan 52

Van Dyke, Henry 61
Venezuelan boundary dispute 17–18, 55
Vest, George G. 8, 51–52, 171*n*12
Victoria, Queen: and Spain-Cuba arbitration 92

Walker, Major 149
Wall Street Journal 116, 127
Walsh, Herbert 145
war crimes 141, 143–44, 147–53
warfare: affects of, on business/economy 116–18; armaments 105; and climate 103; and disease 103; and distance 102–3; economic considerations for 107–8, 113–15; media views of Cuban crisis 101–2; and naval guerrilla (Spain) 106; and naval strengths/weaknesses 91–92, 96–100; and potential for economic growth 115–16; rules of 147; and war crimes 141, 143–44, 147–52

Washington Bee 57
Washington Post 98
Watterson, Henry 43–44
Weekly People 55
Welch, Richard 145
Wells, H.L. 144
Welsh, Henry 152–53
West Indies 131
Westminster Gazette 105–6
Weyler, Valeriano 42, 77
White, Stephen M. 70, 69
Wilhelm II (German Kaiser) 19
Wilkinson, Charles Burnham, "Bud" 67
Woodford, Stewart L. 82, 84, 88, 91, 93, 178*n*19, 179*n*14–15
Woolsey, Theodore 6
World 132

Yale University 52
yellow fever 103
yellow journalism 34, 85–86, 110, 176*n*19

www.ingramcontent.com/pod-product-compliance
Lightning Source LLC
Chambersburg PA
CBHW032059300426
44116CB00007B/809